# SKIRTING THE BOUNDARY

# SKIRTING
## THE
# BOUNDARY
## A HISTORY OF WOMEN'S CRICKET

## ISABELLE DUNCAN

**The Robson Press**

First published in Great Britain in 2013 by
The Robson Press (an imprint of Biteback Publishing Ltd)
Westminster Tower
3 Albert Embankment
London SE1 7SP
Copyright © Isabelle Duncan 2013

ISBN 978-1-84954-546-4

10 9 8 7 6 5 4 3 2 1

A CIP catalogue record for this book is available from the British Library.

Set in Sabon

Printed and bound in Great Britain by
CPI Group (UK) Ltd, Croydon CR0 4YY

*To my father, Andrew Duncan*

# CONTENTS

The burlesque 'Cricket Match Extraordinary'
by Thomas Rowlandson, 1811.

# INTRODUCTION

Not enough has been written about women's cricket. This may have been understandable in the early and middle part of the last century, when women's cricket existed in a twilight world, regarded as a sporting occupation for ladies who could perhaps be most tactfully described as unconventional. Even in the 1960s and 1970s, the era of the great Rachael Heyhoe Flint, the first female cricketer to prove that femininity could still flourish with a bat or ball in hand, women's cricket was treated with little short of derision in many sporting circles. Today, in the first part of the twenty-first century, this attitude no longer has currency, particularly in England, where the national women's team has established itself as the world's number one with the Ashes and two World Cups to its credit. Even our politicians have noticed this.

*Skirting the Boundary* intends to fill this yawning gap in cricket literature. If it will also fill a gap in feminist literature, I cannot emphasise too strongly that I am no bra-burning, man-hating, equality-at-any-price virago. Like the great Rachael, I love the company of men – almost as much as I love cricket (and if the mood and music are right, even more than cricket).

I am not alone. More and more women and girls have taken up this great game in recent years – with the support (at last) of many august cricketing bodies such as Marylebone Cricket Club (MCC), the Cricket Foundation (and its attempts to bring cricket back to state schools), Chance to Shine and amateur cricket clubs all over the world. Even the International Cricket Council (ICC) is recognising the distaff contribution to the greatest game. More and more women are watching cricket, writing about cricket and, of course, playing cricket.

The best place to begin is, as always, at the beginning, when ladies made their first mark on cricket in the late eighteenth century amid frantic betting and rowdy crowd scenes. Then on to the highs and lows of the nineteenth and twentieth centuries, culminating in our twenty-first-century heroines who are dominating world cricket and are on the cusp of turning professional.

Part of my job will be to trace the history of the women's game, delving into its sometimes murky past and examining the recent explosion in its popularity. The last book of any note about women's cricket was published in 1976 – *Fair Play* by Rachael Heyhoe Flint and Netta Rheinberg. There is, therefore, a dire need for a racy update – less of the straight bat and more of the reverse sweep.

This book will contain plenty of photographs – from the frankly amazing portraits of the teams of fifty or a hundred years ago (no ban on pipe smokers) to the frankly sexy pictures of many of today's modern practitioners.

I want to shed light on some of the more remarkable and interesting stories and individuals (females only) who have had some sort of love affair with this great game, on the notable and sometimes controversial figures who have dared to cross the boundary into this male-dominated world.

My own obsession with cricket pervades every part of my life and I don't seem to have time for much else. I have played cricket since forever and I currently captain an otherwise all-male team at Albury Cricket Club in a Surrey league, as well as turning up for a number of nomadic jazz-hat sides including the Invalids, the Heartaches, the Bunburys, the Nomads and MCC.

There are a number of women out there who prefer to play cricket with the chaps, and I am one of them. There are plenty of amusing stories to come out of this and I've got a few of them up my sleeve. Being asked in front of a lot of gawping men whether you wear a box, or being whacked in the boob by a cricket ball are regular occurrences. If the latter, you always get keen offers to rub it better and invitations to join the team in the showers afterwards. Most decent chaps soon forget you're a girl (on the pitch anyway) and treat you with respect once you have shown you can compete on their level. However, one or two remain stroppy...

My work in the cricket coaching arena brings me face to face with grass-roots cricket as I run a coaching company for boys and girls aged four to twelve years old. We travel the highways and byways of Surrey and Sussex bringing the joys of cricket into the playgrounds of state primary schools. The talent and enthusiasm out there from both boys and girls is significant; it is hugely reassuring for the future of the game and it must be nurtured.

My involvement in grass-roots cricket extends into assisting the cricket charity Chance to Shine in some of its endeavours. Chance to Shine is a remarkably successful charity and has worked wonders with girls' cricket – 44 per cent of their 1.8 million children are girls. We have just launched 'Girls on the Front Foot', an initiative aimed at sustaining and developing the charity's work with girls. Our board is littered with distinguished ladies from the sport, business and media worlds, among them Charlotte Edwards MBE (current England captain), Lucy Neville-Rolfe DBE and Clare Connor OBE (ECB Head of Women's Cricket). At Chance to Shine the girls are on an equal footing with the boys, united in the belief that cricket will raise aspirations and develop the values needed for a successful and fulfilling life.

I was lucky enough to be involved in the hoo-ha of MCC finally admitting women within the hallowed walls of the Pavilion at Lord's. Just before the final vote in 1998 I was asked by *Wisden Cricketer* magazine if I would pose for their front cover in an MCC sweater. Controversial stuff, as I was obviously not a member then, but I agreed in the end as I felt it would draw attention to the debate and make people think. I didn't want to appear as a feminist flag-bearer, more as a reminder that we girls were knocking on the Long Room door – girls who loved cricket and who felt we had a right to watch this beautiful game from the best seats in the house. It may be a private club but it's in a public arena with a public responsibility.

I have now been a member of MCC since 2002 and I

play for the Club, sit on a committee and even a disciplinary panel(!), which allows me an intriguing insight into this distinguished bastion of cricket. Some of the 'crimes' of MCC members (usually male, it must be said) are hilarious. In October 2013, Vicky Griffiths and I will join the main MCC Committee for our first term around the big table at Lord's. The only other lady to have graced the sumptuous leather chairs in the Committee Room is Rachael Heyhoe Flint.

So, the girls are here to stay and their cricketing genius is unquestionably destined for universal appreciation and its ultimate rewards. This could not have been better illustrated than in the 2013 Women's World Cup...

The Aussies back on top of the world
in the 2013 World Cup in India.

# PREFACE

It's 8.45 a.m. and England has won the toss. There's some early morning dampness in the air at the Brabourne Stadium in Mumbai and the ball is expected to move around in the first part of the day. England's captain, Charlotte Edwards, knows these conditions will benefit her swing bowlers so she asks Australia to bat. The breaking news is that Australia's star all-rounder, Ellyse Perry, will sit out the match due to a stomach bug, a major blow for Australia and welcome news for England. She will be replaced by seventeen-year-old prodigy Holly Ferling, whose international debut came only a week earlier in this 2013 World Cup against Pakistan.

England's opening bowler, Katherine Brunt, does not disappoint and exploits the conditions with her hostile outswingers. At the other end, Anya Shrubsole torments the opening batsmen, Lanning and Haynes, with exaggerated inswing. She swings it away to the left-hander Haynes who mistimes a drive and gently pushes it back into the hungry hands of the bowler for a soft dismissal. Three balls later, new batswoman Cameron receives a corker from Shrubsole who swings the ball in late to the right-hander and cartwheels her stump out of the ground. A wicket maiden for Shrubsole followed by emphatic celebrations with her teammates. Australia proceed to prod and poke their way to 32 for 5 after only 12 overs. Sthalekar and Coyte, however, rally the innings, putting on 82 together, until bowlers Gunn, Brindle and Colvin finish the job and Australia subside to 147 all out in the 45th over. A paltry score from the titans Australia and the money is on England.

Edwards cracks two fours in the 1st over of the England innings but disaster strikes early when she is given out lbw to Schutt. A poor decision by the umpire, as Hawk-Eye shows, but there are no referrals to the third umpire in this competition to call her back. The rot has set in and Sarah Taylor is next to go with an inglorious golden duck. Much of the middle order fall to ill-judged strokes leaving Greenway (49) and Marsh (22) to keep England's hopes alive with a defiant partnership of 57 in almost 26 overs. New girl Ferling causes the most distress to the England batting attack with her difficult bounce and zippy pace and strikes with her first ball. They collapse to 114 for 9, 34 runs away from victory, but it's a distant horizon with no wickets in hand... The last women standing are Colvin and Shrubsole and the Australian fielders are getting up close and personal; however, the pair sweep aside these intimidatory tactics, creaming five boundaries between them, and by the 48th over they need only 3 to win. An absolute thriller and the crowd are on their feet as Colvin goes back to cut the ball and edges it to the keeper and Australian captain,

Jodie Fields, who takes it with a euphoric scream. It is all over for England but what a terrific crack at a fightback.

These finely tuned athletes, performing in the tenth Women's World Cup, have come a long way from the dawn of women's cricket in Guildford in 1745, where eleven maids of Bramley played eleven maids of Hambledon.

Miss Wicket and Miss Trigger
by John Collett, 1770.

# EIGHTEENTH-CENTURY BEGINNINGS... MAIDS VERSUS MARRIEDS

Or should that be fourteenth-century origins? An illustration by Johann de Grise has been unearthed in the Bodleian Library, Oxford, dated 1344, which reveals a rudimentary form of a bat and ball game in which nuns and monks battle it out; although it is difficult to tell whether the fielders are fielding or actually deep in prayer. However, this illustration bears little semblance even to the earliest accepted versions of the game. We then have a dormant period of about four hundred years with no record of women taking part in any form of the game.

In the early 1700s, cricket was very much in its infancy with only a few villages in England playing a rustic version of the game. This basic sport had no set number of players and the clothing they wore was irregular. The rules were equally erratic and varied from place to place. The bats were curved and tree stumps were used as wickets. Bowling really was 'bowling' as we know it today, the ball being released underarm, at speed, along the ground. It was a rough pastime and these rural players often suffered unpleasant injuries on unprepared and uneven grass playing surfaces. Protective pads would take another hundred years to make their entrance. However, fundamental changes to this primitive game were not too far away.

In 1744 a gathering of noblemen and gentlemen of the London Cricket Club at the Artillery Ground in the City drew up the first known example of the Laws of Cricket. Remarkably, these laws have stood the test of time; they remain the basis of every amendment and additional law applied to the sport, with an underlying emphasis on the spirit of the game and fair play to all. The wicket started life at 22 yards in length, as it is today, and the ball weighed between 5 and 6 ounces. They settled on 4 balls in the over and the bowler could be 'no-balled' for overstepping the bowling crease. And have a look at the ways in which a batsman could be dismissed:

Laws for ye Strikers, or those that are in

If ye wicket is Bowled, it's Out.

If he strikes, or treads down, or falls himself upon ye Wicket in striking, but not in over running, it's Out.

A stroke or nip over or under his Batt, or upon his hands, but not arms, if ye Ball be held before she touches ye ground, though she be hug'd to the body, it's Out.

If in striking both his feet are over ye popping Crease and his wicket put down, except his Batt is down within, it's Out.

If he runs out of his ground to hinder a catch, it's Out.

If a ball is nipp'd up and he strikes her again, wilfully, before she comes to ye Wicket, it's Out.

If ye Players have cross'd each other, he that runs for ye Wicket that is put down is Out. If they are not cross'd he that returns is Out.

Interestingly, there is no law dictating that a bowler must roll the ball, so, in theory, a pitched overarm delivery would have been legal, although it would have caused a serious ruckus! Further revisions were made through the century and it wasn't until 1774 that a middle stump was introduced and the lbw (leg before wicket) law came into being. In 1788, MCC became the custodian of the Laws and remains the sole authority for drawing up the Code and for all subsequent amendments.

The great game really got going in the eighteenth century. That was when MCC was founded and when the first Code of Rules was published. Women were excluded from so many areas of society, and MCC only admitted the fairer sex in 1998, so how on earth could they have had any connection with cricket 200 years before that great day? Well, they did. The first recorded women's match was between Bramley and Hambledon, near Guildford, in July 1745.

The *Reading Mercury*, a local rag, said of that first fixture:

The greatest cricket match that was played in this part of England was on Friday, the 26th of last month, on Gosden Common, near Guildford, between eleven maids of Bramley and eleven maids of Hambledon, all dressed in white. The Bramley maids had blue ribbons and the Hambledon maids red ribbons on their heads. The Bramley girls got 119 notches and the Hambledon girls 127. There was of bothe sexes the greatest number that ever was seen on such an occasion. The girls bowled, batted, ran and catched as well as most men could do in that game.

Another women's match, two years later, was played on the HAC (Honourable Artillery Company) ground, and aroused so much passion that fighting broke out in the crowd. These Sussex ladies must have shown particular talent as it was regarded as a great honour to play at the 'Artillery Ground'. Our equivalent today would be an invitation to play on the hallowed turf at Lord's. The great and the good would also have been in attendance with the Duchess of Richmond, of Goodwood fame, firmly behind the ladies of Sussex; her husband was a great patron of the game. The Duchess is clearly the 'lady of high rank' referred to in this report in the *Whitehall Evening Post* in 1747: 'They play very well ... being encouraged by a lady of high rank in their neighbourhood, who likes the diversion.'

I suspect this grand fixture may have been motivated by money as the entrance fee was raised from twopence to sixpence, an admission charge that was advertised rather apologetically: 'It is hoped, that the paying sixpence of admission to this match will not be taken amiss the charge thereof amounting to upwards of fourscore pounds.'

A freakish exhibition of female cricketers at such a prestigious ground would have been a huge attraction in those days, coupled with the propensity for heavy gambling. The occasion backfired, however, with rowdy crowd scenes ruining the day, and the *General Advertiser* reported:

> In playing the above match, the company broke in, so that it was impossible for the game to be played out, and some of them being very much frightened, and others hurt, it could not be finished till this morning (14 July) when at nine o'clock they will start to finish the same, hoping the company will be so kind as to indulge them in not walking within the ring, which will not only be a great pleasure to them but a general satisfaction to the whole ... And in the afternoon they will play a second match in the same place, several large sums being depending. The women of the Hills of Sussex will be in orange, and those of the Dales in blue: wickets to be pitched at one o'clock, and begin at two. Tickets to be had at Mr Smith's.

These fixtures inspired serious betting and there were clashes between rival supporters; you can even draw parallels with the football hooliganism of more recent times. The stakes were high for these games, with sums of over £1,000 up for grabs. Incredible, you might think, that a few ladies playing cricket could have caused such mayhem.

In fact, such rowdy crowd scenes were not surprising at all. This was a violent age in which the brutal sports of cockfighting and bare-knuckle boxing were popular entertainment. Even executions were treated as days out for the masses; shops were closed and stands were built for spectators. Cricket would not have a civilising influence on society until the Victorian age.

Village cricket blossomed throughout the eighteenth century in the south of England, with villages such as Gander Down, Bury Common, Felley Green, Upham, Harting and Rogate staging many women's matches. Curiously, these games would often be described as 'Married v Single' or 'Married v Maiden' and were followed by spirited social gatherings. The gambling continued and the victorious teams were awarded splendid prizes. One winning team took home eleven pairs of gloves and pieces of lace, and another was awarded eleven hats – even the umpire did not go home empty-handed. In 1765, a typical game is recounted:

A few days since, a cricket match was played at Upham, Hants, by eleven married against eleven maiden women, for a large plum-cake, a barrel of ale and regale of tea, which was won by the latter. After the diversion the company met and drank tea; they spent the evening together and concluded it with a ball.

During the height of popularity of women's cricket, a legendary series of matches was played by the ladies of the villages of Rogate and Harting which attracted crowds of up to 3,000, a number unheard of at the time. Another article in June 1768 read: 'On Wednesday last the third match at cricket between eleven young women of Harting and eleven of Rogate Common, when the game was won easily by the former: they gained 77 notches ahead. They afforded great diversion to near 3,000 spectators...'

The ladies continued to make their mark in the world of cricket for a good fifty years and frequently appeared in newspapers and magazines. In the latter part of the century the women of Bury played in one of the first six-a-side matches and were so successful that they challenged any eleven in the country to take them on for any sum of money. Their legendary exploits even caught the attention of the Poet Laureate, Robert Southey, who penned a few lines about them in his *Common-place Book*.

There is ample evidence, too, that the ladies of the day threw themselves into all sorts of games which included hitting a ball with a stick or a staff and were skilled at throwing. Not all of them chose to spend their leisure hours stuck at home sewing and gossiping, as Netta Rheinberg points out in her book *Fair Play*: 'but many of the feminine sex rode, hunted, hawked and shot and were vigorous in any other ways open to them.'

John Collet's famous painting from the 1770s, *Miss Wicket and Miss Trigger*, reveals how fashion and sport went hand in hand for the ladies from the higher echelons of society as an acceptable pairing. It has been suggested that 'Miss Wicket' may have been a portrayal of a Miss Burrell, a fine cricketer, since she was known to be a batswoman of great beauty and taste.

The 'Ladies of Fashion' came to the fore, as reported in the *Morning Post* in 1777, when ladies of a more elegant and proper demeanour took to the field of play in a match: 'played in private between the Countess of Derby and some other Ladies of Quality and Fashion, at the Oaks, in Surrey, the rural and enchanting retreat of her ladyship.'

It is in this match that we return to the alluring creature Miss Burrell, who made eighteenth-century headlines and became an enduring celebrity. Her beauty, combined with a dazzling batting performance, ensured her fame, as the *Morning Post* described: 'Elizabeth Ann Burrell ... achieved undying fame [by getting] more notches ... than any Lady in the game, and Diana-like, creating [so] irresistible [an] impression ... that the eighth Duke of Hamilton fell in love with her on the spot and married her before the next cricket season.'

Elizabeth was the fourth daughter of Peter Burrell, who was himself a player of great note for the White Conduit Club. Her marriage to the Duke of Hamilton ended in divorce at her request, and, after his death in 1799, she became the third wife of Henry Cecil, 10th Earl and 1st Marquess of Exeter. The Earl only lasted four more years and she survived him by thirty-three, reaching the end of her own innings at the grand age of eighty in 1837.

It is at this point that we encounter Frederick Sackville, the 3rd Duke of Dorset, supporter of Hambledon Club and fervent admirer of the female form. He preferred his ladies to be athletic, sporty and of the 'outdoor' variety. He witnessed the game at the Oaks and instantly became an ardent fan of the women's game, championing their cause at every opportunity and in spite of any resistance they came up against. He wrote in the *Lady's & Gentleman's Magazine* in 1777:

What is human life but a game of cricket? And if so, why should not the ladies play as well as we?

Methinks I hear some little macaroni youth, some trifling apology for the figure of a man, exclaiming with the greatest vehemence, How can the ladies hurt their delicate hands, and even bring them to blisters, with holding a nasty filthy bat?

How can their sweet delicate fingers bear the jarrings attending the catching of a dirty ball?

Mind not, my dear ladies, the impertinent interrogatories of silly cox-combs, or the dreadful apprehensions of demi-men. Let your sex go on and assert their right to every pursuit that does not debase the mind. Go on, and attach yourselves to the athletic, and by that convince your neighbours the French that you despise their washes, their paint and their pomatons, and that you are now determined to convince all Europe how worthy you are of being considered the wives of plain, generous and native Englishmen!

The Duke was no stranger to scandal. He had had a string of mistresses himself, the latest being the Countess of Derby at the time of this celebrated match. It is difficult to tell whether the Duke is genuinely enticing women to take up the bat or if his tongue is firmly in his cheek as he uses his pen to mock those shocked by his affair with the Countess.

It had previously been thought 'unladylike' for women of a certain class to be associated with anything athletic other than riding and shooting, but such an attitude was gradually changing. The next fifty years brought the ladies of the upper classes into the arena of more vigorous sports and it was deemed acceptable in the eyes of their menfolk. They had spent many an hour observing the chaps on the field of play in places like Hambledon and had absorbed a great deal of knowledge. Now it was their turn to show off their prowess in their own cricket matches.

With the onset of the Industrial Revolution there was a marked shift from the more 'rustic set' of the village games to the games of the 'Ladies of Quality and Fashion' of the 'better' classes. Their less fortunate sisters would have been too worn out to play cricket by long hours labouring at machines, and so matches among the female 'lower orders' had all but disappeared by the 1830s.

Another blow to village cricket came with the increasingly strict Victorian moral attitudes that pervaded the upper echelons of society. As Kathleen E. McCrone explains in her book *Playing the Game*, it was considered 'frivolous, non-improving and morally suspect' for the working classes to participate in any sort of sport. This was the final nail in the coffin for women's cricket at this time and by 1838 we have the last reported female game between two teams of Hampshire haymakers at East Meon. Female participation in cricket, even by the upper classes, remained dormant for the next few decades, as McCrone confirms: 'since even it was discordant with the evolving ideal of helpless and fragile femininity.'

A smattering of women's village games did take place in the late eighteenth century, however, and history was made in Surrey when the first recorded century was made by a woman. Miss S. Norcross notched up 107 runs in a game at Felley Green on 11 July 1788, between eleven Maids of Surrey and eleven Married Ladies of Surrey. This wonderful achievement was described by F. S. Ashley-Cooper in 1902 as among the 'curiosities of batting'.

The emphasis on a post-match shindig and celebrations for the victors is reported in the *Sporting Magazine* in 1792 between girls' teams from Rotherby and Hoby, and it appears to have been even more thrilling than the match itself:

A very curious match of cricket was played by eleven girls of Rotherby, Leics., against an equal number of Hoby, on Thursday on the feast week. The inhabitants of all the villages adjacent were eager spectators of this novel and interesting contest; when after a display of astonishing skill and activity, the palm of victory was obtained by the fair maids of Rotherby. There are about ten houses in Rotherby and near sixty in Hoby; so great a disproportion affords matter of exultation to the honest rustics of the first-named village. The bowlers of the conquering party were immediately placed in a sort of triumphant car, preceded by music and flying streamers and thus conducted home by the youth of Rotherby, amidst the acclamations of a numerous group of pleased spectators.

The artist Thomas Rowlandson, better known for his contribution to the world of scurrilous political caricature, produced a cartoon of a women's cricket match in 1811, between the counties of Hampshire and Surrey. He names it *Cricket Match Extraordinary* and his depiction of the spectacle certainly merits the epithet. His voluptuous ladies have a half-dressed, buxom appearance and give more of an impression of a scene in a brothel than a game of cricket. It would seem that for the majority of the crowd, these types of games were seen as bizarre amusements and it was this farcical ingredient that had the greatest appeal. These women were not being taken seriously.

We do, however, have a rather more conservative report of this match in Pierce Egan's *Book of Sports*:

Extraordinary Female Cricket Match

In a field belonging to Mr Storey, at the back of Newington Green, near Ball's Pond, Middlesex, on Wednesday, October 2, 1811, this singular performance, between the Hampshire and the Surrey Heroines (twenty-two females) commenced at eleven o'clock in the morning. It was made by two noblemen for 500 guineas a side. The performers ... were of all ages and sizes, from fourteen to sixty, the young Hampshire had the colour of true blue, which were pinned in their bonnets, in the shape of the Prince's plume. The Surrey were equally as smart – their colours were blue, surmounted with orange. The latter eleven consisted of Ann Baker (sixty years of age, the best runner and bowler on that side), Ann Taylor, Maria Barfatt, Hannah Higgs, Elizabeth Gale, Hannah Collas, Hannah Bartlett, Maria Cooke, Charlotte Cooke, Elizabeth Stocke, and Mary Fry. The Hampshire eleven were Sarah Luff, Charlotte Pulain, Hannah Parker, Elizabeth Smith, Martha Smith, Mary Woodrow, Nancy Porter, Ann Poulters, Mary Novell, Mary Hislock and Mary Jongan.

Significantly, this was the first time that two counties had played each other instead of the usual teams of villages or 'Maids versus Marrieds'. It was also the first time that the names of the players were listed. The two unnamed noblemen ensured that 'a good time was had by all' following the match with a triumphal march to the Angel at Islington.

The thrilling days and dizzying heights of Newington Green in 1811 were hard to match again but village games were still regular occurrences throughout the 1820s, and in 1823 we have the earliest reported match between two female industrial teams. These women emerged from a Kent paper mill and in this fixture fell, once again, into the Married versus Single. By this time we have an established colour scheme of pink and blue ribbons and frills, with detailed attention being paid to the ladies' attire in reports in the press.

The 'Old' were pitted against the 'Young' at Southborough, where the old birds trounced the young fledglings by 55 runs to win, as the *Kentish Gazette* reported, 'three bottles of gin and three bottles of best gunpowder tea'.

The closest we get to the passion aroused at Newington Green were the excitable crowds drawn to a game at Gander Down, near Alresford, Hampshire, on 28 August 1822, as the following excerpts from the *Annals of Sporting* of the same year reveal: 'carriages, and even wagons, were put in requisition on the occasion', and the antics of the game 'excited such intense interest that the roads were literally crammed and covered with crowds hastening to the expected scene of enjoyment'. With the result, 'the matrons exerted themselves to the utmost ... the agility of the maidens prevailed'.

There appears to be only one report in which the ladies allegedly bring shame upon their sex and behave in a scandalous fashion, as conveyed by an outraged reporter for the *Nottingham Review* on 4 October 1833: 'Last week, at Sileby feast, the women so far forgot themselves as to enter upon a game of cricket, and by their deportment as well as frequent applications to the tankard, they rendered themselves objects such as no husband, brother, parent, or lover could contemplate with any degree of satisfaction.'

Strong stuff, but let us not forget that this was written by a man firmly in the grip of stern pre-Victorian attitudes. The party was nevertheless over, for the time being anyway.

Miss Maud Brand, later Dame Maud Bevan of Glynde Place
Sussex, and Miss Madge Thomas, later Mrs Edward Ellice
of Invergarry, Scotland, playing cricket at Glynde 1885.

# THE VICTORIAN ERA

The Victorians, according to Keith A. P. Sandiford in his *Cricket and the Victorians*, considered cricket to be 'a perfect system of ethics and morals which embodied all that was most noble on the Anglo-Saxon character' and 'an exclusively English creation, unsullied by oriental or European influences'.

So how did women manage to penetrate this very English game?

It wasn't until the late nineteenth century that women re-emerged as a force to be reckoned with in the world of cricket. Their participation in the game, which, for the previous thirty to forty years had been on the wane, was reinvigorated when a number of particularly note-worthy women took the helm. Gone were the days of outlandish women's cricket matches played purely for the amusement of spectators: in came ladies who had a genuine passion for the game. They not only loved playing cricket, but they were a knowledgeable breed and sowed the seeds of a more serious venture into the game.

The cricket women of the 1880s and 1890s burst onto the scene in many places: in schools, colleges, villages, in the great country houses, and in the colonies, and a professional women's cricket team even toured the country. Such games featured in the pages of the satirical magazine *Punch* and in the writings of J. M. Barrie, himself a noted aficionado of the game. Indeed, all of this is set against the background of the fascinating history of women's progress in many fields of endeavour.

It was around this time that women were taking their first steps into professional life and forging their own careers. They were seen in public on tennis courts, even though they were still dressed in the awkward long skirts and sleeves of the day. Ladies took to their bicycles wearing bloomers and shocked the nation. The female talent for sport was, however, at last being noticed. The publication *Modern Society* wrote: 'Batswomen is quite a new expression in cricket parlance. This is essentially, though, an age of muscular Christianity, and its apostles will not be displeased at the latest addition to its lexicography.'

By 1895, *Cricket*, the sport's official journal of the day, reported: 'The New Woman is taking up cricket, evidently with the same energy which has characterised her in other and more important spheres of life.'

Legend has it that the invention of overarm bowling is down to one of those 'new women'. In the early nineteenth century, this action came about purely by chance in a barn in Tonford, near Canterbury, where John Willes and his sister Christina were in the habit of practising. Christina, being a practical girl, discovered it was much more effective to lob the ball at her brother with a round-arm action. The skirts of this period were cumbersome and voluminous and so handicapped her underarm bowling that she had come up with the perfect solution.

John Willes recognised at once the potential and effectiveness of this action and adopted it himself for the rest of his playing days. He was, however, thwarted at every turn and was even no-balled by the umpire at a well-known match at Lord's in 1822, playing for Kent against MCC, whereupon, as Nancy Joy notes in *Maiden Over*, 'He threw down the ball, jumped on his horse and rode away, out of Lord's, declaring he would never play again.'

Willes abandoned his great love from that day on but his endeavours bore fruit when his sister's invention was enshrined in cricketing law six years later. He, however, rather than his sister, is given full credit for this brainchild, in the immortal words engraved on his tombstone: 'He was the first to introduce round-arm bowling in cricket.'

The second lady of note is the most renowned of all cricketing names, Mrs Martha Grace. Her encouragement and influence on her clan of five sons and three daughters knew no bounds. She was, by all accounts, a true and influential cricket lover: a trio of Graces, E. M., G. F. and W. G., playing for England in the first Test in this country against Australia, at The Oval in 1880.

Martha Grace was a regular spectator whenever her sons were playing and spent many a fine afternoon coaching and playing with the children and their dogs in the orchard of the family home in Gloucestershire. Her knowledge of cricket was faultless and she could match any man in conversation on the finer points of the game. An imposing presence at matches, her booming voice could often be heard making astute comments about a player's prowess or, more usually, lack thereof. One story describes W. G. being caught at square leg for a low score following a half-hearted heave, where his mother was heard to berate him: 'Willie, Willie, haven't I told you over and over again how to play that ball?'

We owe a great deal to this 'Mother of Cricket' who thrust her son W. G. to the very top of the game and gave England a true sporting legend.

In 1887, in an attempt to regulate the rather haphazard female involvement in cricket, the White Heather Club was formed. Members of the club comprised ladies of aristocratic birth who bore all sorts of lofty titles. They were of independent means and their position in society, both socially and politically, would have carried great weight. The copper-plate inscription on the cover of their extravagant leather scorebook reveals the prominence of its original members:

The Club was started at Nun Appleton, Yorkshire, in the summer of 1887 by the following eight ladies: Hon. M. Brassey, Hon. B. Brassey, Lady Milner, Lady Idina Nevill, Lady Henry Nevill, Hon. M. Lawrence, Miss Chandos Pole and Miss Street.

It was thought advisable to start a Club in consequence of the large amount of cricket at Normanhurst, Glynde and Eridge.

Normanhurst was the country seat of the Brassey family and Eridge the seat of the Nevills, and these founding members from the nobility spread their enthusiasm to their families and friends and ensured the club remained an elite group within high society. Mrs B. Stacy, secretary of White Heather for a long period, the Duchess of Richmond and Mrs Leveson-Gower were all members of the Brassey family. Lady Camden, Lady Cantelupe and her sisters all belonged to the Nevill clan.

These ladies of means were exquisitely turned out on the field of play with pink, white and green splashed across their silk ties, boaters and the braid on their blazers. Whatever the standard of play, they must have been a sight to behold for any spectator.

The club prospered, growing from a modest eight members to an impressive fifty by 1891 in only four years, and continued to flourish until its eventual demise in the 1950s. This bold move into a sacred male domain proved there was a demand out there and thus the foundations for women's cricket were laid.

We cannot continue without mentioning the White Heather's most lauded member, Miss Lucy Ridsdale. In 1892 she averaged 62 with the bat and (almost as notably) went on to marry the future Prime Minister, Stanley Baldwin. In conversation with the captain of the Australian touring team, Mr H. L. Collins, in 1926, recorded by the White Heather Club Scorebook, she confided how she conquered her nerves at the crease: 'One strange thing about my batting was that I was frightfully nervous when I went in. But, when I became engaged to Mr Baldwin, I lost all my nervousness and it was in the year I was married, that I made my best batting average, 62 runs for the season.'

In the same year, during the General Strike, Lady Baldwin invited the White Heather Club to No.10 Downing Street for their Annual General Meeting. Not only did she bring much needed publicity to the crusade of women's cricket, but her devotion to the game was unsurpassed. She didn't miss a Varsity game at Lord's for forty years. Her passion spills out on to the page in a letter she wrote to the editor of *Women's Cricket*, a magazine produced by the Women's Cricket Association, in 1930: 'Cricket is to me summer, and summer cricket ... The crack of bat against ball amid the humming and buzzing of summer sounds is still to me the note of pure joy that raises haunting memories of friends and happy days. The one game in the world for me.'

In direct contrast to the high-born ladies of the White Heather Club, a professional women's enterprise material-ised in 1890. For the first and the last time in the history of women's cricket, two professional ladies' cricket teams were formed and the Original English Lady Cricketers was born. A handful of entrepreneurial gentlemen from the 'English Cricket and Athletic Association' wanted to cash in on the growing popularity of women's cricket and felt there was commercial profit to be made. Advertisements were placed in various London newspapers and the players were specially selected. An announcement was made in all the leading publications of the day:

With the object of proving the suitability of the National Game as a pastime for the fair sex in preference to Lawn Tennis and other less scientific games, the English Cricket and Athletic Association Ltd have organised two complete elevens of female players under the title of the Original English Lady Cricketers.

The *James Lillywhite's Cricketers' Annual* for 1890 agreed with this sentiment and published a photograph of the team and a short article:

As an exercise, cricket is probably not so severe as lawn tennis and it is certainly not so dangerous as hunting or skating; and if, therefore, the outcome of the present movement is to induce ladies more generally to play cricket, we shall consider that a good result has been attained.

These players emerged from the lower middle classes and assurances were given by the Association that they were 'enterprising and decent' young women. They were properly coached by professional county players George and Alec Hearne of Kent, Maurice Read of Surrey and Fred Bowley of Worcestershire, and embarked on a series of exhibition matches at major grounds around the country. This novel collection of women attracted large, gawping crowds, with 15,000 spectators at the Public Athletic Ground in Liverpool, where the curious art of overarm bowling was on display. The write-up in the *Liverpool Post* stated that the crowd 'came to scoff and remained to praise'.

In order to protect their reputations, however, women were forbidden from using their real names and were chaperoned wherever they went by a 'matron'. The teams were named the Red XI and the Blue XI and the Association wrote that they would be 'elegantly and appropriately attired' by Lillywhite, Frowd and Company. There was talk of a tour to Australia but the players' parents would not give their approval and in the end the whole enterprise collapsed when their managers (all men) did a runner with the profits.

The stark social contrast in cricket between the 'professional' of the lower orders, who was remunerated for his sport, and the 'amateur' of noble stock (who was not) was now apparent in the women's game. The lofty lady amateurs, who rather looked down their noses at the professionals, the Original English Lady Cricketers, were apparently overheard saying, 'They might be original and English, but they were neither ladies nor cricketers.' Those in the amateur camp viewed the whole operation as a stunt and even W. G. Grace remarked that the venture was a failure. Not all views, however, were unfavourable. The *Illustrated London News* was more supportive with its description of the OELCs as 'a social novelty illustrative of the disputed notion that women can, may and will do everything quite as well as men'.

The *Buckinghamshire Examiner* of Chesham was even complimentary of the ladies' clothing on the field, stating that their 'dress has been designed with all possible regard to freedom of movement, and is by no means unbecoming'.

Other publications chipped in with positive comments and the only stark omission in the press was made by the pamphlet *Cricket*, which completely ignored the existence of the Original English Lady Cricketers. On the whole, though, the creation of the OELCs was not hailed as a success. These ladies were viewed with an ingrained chauvinist suspicion by the men who mattered.

The idea of professional lady cricketers now appeared to be dead and buried, but in fact other amateur ladies' clubs sprang up and enjoyed a short-lived existence. Although not in the same league as the blue-blooded White Heather Club, these clubs, including the Dragonflies or Derbyshire Ladies, the Clifton Ladies and Severn Valley, showed true grit and talent on the field of play. W. G.'s daughter in particular, Miss Bessie Grace, who played for the Clifton Ladies, appeared to be cut from the same cloth as her father and was renowned for smashing the ball all over the ground.

Now and then, women's heroics with the willow and leather would creep into the public eye. Another Miss Grace, no relation to W. G.'s clan, hit 217 facing only men's bowling at Burton Joyce, Nottinghamshire, in 1887, and a Miss Wright knocked up mammoth scores of 106 and 142 at Sidmouth. The most notable heroine to make the front pages was a Miss Mabel Bryant, who scored a staggering 224 not out in only two and a quarter hours for the Visitors to Eastbourne versus the Residents in 1901. She put the icing on the cake by taking five wickets in each innings. One male spectator observed:

I saw her make five consecutive fours to the boundary, three cuts between point and slip, an off-drive and a leg hit. She also obtained five wickets in each innings. On one occasion, in bowling down a wicket, she smashed a stump, and carried away a portion of it as a memento!

Surprisingly, in 1893 we stumble upon one Richard Daft, who, in *Kings of Cricket*, recommended a lighter ball and bat and a shorter pitch for the ladies' game, in order that 'the game might be played to advantage' and 'more wrist and elbow work would be seen in their batting'. Despite the fact that Mr Daft was unconvinced by women's cricket he was still prepared to make these suggestions and, in this respect, was a man ahead of his time. In 1897, Alfred Reader, a manufacturer of cricket balls, took note of Daft's ideas and produced a 5oz ball, tailor-made for the ladies' fair hands. His fatal mistake was to give it a feminine touch by colouring it in a clear blue. This colour, of course, proved impractical, as it invariably disappeared into the green grass and the blue sky and the players were forced to abandon it as lost. It wasn't until 1929 that the weight of the ball was finally standardised and it took another three decades for the ladies to exchange their cumbersome lumps of willow for lighter and smaller models.

The Victorian age was an important one for schoolboy and schoolgirl cricket in England. The boys' Victorian public schools looked upon cricket almost as a new religion, since it was considered to epitomise all the qualities to which all young chaps of the day should aspire. The first girls' public schools were not established until the 1860s and it was felt in some quarters that physical sports would be just as beneficial to girls as it was to their brothers. Girls, too, could learn from cricket's true sporting values and it should not be just a male preserve. In *Playing the Game*, Kathleen McCrone explains the beliefs held by the reformers of female education: 'Games-playing, they insisted, would improve girls' health and child-bearing potential, counteract mental overstrain, stimulate study and aid discipline. Above all it would impart valuable moral qualities, like honour, loyalty, determination, resourcefulness and courage, that had previously been ascribed exclusively to males.'

Fresh-faced female teachers who had been drawn to sports such as cricket at their colleges were keen to pass on their passion to their girls. By the end of the nineteenth century, cricket was very much a part of the sports curriculum of many of the major girls' public schools, as well as women's universities and physical training colleges. Well-known schools such as Roedean, Wycombe Abbey, Clifton Ladies and the Royal School, Bath, embraced the game with zeal. The girls' public school phenomenon was driving full steam ahead, as McCrone notes, and they hoped to achieve for their charges 'male academic standards and the constraints of ladylike behaviour'.

Roedean, in Brighton, was particularly focused on providing an 'Eton for girls' and by 1897 it fielded eight cricket teams from its one hundred pupils. The three sisters, Penelope, Millicent and Dorothy Lawrence, who ran the school at the time, put sport at the top of their agenda and were keen for their girls to get out in the open air for two to three hours a day for exercise and games. The school magazine was littered with batting and bowling averages and even referred to its players as 'men'! The townsfolk of Brighton, however, who were still in the grip of unrelenting moral attitudes, disapproved of these girls gallivanting about playing sport. One old girl, Ruth Mackan, quoted in Judy Moore's *Memories of Roedean*, recalls that they were 'so shocked by the girls showing their ankles that they used to draw their curtains as they passed'.

The team photographs of the Roedean 1st XI in 1888 and 1891 reveal the austerity of their clothing, consisting of long-sleeved heavy blouses and full-length gathered skirts; it was a miracle they could move at all. Things improved slightly by 1900, however, when lighter material was introduced and skirts were lifted to the calves.

Despite the enthusiasm for girls' cricket during their school years, it was generally not encouraged once they had completed their education. Jane Dove, headmistress of Wycombe Abbey, appreciated that cricket was an invaluable experience for her girls, but we can see from her writings on *Occupations for Girls* that cricket would not be taken seriously beyond their school years. She felt that cricket would allow 'a girl to play with her young brothers and sisters in the holidays and to take an intelligent interest in her brothers' pursuits'.

If she went on to the back foot when describing the ineptitude of girls' cricket in her *Cultivation of the Body* – 'I am well aware that most real cricketers would laugh at the idea of girls attempting the game' – she actually championed the game for her girls, saying that the courtesy, strength and determination demanded by the sport were exactly the attributes her young ladies would need to break out from the four walls of their home and be the female pioneers of their age.

Cricket for the women and girls of the Victorian age was confined largely to the middle classes. Before the birth of the White Heather Club in 1887, the only cricket played outside the school walls took a rather frivolous form, as at informal garden parties, hidden away on the lawns of country houses. It was a fashionable and private affair where mixed matches were often staged and gave the ladies a marvellous opportunity to fraternise with the opposite sex, which, no doubt, was the main objective of the day. Indeed, as expressed in *A Punch History of Manners and Modes 1841–1949*, ladies were encouraged to, 'Get yourself bowled first ball so that you can spend the rest of the time at tea and flirtation with the five fielders who have been withdrawn from the field to give the ladies a chance.'

This patronising and mocking view of ladies' cricket is further affirmed by the chaps playing left-handed with broomsticks and poking fun at the ladies' ignorance of the laws, lack of concentration, useless and absurd fielding, poor running and wild throwing. There was not an ounce of seriousness in these games but no one seemed to mind as titillation ruled the day.

The all-women games of the 1870s appeared to support the misapprehension that these ladies had no ability and were generally ignorant as far as sport was concerned.

In 1873, Mr Punch makes this comment on 'Pretty Batswoman', revealing the deep male suspicion of women playing 'male' sports:

> Irrepressible Woman is again in the field. 'Ladies' Cricket' is advertised, to be followed, there is every reason to apprehend, by Ladies' Fives, Ladies' Football, Ladies' Golf etc. … It is all over with men. They had better make up their minds to rest contented with croquet, and afternoon tea, and sewing machines, and perhaps an occasional game at drawing-room billiards.

Male supporters, or in fact any supporters, of women's cricket during this period were few and far between and were tarnished with elements of prejudice. It was felt that women's physical and mental make-up would never allow them to play as well as the men, yet they defended the belief that women were capable of playing technically correctly and to a reasonable standard. These proponents recognised that cricket was a game of grace, balance and quick reactions that didn't have to depend on brute force and would therefore suit the female nerves and delicate muscles. They even argued that cricket was less physically damaging than other sports and was unlikely to harm the female moral character as much as flirtation!

Unfortunately, despite growing support, women's cricket was still regarded with disapproval. On the whole, women cricketers were ridiculed and their games treated as freak shows. Even the medical world got involved, warning that the structure of the female shoulder blade would prevent women from bowling overarm properly. They were advised to stop trespassing on men's games and to stick to what they were best at: staying behind the scenes, supporting their menfolk and adorning the crowd of spectators with their fashion and beauty.

This nonsensical approach is highlighted by a discussion held at a meeting of the Birmingham Teachers' Association in 1881, in which the subject of women playing cricket was raised and presently taken up as a story by the *Birmingham Daily Mail*. The meeting came up with the absurd argument that women's femininity and physical and moral health were at stake when playing men's sports, which:

> ... though harmless in themselves, are unsuitable for girls. Cricket is essentially a masculine game. It can never be played properly in petticoats ... If cricket is to become a recognised game at ladies' schools, we can expect football to be introduced, and then single-stick, and no doubt the dear damsels will finish up with boxing ... the girls of the future will be horney-handed, wide-shouldered, deep-voiced ... and with biceps like a blacksmith's ... Let our women remain women instead of entering their insane physical rivalry with men. They can get all the exercise that is necessary for them in games far more suitable to their strength, and far more in accordance with feminine tastes. The line must be drawn somewhere, and it might just as well be drawn this side of those violent athletic pursuits which have hitherto been considered fit only for strong and active young men.

Some women, however, did manage to break out of these chains of prejudice for a brief time and cobbled together a game in a suburb of Birmingham. However, their efforts were soon quashed by a local newspaper belittling their game as a 'pretty little burlesque', noting that if this travesty were allowed to continue it would have dire consequences as, 'the man of the future will be the stocking-mender, and the children's nurse'.

Lacrosse and hockey were less of a threat because the men's and women's games were recognised as separate entities, while netball was seen as the ultimate team game as it was a non-contact sport and was only played by girls and so did not pose a problem to the purity of men's sports. Cricket, on the other hand, was in a class of its own as the number one national sport, with Lord's and The Oval as its headquarters. The idea of women encroaching on this noble sport was abhorrent to most men, threatening as it did their (as they saw it) God-given right to and dominance of athletic power and privilege. Women's cricket challenged these independent spheres of men's and women's sports and Victorian public opinion was not about to be uprooted. The message was simple: women belonged at home and had no business interfering in the sacred domain of manly games. In *Playing the Game*, Kathleen McCrone sums up the prevailing attitudes of the era:

> Just as female university students were regarded as threats to the integrity of the 'learned craft' and the survival of the race, just as a female electorate was portrayed as the thin edge of the wedge that would lead to female judges,

generals and bishops, so female hockey players and cricketers were presented as degraders of sport and precursors of
the intolerable – female boxers and footballers.

Women's exploration into the field of sports was critical to
the women's rights movement and inspired the campaign
for female higher education. Women's colleges started to
appear in the 1860s and their focus was not only on improving the intellect but also the encouragement of games and
exercise as a relief from academia. The predominant view
of the time was that women were simply too weak to cope
with higher education. These reformers of female education
had a real battle on their hands as the medical profession
firmly upheld this belief in the 1870s. As highlighted in *Sex
in Education* by Edward H. Clarke (1873), a number of
eminent doctors felt that a university education was 'out
of harmony with the rhythmical periodicity of the female
organisation' and could result in underdeveloped sex
organs which would be 'no less than a crime against God
and humanity'.

In other words, women pursuing a university education
would be drained of all energy, causing untold damage
and would therefore be of grave danger to the future of the
human race!

The pioneering heads of women's colleges were aware of
the scrutiny under which their students found themselves,
and so were particularly careful that all sport and exercise
should be concealed from prying eyes. They didn't want to
risk the house of cards collapsing, as it were, as a result of
accusations of unladylike behaviour, so games of cricket

and other sports were discreetly carried out away from the public gaze. Conversely, they also needed to prove their critics wrong in the suggestion that women were too weak to handle higher education. Women on the sports field revealed their true capabilities and were made stronger for academic success. These women's university colleges eventually developed into 'centres of athletic pioneering as well as intellectual advancement', as referred to in McCrone's *The Lady Blue*.

In the early nineteenth century, cricket and country pursuits had been the dominant pastimes of male Oxbridge undergraduates, and games became more structured by the end of the century thanks to the birth of organised sports in public schools. Oxford and Cambridge were the first universities to establish successful women's colleges and thus set the example for other universities to follow. Women's collegiate sport at Cambridge had humble origins, beginning when Emily Davies opened Hitchin College in Hertfordshire in 1869 with initially only five female undergraduates. In *Playing the Game*, McCrone describes Davies's mission to concentrate on both physical and mental development and how she encouraged 'students to take long country walks, properly chaperoned of course, and to play croquet, fives and a crude form of cricket in the seclusion of the college garden'.

In 1873, Hitchin College transferred to Girton on the fringes of Cambridge and it was here that, by 1893, a cricket club was formed. Girton College's records reveal that their cricket was fairly light-hearted but they did play matches on the hockey ground, and later on the golf course, between students and sometimes against lecturers. Fixtures against other universities did not feature at Cambridge until after 1914. The club thrived during this era and, according to the *Girton Review*, even went as far as engaging a professional coach with the 'highest testimonials'.

The young ladies at Oxford were not as fortunate as their Cambridge counterparts, however, as cricket was banned in the mid-1880s and the spoilsports at Somerville College would not give permission to the ladies of Lady Margaret Hall to use their grounds to play cricket. Later, in 1901, the college logbook reveals that the female students made a second attempt at approaching the powers that be and asked the hall council at LMH if 'they might be allowed to play cricket with the High School Games Club or any other Ladies Clubs in Oxford'.

The council turned them down, and even the principal of Lady Margaret Hall, Miss Elizabeth Wordsworth, was against it, considering the game far too masculine for *her* young ladies. Sadly, cricket did not feature in any of the Oxford women's halls until 1914. St Hilda's and the Home Students' Society produced a glimmer of hope, however, by allowing individual women to play with local clubs.

This lack of activity at Oxford was in stark contrast to the flourishing ladies' cricket clubs at Cambridge and this, no doubt, had a lot to do with the numbers of female students at each university. The numbers of students at Newnham and Girton at Cambridge had swollen to approximately 165 in each college by 1913, while Oxford housed about 47 at St Hilda's and 110 at Somerville.

Both universities produced an array of talented and athletic all-round sportswomen, among them the future explorer, archaeologist and Middle East expert Gertrude Bell at Lady Margaret Hall, who swam, rowed, fenced, walked and played tennis during her time there in the 1880s. Others included Violet Cooper of Girton, another wonderwoman, who played golf, tennis, cricket, hockey and cycled from 1906 to 1909, as well as the four Martin-Leake sisters, all of whom were great tennis players at Girton between 1882 and 1899. Importantly, these ladies of distinction and other enthusiasts of sport would sometimes go into teaching and so pass on their passion to their pupils in schools and this had an acute effect on the development of girls' cricket.

This was a time of great significance for women who felt stirred to push the boundaries of Victorian preconceptions and seek the freedom previously denied them to explore intellectual pursuits and sports. The university environment, especially, provided an ideal breeding ground for these ladies to pursue their ambitions. Cricket, among other sports, went a long way to proving to the world that women were not weak and feeble creatures but possessed great self-determination as well as physical and mental power.

We should not, however, neglect what was happening to the men's game alongside the slow development of the women's. This was an important time of transformation, with changes in equipment and technique, standardisation of rules, the formation of an organised system of local and county teams and the introduction of club cricket. Cricket had become the first major organised sport in England with Marylebone Cricket Club at Lord's as its headquarters. It represented 'manliness, self-dominion and modesty' and the 'gentlemen's code of honour' and was considered the best sport for athleticism and manly virtues. No wonder women met with such resistance when trying to prove themselves at this game in the face of such male fervour.

Women cricketers on Victor Park cricket ground, St Lucia, 1928.

# THE EMPIRE

From its small beginnings in rural southern England, cricket spread across the world and Test cricket is now played in more than ten countries. Wherever the British Army and Royal Navy went, cricket went with them, and when the forces left, cricket often stayed behind. By the early 1800s cricket was making its mark around the world: at St Anne's Cricket Club in Barbados; in Sydney, Australia; British prisoners of war in Argentina managed to cobble together games; the first recorded century was amassed in Calcutta, India, in 1806 by R. Vansittart representing 'Rest of Calcutta' versus 'Old Etonians'; in 1808 officers in Cape Town took to the field and even Boston in the United States had its own cricket club.

Europe, too, saw its fair share of action when officers of the Brigade of Guards warmed up for the Battle of Waterloo in June 1815 by playing a match near Brussels with the Duke of Wellington among the spectators. A club in Naples was formed, drawing French and Neapolitan members. And, further afield, evidence of leather on willow could be found in Ontario, South Carolina, Valparaiso (Chile) and Tasmania.

We have to start with the men who spread the gospel of cricket overseas in the eighteenth and nineteenth centuries, as the women, at this stage, had little to do with it. Women's social constraints did not permit them to travel and so there was no way they could have been a part of this pioneering movement.

The tentacles of cricket reached far and wide, initially via the major sea routes and then advancing inland through rivers, roads or railways. Once the military had established itself on new territory they clubbed together with the settlers and traders to promote the game. This pattern emerged in countries such as Australia, New Zealand, India and South Africa and almost all the other British Commonwealth countries.

Exclusivity went hand in hand with this British invention and the local and indigenous populations were seldom involved in the game. The British formed their own separate clubs of military and civilian members with their own distinctions of social class and occupation. For their part, not all occupied countries were overjoyed by this imperial game played by their masters and (even if they were able to) locals were sometimes discouraged from joining in. Such an example is the Gaelic Athletic Association in Ireland, which from the 1880s actually forbade any person to join if they had taken up cricket. Hurling and Gaelic football were encouraged as the national sports and this ban was not lifted until as late as 1970.

The British, however, needed administrators and so cricket was established in local schools and the grass roots were put in place. In this way, cricket found a permanent home in the Caribbean, India, Sri Lanka, Pakistan, Fiji and South Africa. By the late nineteenth century the British were playing matches against local sides and playing cricket was recognised as an effective way of climbing the social ladder. Wealthy patrons emerged from these local communities, among them the maharajas in India, many of whom fell in love with the game and competed with each other to get the best players for their teams.

In other parts of the world, the adoption of cricket was more straightforward, where the local population absorbed this initially bizarre British game first from observing it and then replicating it for themselves. This was probably what happened with the Greeks in Corfu in the 1830s and the Parsees in Bombay. A particularly obscure example of the game is the 'cricket traditionnel' of the South Pacific with its teams of fifteen to twenty players that has mainly been adopted by women. More of this peculiarity later. An example today would be the Afghans discovering and taking up cricket in the refugee camps in Pakistan. A snippet from John Major's book *More Than a Game* speculates on the reasons behind the Parsees' passion for cricket:

No one knows why the Parsees took to cricket with such enthusiasm. A cynical interpretation would be that they saw the game as an effective way to steal a march on the haughty Hindus by ingratiating themselves with the ruling

British. Early matches must have been an ungainly spectacle, as the Parsees' traditional tunic shirts impeded batting and bowling alike; but whatever their motivation, they became devoted to the game.

The British did not successfully manage to establish cricket throughout the Empire. If a strong foundation was not laid by the locals, the game disappeared once the British moved on. This happened in Shanghai, China, and Montevideo, Uruguay. East Africa suffered, too. Once independence was granted to much of East Africa in the 1960s and the British and Asians departed, cricket survived only in the cities.

Women's cricket could only flourish where the men's game had established itself in the heart of the sporting culture. There was little financial support and men were mostly unenthusiastic, but cricket was introduced to girls' private schools and clubs were formed in some countries. Where there were small numbers of female cricketers it was an arduous task to get anything off the ground. Until recently, due to male prejudice towards the women's game and possessiveness of the 'male preserve', female cricket struggled to survive in the Indian subcontinent, South Africa and the West Indies. Cricket for women overseas is a relatively new phenomenon which has only developed significantly throughout the last few decades. The one exception is the Netherlands; there it comes up trumps with women's cricket taking guard as early as the 1930s.

This is not to say that nothing happened before the 1930s. Pockets of activity would occasionally appear around the globe as early as the nineteenth century when, in 1894, a women's league was formed in southern Tasmania. The driving force behind this was a young schoolteacher named Lily Poulett-Harris. Lily founded the Oyster Cove team and went on to become its captain. She was quite a character, it seems, and when she died *The Mercury* (Hobart, 27 August 1897) gave her an affectionate send-off:

> Quite a gloom was cast over our neighbourhood when it became generally known that Miss Lily Poulett-Harris had succumbed to her painful illness on the night of Sunday the 15th inst. Miss Lily was of a mirthful and happy disposition, ever endeavouring to make those with whom she came in contact – and those not a few – cheerful and happy also. She was a great admirer of athletic exercises, firmly believing that it was very necessary to develop the physical as well as the mental part of our nature. Cricket had her warm sympathy and support, and when the ladies in the district formed a club – the first, I believe, in the colonies – Miss Lily was unanimously elected captain, and she was remarkably successful in piloting her team to many a victory. I might also add that she was a good horsewoman and cyclist. Fear, it is said, was a thing unknown to her. When scholastic duties permitted her to visit her home at the Cliffs she was always welcomed by young and old alike. One old man tells how she stopped and obliged by cutting up some tobacco for him, and by many of such little acts and kindnesses Miss Lily endeared herself to the whole community. Much sympathy is felt for the bereaved family.

On the mainland, the Australian ladies were not far behind in founding the Victorian Women's Cricket Association in 1905 and the Australian Women's Cricket Council in 1931. In fact, they were ahead of the game in organising themselves – the English ladies did not form any sort of an Association until 1926. It is generally thought that the first recorded women's cricket match in Australia was played in April 1874 at Bendigo, Victoria, although a lady player of the time, Mrs E. J. Cordner, describes a game that took place in 1855 between two mining towns in New South Wales. This may well have been a lucrative match for these ladies as it was the habit in those days for miners to reward players with a sovereign for each run scored.

New Zealand's indigenous women were keen to take part in the early days and, in 1886, eleven Marahua girls challenged eleven Riwaka girls to a match, as quoted in the *Motueka Herald*, 'anytime they like. Dinner and Dance provided. All Welcome.'

Sadly, any further references to women participating in the game in New Zealand for the next fifty years are thin on the ground, although there was a kindling of interest in Picton and Waipawa in the 1890s. Women's hockey appears to attract more attention during this period and the women played their debut match in Nelson in 1897 when a team of local Maori girls took on their European sisters. This inspired the formation of New Zealand's first women's hockey club, the Wakatu Maori Ladies' Club, and Nelson College for Girls soon followed. It is refreshing to see that social inhibitions seem to have been brushed aside as these indigenous women played side by side with their colonial mistresses.

Although no scorecards can be found as evidence, eleven English ladies made a trip to Cork in 1888 to challenge the ladies of Ireland. The Irish damsels had already been victorious over a men's team, winning by one wicket, in a game at Strabane, County Tyrone, in 1884.

The beginnings of women's cricket in South Africa were short-lived because of low numbers but evidence does exist of games played in Cape Province during the 1880s and 1890s. It was mainly the African and coloured women who took to the game rather than their European sisters.

These early stirrings into cricket are sporadic and never really prospered, lasting only a few years. Most of these countries had to wait a long time for its revival.

## Australia

The game at Bendigo, Victoria, in 1874 attracted the attention of the press, although the write-up in the *Melbourne Argus* focused on the frills and thrills of the ladies' fashion rather than the game itself. Despite this, these ladies were determined to take it seriously and underwent special training for this charity match. The women of Victoria and New South Wales had caught the bug and, although there are no records, there must surely have been some matches played over the next few years. They would also have witnessed, heard or read about the male cricketing heroes of the day by this time since by 1886 the men had played England in Australia five times. Such names as Fred Spofforth, Percy McDonnell, George Palmer and Charles Bannerman would have filled them with desire to return to the field. The next surviving scorecard is that of a match played at Sydney, in

March 1886, where two scratch teams battled it out. The well-known publication *Cricket* had this to say about it:

> There were considerably over a thousand persons at the Sydney Association Cricket Ground on Monday afternoon, the majority of those present being ladies ... The two elevens were called Siroccos and Fernleas respectively, the former wearing a cardinal and blue costume, while the latter were attired in black and gold. Play began at 2 p.m. and continued until half-past six o'clock. The Burwood band played selections during the afternoon. Miss L. Gregory captained the wearers of the yellow and black, while her sister Miss Nellie led on the amazons of the scarlet and blue...

Still the obsession with their clothing! Nellie, Lily and Alice Gregory, all of whom played in this match, were the daughters of E. J. Gregory, who played for Australia in the first Test match in 1877, and their brother Syd was also a great player. It was clearly in the blood and this cricket clan were an impressive influence on the game. *Cricket*, at last, refers to the actual game and adds:

> The palm for all-round cricket must be awarded to Miss R. Deane, who displayed such excellence in all departments of the game that many players in our senior clubs would envy. The misses Gregory and Englestoff also shone to great advantage, evincing a thorough knowledge of the intricacies of the game. The wicket-keepers Miss L. Gregory and Miss Jeffreys were very smart behind the sticks, and at times fairly brought down the house with dexterity. The fielding

was generally good, but the ladies with several exceptions could not throw. Their bowling was mostly round-arm, the obsolete grubber being resorted to only by one bowler.

Miss Rosalie Deane went on to greater feats when she knocked up a century in each innings, scoring 195 and 104, at a match in Sydney in 1891 for the Intercolonial Ladies' Club versus the Sydney Club. Once again, this match attracted much publicity and Miss Deane was awarded the unprecedented honour of being the first female to be recorded in *Wisden Cricketers' Almanack*. This was a woman impossible to ignore.

The terrific successes of the 1880s helped the game take off and by 1900 women's cricket had been played, and was blossoming, in Victoria, Tasmania and New South Wales. New women's club sides were popping up all over the place and were starting to employ professional coaches. In 1897 a Victorian team, the Seafoam Ladies, went as far as training for five weeks with John (Jack) McCarthy Blackham, considered the world's best wicketkeeper at the time. He, incidentally, had kept wicket in the first ever Test match in 1877 against England and in the legendary Ashes Test of 1882 at The Oval, when Australia beat England and prompted the mock obituary from the *Sporting Times* lamenting the death of English cricket. It was no surprise that the Seafoam Ladies convincingly beat the Forget-me-Nots at Warrnambool in the Friendly Societies Park. Undeterred by their defeat, the Forget-me-Nots took on the chaps in the shape of a Victoria parliamentary men's team in 1898. The men failed to reach the ladies' total and gold medals were dished out to the top scorers, Miss Ethel Dallimore, with nineteen notches, and Mr W. A. Wall, with eleven.

Once the Victorian WCA was founded in 1905, they had twenty-one clubs signed up by the end of the year and competitions were organised for an oak and silver shield. Mrs Harry Trott, wife of the former Australian Test captain, led one of these sides and she was influential in introducing competitive matches to the Association. They needed some heavy hitters on their side. She wrote of her support for cricket: 'My brothers all played county cricket, and my sisters also played, so I just lived in a cricket atmosphere. My grandfather was a good wicketkeeper in England, and a nephew, Harry Paternoster, organised the Men's Country Week Cricket Association and was secretary for years.'

Another weighty addition to the board was the first president of the Victorian WCA, Miss Vida Goldstein, who was also the first woman in the British Empire to become a parliamentary candidate. She remained president from its inception in 1905 until 1912 and attended one VWCA meeting in its first year. Her presence at this meeting was a firm expression of her support for this official body of women in a sport that had previously been considered a male-only domain. The struggle for women's liberation was high on her agenda and she was certain to pick up a good number of votes from this female membership.

The inaugural interstate match was played on 17 March 1906 when a chaperoned team of ladies from Tasmania visited Victoria and were beaten by six wickets at Collingwood. The tradition of raising money for worthy causes continued and a donation was made to the 'Bushfire Relief Fund'. More interstate matches followed over the next few years and these generous ladies made further donations to testimonials for Victor Trumper, Jack Blackham and Monty Noble. Sadly, a few years down the line, this generosity was not reciprocated when the VWCA were in dire financial need and appealed to the chaps at the Victorian Cricket Association for help. The mean-minded VCA gave them a derisory two guineas which even the press commented 'was hardly enough to purchase a lady's hat'.

New South Wales made their debut tour to Victoria in 1906 and played six matches. The entertainment was lavish, with outings to the Opera House and Theatre Royal, as the VWCA was well connected through its august patrons and families such as the Paternosters.

The cricket in those days was particularly hard work and runs were difficult to come by on unpredictable, uncovered pitches. Boundaries had yet to be introduced and everything had to be run unless the ball hit a tree, but these were hearty and robust ladies and a number of tough centuries were made. On one occasion, Mrs Cutter, Victoria's president, made a hundred in each innings – a remarkable achievement.

In the light of all these cricketing heroics, it is all the more tragic that the women's game in Australia suffered such a rapid decline after 1910. The reasons for this are mixed: the petty chauvinism of the time would have discouraged girls from taking up the game; many ladies married and drifted away from playing; funds were short and, with the threat of war on the horizon, it was a disturbing time. Women's cricket had thus dwindled to almost nothing, with only five clubs functioning by 1914, including the Coldstream, Brunswick and Tartan Clubs. Once the war broke out, it put the kibosh on cricket altogether.

After the war the women had to start from scratch and they were swiftly out of the blocks. New associations were born all over Australia: in Victoria (1923), New South Wales (1926), Queensland (1930), South Australia (1934) and Western Australia (1935). For the first time, a national HQ was founded to give all these Associations a structure in the form of the Australian Women's Cricket Council (1931).

The pre-war cricket heroines of the 1900s were not going to be left behind, and in the same year they clubbed together to create the Pioneers Association so the young could have the support of these fine ladies.

The 1930s was a golden age for men's and women's cricket and the women tended to mirror the successes of the men, enthusing girls to take up the game. The Australian Women's Cricket Council wasted no time in organising an interstate tournament in 1931 and this provided the perfect format for selectors to pick their national team. The England ladies arrived on Australian shores for their tour of 1934/5 and the Australian public sat up and took note. Women were now playing cricket seriously, they were given more support and standards shot up. This tour was hailed an all-round success, even financially, and Australia then sailed over to England in 1937 for their first international victory. More detail will be devoted to these historic tours in the next chapter, where the games and players jump out of the page with spine-tingling performances, fierce rivalries and colourful off-field antics...

Once again, however, a world war interrupted all cricketing progress. The women's game all but fizzled out, apart from the true lady stalwarts, in both England and Australia, who were determined to carry on playing on Saturday afternoons through the summer months. The war was not going to ruin their cricket.

The Second World War brought the American Armed Forces to Australia and with them came softball. The US Army Nursing Service played it to let off steam and the game was an instant hit with the locals, spreading like wildfire all over Australia and New Zealand. Cricketers tended to play this game in the winter to keep themselves in shape for the cricket season but some players were lost to softball permanently.

The international game was resumed once more in 1948 when Australia toured New Zealand, playing one Test match and seven other games. The Kiwis were well and truly outplayed, losing all the matches with the exception of one draw. Australia were on a roll and were victorious over England in three Test series in the late 1940s and early 1950s. The legendary Betty Wilson contributed a lot to these victories and more ink will be devoted to her in the chapter entitled 'Superstars'.

Plenty of young talent was now coming up through the ranks, and by 1957 these girls were ready for the international arena, where their youthful vigour would blend successfully with the experience of one or two of the old guard. They proved themselves against New Zealand by winning the Test by an innings and 88 runs. This young, thrusting team inspired hundreds of schoolgirls to play the game and the arrival of the England team in 1958 only added to their passion. The 1960s brought a handful of drawn matches with one series defeat in England at The Oval in 1963.

Despite the exuberance of youth, lack of funds and low public interest caused the women's game, once again, to decline. However, a handful of dedicated players and administrators managed to keep women's cricket afloat and, through their efforts in schools and junior clubs, the 1970s saw the women's game soar in popularity once more.

One such devoted woman was Mary Allitt (now Loy) who captained the side for the 1963 tour to England. Since then she has been showered with awards for her lifelong commitment to the game. At the age of eighty-one, in June 2007 she was awarded the Medal of the Order of Australia (OAM) in the Queen's Birthday Honours, to add to her Australian Sports Medal and Centenary Medal. The team attracted sponsors with the help of the first Women's World Cup in 1973, and the number of tours increased both overseas and at home. Things were looking up. Their healthy finances allowed them to invest in more suitable training and coaching, which paid off in spades with world domination by the 1980s. These queens of cricket reigned over the globe up until the early twenty-first century, winning 80 per cent of their one-day international games and taking home the World Cup six times out of the ten competitions played so far. Belinda Clark, the golden girl of the 1990s, captained Australia and received the great honour of being selected as one of *Wisden Australia*'s five Cricketers of the Year in 1999. England has exacted its revenge since then, but more of that later...

The men and women of Australia ruled the world of cricket in both Test matches and one-day internationals throughout the 1990s and early 2000s. Their highly competitive and aggressive approach to the game took them all the way to the top and, annoyingly, they stayed there for a very long time.

## India

Once again, the British colonialists did a grand job of importing cricket to foreign shores in the late 1700s. In 1792, the Calcutta Cricket Club was formed for Europeans only. The Parsees were soon drawn to the game and established their own Indian cricket club in Bombay in 1848. By 1877 the Parsees had beaten the Europeans, which must have been a humiliating experience for the inventors of the game! On the back of this success they toured England but only managed to win one game. In 1928, India felt ready to play Test cricket and so formalised themselves into the Board of Control of Cricket in India to show the ICC how serious they were. They made their Test debut against England in 1932 and the rest is history.

The women, however, had a longer wait on their hands, with the Women's Cricket Association of India being formed as late as 1973, despite India owning more than 250 years of cricket history as a man's sport. The girls had been confined to knockabout games with their fathers and brothers but the late 1960s and early 1970s saw the more talented among them break through into boys' club cricket. Even though only a handful of girls' schools played cricket and money and facilities were lacking, women's cricket gained great momentum in the 1970s thanks to widespread enthusiasm for the sport.

The roots of domestic women's cricket in India were firmly planted in Delhi in the 1950s with plenty of tournaments taking place; one local newspaper described these cricketing girls as 'visible music between the wickets'.

By the 1960s women's cricket was catching on in Madras, Bombay, Delhi and Calcutta. The Albees Club in Bombay, founded in 1969, was an impressive women's club with prestigious and fruitful connections to the men's game. Various Indian Test players, such as Vijay Merchant and Polly Umrigar, supported the Albees, and one of their best players, Nutan Gavaskar, was sister of the cricket megastar Sunil Gavaskar. Tina Lalo, the first Albees wicketkeeper, was a cousin of Farokh Engineer who kept wicket for India and Lancashire in the sixties and seventies.

The year 1975 brought the first touring women's cricket team to India at the invitation of the Indian WCA's secretary, Mahendra Sharma. The Australian U-25 team's visit was a raging success in India with an astonishing 35,000 spectators turning up to some games, outdoing the crowds for men's games back in Australia. Cecilia Wilson, of New South Wales, led her troops 8,000 miles round India, playing in the international stadiums of Poona, Delhi and Calcutta. All three Tests were drawn and the India women put up a decent fight despite their lack of experience.

Some first-rate talent emerged from these Tests in the shape of Shanta Rangaswamy, one of seven sisters, a superb bat and medium-pace bowler and without doubt India's number one all-rounder at that time. Diana Eduljee from Bombay was loved by the crowds for her left-arm spin and aggressive batting and, despite losing four front teeth to the game, she remained dedicated to the cause. Probably the youngest ever wicketkeeper in a Test side at that time, the sixteen-year-old Fowzieh Khalili kept tidily behind the stumps and was a useful bat.

Their matches were given ball-by-ball commentary on the radio and some were even televised, an honour never before bestowed upon the players from Australia and New Zealand.

The country was by now firmly behind them and the Indian WCA even paid the airfares for the New Zealand girls to tour there in 1976. This was unheard of in women's cricket and showed just how far the women's game had come in such a short time. The Indian women were in an enviable position, attracting huge crowds and receiving media attention, and this just accelerated the interest in women's cricket in India. Mrs Gandhi, the then Prime Minister, was a firm supporter and met with members of the Delhi WCA and the Australian and Indian women's Test teams. Mrs Gandhi perceived cricket as an opportunity for women to broaden their horizons beyond the four walls of their homes. The *Times of India* expressed the public's devotion for the women's game, despite the slightly condescending language used: 'The matches between Bombay and Maharashtra attracted large crowds. The women in particular sat there in the hot sun for hours watching their species in action for the first time on the cricket field, playing the game not with a tennis ball but in the complete outfit and style.'

In 1978 the Indian women had impressed the International Women's Cricket Council enough to be asked to host the Women's World Cup, and England, Australia, India and New Zealand battled it out, with Australia ultimately taking home the silverware.

India has always been Asia's strongest team, having won every Asia Cup tournament and reached the final of the World Cup in South Africa in 2005. They are considered to be one of the top four women's cricket teams in the world. They are ahead of the game in that they are the first and only country to employ professional female players in companies which have their own cricket clubs. Diana Edulji worked and played for the railways and became the first Indian woman to be awarded a benefit match. India also has great wealth on its side. The Board of Control for Cricket in India is the world's richest and this allows them generous funding and high-profile exposure. The Women's Cricket Association of India merged with the BCCI in 2006.

India have produced the fastest female bowler in the world in Jhulan Goswani. She whips the ball down at speeds of up to 120kph, which is approximately 75mph – enough to knock the stuffing out of most mortals!

## Ireland
In Ireland, both men's and women's cricket have had a rocky past, mirroring, if you like, the country's turbulent

political history. The sport was dealt its first blow by Oliver Cromwell in 1656 when, in true Puritan spirit, he issued an edict to destroy all bats and balls in Dublin. It is likely that Cromwell's Commissioners had confused hurling with cricket since all evidence points to the English introducing cricket to Ireland in the late eighteenth century. It was mainly played by the British military and the Irish aristocracy and was not embraced by the rural population of Ireland.

Women's cricket in Ireland had a promising start in the late nineteenth century and a match recorded in 1884 reveals Claudine Humphreys and her women's XI beating an all-men's XI by one wicket at Strabane. In the 1890s the first known all-women's match was played in Cork. The top girls' schools in Ireland, particularly Sion Hill, Holy Faith and Glasnevin and Glengara Park took to the game, and an Irish schoolgirls' XI was selected to play against a touring English schoolgirls' team in 1908. These spurts of activity, however, were purely local and it would be a long time before cricket became a national sport for women.

The First World War put a stop to all cricket and all went quiet on the women's front until the late 1930s. The Leinster Women's Cricket Union was established and a thriving evening league competition was set up for six clubs in Dublin. Women were playing in other parts of Ireland, too, although not in any organised competitions.

Men's cricket in Ireland, before and after the Second World War, was in a good position, with international matches against visitors from Scotland, the West Indies, India and Australia throughout the 1920s and 1930s. At the same time, however, the women's game was falling apart and outside influences played a large part in its decline. The Second World War and a shortage of petrol led to the closure of many clubs. Leinster, the hub of Irish women's cricket, was left with only Trinity College, Clontarf and the Railway Union clubs. Male attitudes did not help either and the Trinity women were forbidden to play on the men's ground at College Park and were banished to Dartry, a suburb of Dublin.

Northern Ireland was in on the act, too, and the Northern Women's Cricket Union of Ireland was formed in 1948, with Lady Brooke at the helm as its first president and five member clubs in Belfast, Holywood, Lisburn, Muckamore and Newtownards. These ladies played regularly up until 1957, by which time most of the clubs had folded.

By the 1970s, women's cricket had crumbled to almost nothing with only Ulster hanging on to a few games, but by 1972 even Ulster had fallen away thanks to sectarian troubles. The women's game did not lie dormant for long, however, and with the men's game attracting much more public attention, the women were stirred into action. By 1980, Leinster Women's Cricket Union had re-emerged from the ashes and a new league involving seven clubs was set in motion. Cricket made a comeback in the leading girls' schools and the areas of Ulster and Munster underwent a revival.

Once the Irish Women's Cricket Union was formed in 1982, the national team made their first outing to foreign fields, competing in a quadrangular tournament in the Netherlands. The Irish ladies were leaving the men behind, with their debut in the international arena a good nineteen years before the chaps played their first one-day international. They played a three-match series of ODIs against a tough Australian team in 1987 in Australia and, not surprisingly, were rolled over by the best team in the world at that time. However, they were still invited to take part in their first World Cup in Australia in 1988. There were no great successes in the 1980s but they had gained international status and were on the up.

The 1990s brought more World Cups and European Championships and they finished runners-up to England in the latter competition on three occasions. The best they managed in the World Cup was to reach the quarter-finals against New Zealand in 1997.

Their first Test match took place in 2000 in Dublin against a weak Pakistan side, and Ireland despatched them by an innings within two days. They also polished off the ODI series with a 4–0 whitewash. Confidence was high and in 2001 they followed through by winning the European Championships, beating England for the first and only time. Two years later and 2003 brought the amalgamation of the Irish WCU into the Irish Cricket Union with the hope of more funding, sponsorship and coaching. These resources did not appear to be forthcoming at first and there was a concern that the women would be sidelined by the success of the men's game. Their domestic presence has improved, however, with the Irish senior women's team competing in the Leinster men's league and achieving promotion a number of times. While Dublin remains the hub of women's cricket in Ireland, Northern Ireland has enjoyed a resurgence in popularity and cricket is being played in an increasing number of schools.

The Joyce family deserve a special mention as they have produced a prodigious number of cricketing internationals. Starting with the girls, Isobel Joyce is a current Ireland player and she and her twin sister Cecelia form an almost preternatural batting partnership for their country. This dynasty extends to her brothers Dominic, Ed and Gus, who have all turned out for Ireland; Ed Joyce is particularly distinguished, having also played for England and Middlesex. 'Izzy' took over the captaincy in 2008 when Heather Whelan had to stand down due to falling pregnant.

Ireland has also been competing in the ECB LV Women's County Championships since 2009, which has helped to attract sponsorship. Major international sides such as Australia, India and South Africa have toured Ireland over the last few years, putting them firmly on the map of world cricket. They have yet to overcome Australia, New Zealand, India or South Africa, but their record against the Netherlands, Denmark, Scotland and Pakistan is something of which they can be proud. Ireland qualified for both the 2005 and 2010 World Cups and has played in five of these tournaments in their short history.

## The Netherlands

Cricket was a popular sport for the Dutch community in Rome in the 1790s so it is reasonable to assume the game had a firm foundation in the Netherlands by the late eighteenth century. In the latter part of the nineteenth century, a number of exclusive cricket clubs existed with restricted membership, and they often adopted their own quirky rules which did not resemble those of MCC – for example, one club felt it unfair to score runs behind the wicket!

The Dutch women eventually became part of the scene in the 1930s. Women's hockey had its roots in Haarlem and it was a natural transition for them to play cricket in the summer months. So, the first women's cricket club was born there and a handful of clubs followed around the country. These original three or four clubs got together and formed the Nederlandse Dames Cricket Bond in 1934 and a league was quickly set up. The male cricketers did nothing to help the cause but the WCA in England were eager to assist in improving standards. In 1937, the Australian Women's team tagged on a brief visit to the Netherlands following their tour of England, where they played on matting wickets as the soil was considered too sandy for cricket. It took the Nederlandse Cricket Bond another seventeen years to persuade the Australian men's side to pay them a visit! The Dutch ladies were inevitably pummelled by the Australians but they did gain valuable experience.

The women's game made a comeback after the Second World War but did not expand beyond its 1930s legacy until the 1980s. The German occupation in 1940 caused cricket to grind to a halt with no access to equipment and this sorry state of affairs remained until 1947. The Dutch ladies continued to enjoy a harmonious relationship with the English ladies during the 1950s and 1960s, however, and cricket clubs from both countries sailed across the water for tours. The English WCA sent their first official team to Holland in 1959 to celebrate the Silver Jubilee of the Nederlandse

Dames Cricket Bond, and a dynamic young Rachael Heyhoe went with them, making her debut WCA tour.

In the spirit of ambition, the Dutch women's association even published their own cricket magazine, *De Cricketster*, for a short time in the 1960s, but interest in the game dwindled and by the end of the decade new players were few and far between.

The women's domestic league got going again in 1976 and in 1984 the Dutch women made their international debut against New Zealand in an ODI. Once again, the women were outshining the men on the international stage, and it would take another twelve years before the chaps played their first ODI. They lost to New Zealand by 67 runs and in 1987 they lost to Ireland in their first and only two-innings match.

The Dutch ladies have not had an easy ride, hampered by little encouragement from the men's national body, lack of facilities and match practice and a limited number of players. Success has been hard to come by, although they have infrequently triumphed over Denmark, Japan, Pakistan and Scotland.

They finished in last place in their first World Cup in 1988 and third in the European Championship the following year. Unfortunately, the 1993 World Cup was a disappointment, too, resulting in another last-place position. The 1990s ushered in a decade of globe-trotting for the Dutch team when they won their first, and to date only, ODI series against Sri Lanka in 1997 (2–1). That same year they avoided the familiar wooden spoon in the World Cup by getting as far as the quarter-finals where they lost to

Australia. There were a couple of trips to Germany to play ODIs against Denmark in 1997 and 1998, and another long-haul tour to Sri Lanka in 1999 where they lost the ODI series, being whitewashed 5–0.

Overseas travel continued with the World Cup in New Zealand in 2000 where they were once again in the doldrums, finishing in last place. This was to be their final appearance in the World Cup as they failed to qualify for the 2005 tournament. In 2001 they bravely ventured to Pakistan for a marathon seven-match ODI series, with the home side taking the first four matches and sealing the series. Although the Netherlands won the last three games, it was too late for them to salvage anything. An ODI series in New Zealand (2002) and Ireland (2006) ended in more heavy defeats. There was a ray of sunshine for the Dutch team in 2006 when the ICC announced that the top ten women's teams in the world would have Test and ODI status and, unlike their male counterparts, the Dutch women made the grade. They hung on to their status by reaching the semi-final of the Women's Cricket World Cup Qualifier in 2008 but later lost it when they finished seventh in the qualifying tournament in Bangladesh in 2011.

They played their first Test match when South Africa toured the Netherlands in 2007 but, as so often, were outclassed and lost by 159 runs.

On the domestic front, the Netherlands has two thriving women's leagues with a 45-over and 35-over format. In 2009 they embraced Twenty20 cricket and the national team won the European title in both the T20 and 50-over competitions in 2011.

## New Zealand

Immigrants from England were intent on promoting Britishness throughout their burgeoning settlements from 1830 to 1880. Although the non-Maori population of New Zealand only amounted to roughly 10,000 people, while the total population – Lieutenant Governor William Hobson's 'one people' – numbered between 100,000 and 200,000, cricket had already made its presence felt among the indigenous folk. New Zealand became part of the British Empire in 1840 but before then the missionaries had played their part in spreading the gospel of cricket. Charles Darwin noted in *The Voyage of the Beagle* a game of cricket played between young Maoris and the children of missionaries in 1835 at Waimate in the Bay of Islands.

Except for that earlier reference to the eleven Marahua girls challenging eleven Riwaka girls to a game of cricket in 1886, all went quiet for the next fifty years, as austere Victorian values dominated society and the powers that be in the all-male cricket administration had a strong aversion to women playing the game.

The earliest evidence of a women's match in New Zealand was in 1867 at Greytown, but interest was short-lived with only the odd game referred to in Waikato in the 1880s and in Auckland in the 1890s. Only the elite girls' public schools such as the colleges of Mount Eden, Auckland and Wellington included the game in their school life. An isolated group of ladies were brave enough to play the game before the First World War but they were persistently mocked and dismissed as unrefined.

The women's game began to make gradual progress in the 1920s and 1930s as more girls' secondary schools took it up, particularly in Auckland, where cricket was also adopted at a teacher training college. Fixtures were regularly organised between schools, culminating in the Auckland Women's Cricket Association in 1928. Other areas were slower to embrace the game but, by 1932, Wellington, Otago and Canterbury included cricket in their girls' schools' sports curricula and had established women's associations.

Their finest hour came with the arrival of the England women's team in 1935 where they showed a scornful public that they could play with skill and finesse and should be taken seriously. The New Zealand Women's Cricket Council had been formed in 1934, revealing to the world that the NZ Women's cricket team, aka the 'White Ferns', meant business and wanted to attract other cricketing nations. Their inaugural Test match against the mighty English was played at Christchurch: they were duly thrashed by an innings and 337 runs. This was no surprise because of their very limited experience but it nonetheless led to an invitation in 1938 from the New South Wales Women's Cricket Board to visit Australia to celebrate the 150th anniversary of the founding of the state. This was the start of something special, creating a healthy rivalry between the two sides, and more tours followed.

The Second World War once again put a stop to cricket (and to so much else) for a number of years, and the ladies did not resume international matches until 1948, when Australia pitched up in Wellington for the first of eight matches and took no prisoners. They beat the New Zealand women in the only Test match by an innings and 102 runs with Una Paisley, the queen of the cut shot, playing a match-winning innings of 108 for Australia. The England women quickly followed, touring New Zealand in early 1949, and these intense few months did wonders for the Kiwi ladies, lifting their standard and converting their rather flimsy batting attack into sterner stuff.

In stark contrast to the pre-war lack of co-operation from their male counterparts, the New Zealand government awarded its women's team a £1,000 grant towards their 1954 tour of England. The ladies still had to reach a target of £5,000 to cover their travel costs, uniforms and equipment, however, and they pulled out all the stops to achieve this, with one particularly enterprising Kiwi being singled out in *Fair Play*: 'One member, Peg Batty, a double hockey and cricket international, entered as Queen in the Auckland Carnival to augment her finances, and the New Zealand Rugby League gave permission to the Auckland women to take a collection at the third Test at Carlaw Park.'

New Zealand had a cracking time of it in England, winning ten of the nineteen matches and losing only one of the three Test matches, at Headingley, where they lost by six wickets. Yorkshiremen probably won't want to hear this, but it is believed that women were actually the first to grace the pitch here in the late nineteenth century! The woman of the series for New Zealand was undoubtedly Phyl Blackler who hit two centuries, topping the batting averages and achieving the second best bowling figures.

The English weather was not kind to them and, thanks to this, a lack of publicity and sparse crowds, the tour was not a financial success. But it was a hit for the Kiwis in every other way – they gained the taste of victory to whet their appetites and important bonds were made with the English.

The New Zealand ladies were now getting noticed and the Prime Minister, the Hon. Walter Nash, together with a crowd of cricket celebrities, turned up to a Women's Cricket Week at Wellington to celebrate the Silver Jubilee of the Women's Cricket Council in 1959. This was not the first bit of good fortune in relation to a political figure, for Dame Elizabeth Knox Gilmer, daughter of the charismatic Right Hon. Richard Seddon, a former Prime Minister, was an ardent supporter of women's causes and a cricket fan, and she gave a send-off lunch for the New Zealand women's team before they sailed for New South Wales in 1938. She even paid the hotel bill for the England women when they stayed in Wellington in 1935. A good egg by all accounts.

The 1966 team to England still contained the veteran star Phyl Blackler, who was to make her last international outing. Once again, the great British weather severely hampered the tour and two matches were abandoned altogether. The Kiwis, however, played competently with a strong bowling attack. The performance of Jocelyn Burley with the new ball was a great asset in particular and they managed to draw all three Tests, despite having to face an indestructible Heyhoe Flint at the helm for the first time. Jos Burley still holds the record in her country for 'best innings bowling' with 7 for 41 in the final Test of that series at The Oval.

The Kevin Rothman Sports Foundation and the New Zealand Sports Council did much to help the cause of schoolgirl and youth cricket at this time, and with satisfying results. The investment and hard work paid off during England's tour of New Zealand in 1968/9. They drew the first Test at Wellington, playing with patience and concentration, with New Zealand's captain, Patricia McKelvey, hitting 155 not out in a marathon five and a half hours, breaking the record, by a mile, for the highest score by an NZ female player at that time. The previous record had been held by wicketkeeper Beverley Brentnall, who scored 84 not out going in at number eight at Edgbaston in 1966. In that same series, Bev Brentnall conceded only one bye in three matches. Her magic with the gloves cast a spell over the Test at Auckland in the 1968/9 tour when she nabbed five batsmen – catching three and stumping two in just one innings. The England keeper Shirley Hodges was not to be outdone and followed suit with three stumpings and two catches in New Zealand's second innings. Between them the pair bagged twelve of the thirty-three wickets in the match. England won the series 2–0 but this did not take the gloss off Judi Doull's composed innings of 103 in just over four hours at Christchurch.

On the subject of wicketkeepers, we should not forget the tough and athletic Ingrid Jagersma who twice dismissed the England captain, Jan Southgate, in England in 1984 with two breathtaking one-handed diving catches. She was named Player of the Series and was right up there with the best wicketkeepers in the world. Another wicketkeeping feat held by a New Zealander is Sarah Illingworth's six dismissals with the gloves in a 1993 World Cup match, together with India's keeper, Venkatacher Kalpana, who achieved exactly the same thing on the same day. These two ladies beat the men to it with this new record in ODI cricket.

The 1971/2 season was a golden one for New Zealand, kicking off with their first ever Test match win against Australia at St Kilda, Victoria. Pat Carrick claimed 6 for 29 and New Zealand won by an impressive 143 runs. In a more stationary position, Pat Carrick owns the distinction of being the first woman to umpire a first-class men's match in 1988. In the same month of the Australia Test, New Zealand jetted off to South Africa to clinch a three-match Test series 1–0. McKelvey and Doull were once again prolific run scorers and McKelvey amassed her second century at Cape Town. Their victory came in Durban, beating South Africa by 188 runs.

New Zealand continued to play Test cricket against Australia, England and India up until 1996 but they have yet to return to the glory days of 1971/2, having not won a Test since. Kirsty Flavell achieved a double whammy at Scarborough in 1996 when she broke Patricia McKelvey's highest individual innings score of 155 not out with a remarkable 204 against England, and was also the first woman to score a double century in a women's Test match. Apart from one Test match against England in 2004 that was drawn, the New Zealand women appear to have abandoned the Test arena to focus on ODIs and the Twenty20 format.

The first Women's World Cup one-day competition was held in England in 1973 and New Zealand sent a team off to do battle with the hosts, Australia, Trinidad & Tobago, Jamaica, an International XI and a Young England XI. The English skies delivered their usual downpour and the first match between New Zealand and Jamaica at Kew Green was completely washed out. Rain, however, is not always the enemy as it assisted New Zealand to a surprise win over England at Exmouth. New Zealand finished in third place and held that position for the next three World Cups. Their greatest achievement was when they won the 2000 World Cup in their own country with a tantalising final against Australia. The crowd were on the edge of their seats as New Zealand, led by Emily Drumm, narrowly beat the Aussies by four runs.

New Zealand has played 257 ODIs to date, winning 128 and losing 121 with two tied and six no result. Their first tie in an ODI was against England in the 1982 World Cup – the first tie ever in any ODI for men or women. Strangely, they went on to tie against Australia later on in the same competition. A high point of their ODI history came when New Zealand pulverised Pakistan, scoring a tremendous 455 for 5 at Hagley Oval, Christchurch. This still remains the highest team score in ODIs.

The New Zealand ladies were given a well-earned boost when the NZ men's cricket board took over the women's game in 1992. New Zealand was the first country to do this and set a precedent for the rest of the world to follow. The women's game improved in leaps and bounds from this union, climaxing with their World Cup victory in 2000.

More recently, international cricket has become immersed in the Twenty20 phenomenon and women's cricket has embraced this wholeheartedly. The ladies, once again, beat the men to the record books when the England women took on the New Zealand women at Hove in 2004 in the first international Twenty20 match. The White Ferns are now a force to be reckoned with in Twenty20 cricket, having reached the finals of both the 2009 and 2010 ICC World Cups. They showed their grit and competitive spirit by scoring the highest total of the 2012 Twenty20 World Cup in Sri Lanka against South Africa with 151 for 5, but were later knocked out in the semis by the favourites, England.

New Zealand finished fourth in the 2013 Women's World Cup in India and their captain, Suzie Bates, was named Player of the Tournament as the leading run scorer. The 25-year-old went on the rampage with the bat over the eighteen-day campaign with a resplendent century and three half-centuries in only seven innings. This dual inter-national athlete is also a star of the basketball court and is a Beijing 2008 Olympian. She has now taken the tough decision to focus solely on cricket, recognising that playing two sports in parallel at the highest level has taken its toll on her mentally and physically. She justified her decision saying, 'I reached a stage where I didn't feel I was doing either [game] justice. I was inconsistent with my cricket and not as good at basketball as I could have been.'

## Pakistan

It didn't take Pakistan long after the Partition of India in 1947 to be accepted into Test cricket by the Imperial Cricket Conference in July 1952. Since then, the Pakistani men's team has ridden an emotional roller-coaster from the dizzy heights of World Cup glory to lows of diabolical and astonishing defeats. The Pakistan Cricket Board set up a national first-class championship in 1953 but this has been racked by inconsistency in policy by the PCB and in reality is a shambles.

The men's international history is chequered, to say the least. It had promising beginnings but was later marred by endless infighting between the Board and the government over selection and bickering between the members of the PCB. Imran Khan came to the rescue in the 1980s as an inspirational captain and led his team to World Cup triumph in 1992. More recently, the men's game in Pakistan has been held back by security issues and tarred with allegations and convictions in match-fixing.

Religious fundamentalism attempted to dish out its doom and gloom over women's cricket when two sisters from Karachi introduced the concept in 1996. The government immediately clamped down on them by banning women from playing sports in public and refused them permission to play India in 1997. They were even met with court cases and death threats. Shaiza and Sharmeen Khan are a determined duo, having been brought up on a diet of cricket with their brothers in the 1980s and continuing their passion at boarding school in England. Their university years were filled with cricket at Leeds and they also turned out for Middlesex women. They wanted to continue to play the game they loved in their own country and so founded the Pakistan Women's Cricket Control Association in the mid-1990s.

Despite the predictable opposition from the miserable

mullahs and tiresome men in general within the PCB and the government, these women got a national team together and played against New Zealand and Australia in 1997. They lost all three ODIs but they had made it to the international stage and were ultimately invited to play in the Women's World Cup in India in the same year. Unfortunately, they lost all their games and finished last. Their disappointing result had something to do with what appears to be an enduring Pakistani characteristic, 'squabbling' in the ranks. A group of women players took umbrage with these so-called 'super-rich sisters', who were sponsored by their father and his carpet business, and formed a rival organisation, the Pakistan Women's Cricket Association, and even this split into two factions. All of this had a detrimental effect on the selection process for this World Cup and a weakened side was sent off to India.

The in-house fighting continues but these warring women have managed to get their act together on the domestic front with six teams competing annually for the Fatima Jinnah Trophy. A positive step has been made at grass-roots level as cricket is now a compulsory sport in all girls' secondary schools in Pakistan.

The noughties brought more good news when the ban on the women's team playing international matches at home was lifted. An invitation was swiftly despatched to the Netherlands to come and tour Pakistan in 2001/2. Miraculously, the PCB allowed the women to play in the National Stadium in Karachi and promised television coverage for the first time. They failed to follow through with the coverage and sponsorship, however, and the Khan sisters' hugely generous father had to pick up the tab. In the end it was all worthwhile as the Pakistan women had their first international victory and won the seven-match ODI series 4–3. By this stage Pakistan had reached the standard of Scotland, the West Indies and the Dutch, an impressive leap after such a troubled past.

Pakistan faced their first Test-playing nation, the West Indies, in 2004 and despite losing the one-day series 2–5 they drew the all-important Test match. This inaugural Test was a huge success with new records aplenty for the Pakistan women: highest team score of 426 for 7 declared, highest batting score of 242 for Kiran Baluch and best bowling figures of 7 for 59 for Shaiza Khan, who went on to take the best bowling figures in a match with a grand total of 13 wickets for 226 runs. All of these records still hold. This match was staged in the National Stadium and was a tremendous confidence boost for the Pakistan ladies.

Two more records belong to Pakistan's Sajjida Shah who, at the tender age of twelve, played against Ireland and became the youngest player to appear in international cricket. And she doesn't stop here ... Her remarkable off-spin bamboozled the Japanese women in Amsterdam in 2003 and she cleaned up with the best bowling figures in a one-day international, taking seven wickets for a mere four runs, with 8–5–4–7.

The ICC have been consistent in their support of the Pakistan women and insisted that men's and women's cricket be unified under one governing body to force the PCB to recognise the work of the PWCCA. As a result, the PCB reluctantly took on the responsibility to run women's cricket in 2005 but it remains to be seen whether they will do more than the bare minimum to promote the women's game. The PCB has behaved woefully in the past and attitudes were not going to change overnight.

Since then, the Pakistan women have hosted the 2005/6 Women's Asia Cup, which featured the first match between the Indian and Pakistani women's teams. Their form took a dip and they lost all their games. However, they qualified for the 2009 World Cup and finished in sixth place, having entered the competition ranked eighth in the world. They continued in this positive vein by winning the gold medal at the 2010 Asia Games with an emphatic 10-wicket victory over Bangladesh. The Pakistan captain, Sana Mir, stressed that their 'historic Asian Games gold medal was welcome good news for a country where the men's game is mired in scandal'. She went on, 'the way the women's team has played and the way they have handled themselves on and off the field is really wonderful for Pakistanis living in Pakistan and abroad'.

She credited their success and freedom to play cricket to powerful female role models such as the late former Prime Minister, Benazir Bhutto. Even the current PM (a man), Asif Zardari, congratulated the team, describing the women's gold medal as 'a gift to the nation riding on a series of crises'.

The Pakistan women, as with all cricket-playing nations, have embraced the Twenty20 game with enthusiasm and have appeared in the ICC World Twenty20 tournaments.

More recently, attitudes towards women's cricket in Pakistan has softened considerably and cricket is seen as a form of progress for women's rights. The PCB has come a long way in recognising the development in women's cricket, as is evident in their announcement in August 2012 that they would issue seventeen women players with Central Contracts. The women really have proved themselves in all kinds of adversity and they now enjoy travelling the world playing all formats of the game.

## South Africa

The origins of women's cricket in South Africa seem to lie in Cape Province in the late 1880s and 1890s. Interestingly, it was the black and coloured women who took to the game rather than the European maidens. These African ladies had established a handful of cricket clubs in Kimberley by 1909; and in Port Elizabeth, even earlier, in 1884, a women's club was formed as a spin-off from the ladies' croquet club. Another club appeared in Pietersburg in the Transvaal in 1894. In Andre Odendaal's *A Short History of Women's Cricket in South Africa*, Harry Cadwallader provides us with an insight into lady cricketers in 1888 when he observed 'a number of the fair sex indulging in practice ... and they showed they are possessed of not inconsiderable talent...'

In 1889, male students from the South African College were given an absurd handicap in a match against a Ladies XI whereby they all played left-handed and batted with the handle of a pick-axe. The ladies made short work of these unnecessarily tame conditions and won by an innings. The numbers involved in women's cricket at this time were scanty and most of the clubs that did exist only managed to survive a few years. The 1920s, however, saw a revival of the women's game thanks to a Mrs Winifred

Kingswell who got women's cricket going again in a more official capacity. In 1922 she formed the Peninsula Girls' School Cricket Union and was the first president. When the Peninsula Ladies' Cricket Club was founded twelve years later they became affiliated with the WCA in England, since they did not have a national governing body at the time. These Peninsula ladies ditched the patronising traditional handicaps given to the male players in the past and played regularly against the chaps on an equal footing, and with some success.

Sadly, such initiative was confined to the Western Province and little progress was made to develop the women's game nationally by either whites or blacks. Predictably, cricket was further hampered by the outbreak of war, and it wasn't until 1947 that these enthusiasts were able to take guard again. Transvaal joined Western Province as an official association and in the same year a thirteen-year-old schoolgirl, Eileen Hurly, scored the first century in a women's league match in Johannesburg. More of Eileen later. Seven other provinces followed suit by 1950 and formed associations, and an inter-provincial competition was established. At this stage only white cricketers were playing, and this still pertained when the South African and Rhodesian Women's Cricket Association was established in 1952.

True to form, male cricket organisations were unwilling to help out the women's game, but enlightened individuals such as Eric Rowan, a former South African opening batsman, Pat Goulding and Harry H. Winrow did offer their support and sat on the panel of national selectors for women's cricket.

In 1953 Eileen Hurly was back dazzling the crowds with another century, this time 106 not out, for Southern Transvaal, and her performance was matched by the bowling of Sheila Nefdt (soon to be captain), who took an outstanding double hat-trick in Cape Town for Western Province in the same year.

South Africa was now ready for the international scene and in 1960/61 England arrived to do battle. It was a busy match schedule with nine other fixtures in addition to the four Test matches. Now, along with England, Australia and New Zealand, South Africa was the fourth women's Test-playing nation. Their first Test venue was St George's Park, Port Elizabeth, a historic ground which had seen the first men's Test match played in 1889. Eileen Hurly distinguished herself by scoring an unbeaten 96 for South Africa and the match ended in a draw. The press were enthralled by the women's performance in this first Test: 'Two thousand spectators, mainly men, loudly applauded some excellent fielding and throwing by the English girls and some classic batting by South Africa's middle batsmen at St George's Park.'

In the second Test, South Africa clung on to draw at The Wanderers in Johannesburg, when England posted a colossal score of 351 for 6 in their first innings. England stole the show at Durban, however, clinching the third Test by 8 wickets, thanks mainly to a glorious innings of 126 by Helen Sharpe, the England captain from Middlesex. The South Africans had their time in the sun, too, when all-rounder Jean McNaughton gave a marvellous performance with the ball, ending up with figures of 6 for 39 in 19 overs in England's first innings of 269 for 8 declared.

Newlands, nestling at the foot of Table Mountain in Cape Town, was the next port of call. South Africa's Lorna Ward, from Port Elizabeth, came of age when she took 5 for 18 in 14 overs with her seam-up pace bowling, restricting England to 223 all out. Left-hander Yvonne van Mentz then wowed the crowds by becoming the first woman in South Africa to score a Test century with a composed 105 not out during South Africa's first innings of 266 for 8 declared. And she managed all this without wearing batting gloves! The match was drawn and England went home with a 1–0 series victory.

South Africa had gained invaluable experience against England and had proved themselves in international cricket. Eric Rowan expressed his pride in their achievements and in the way they handled themselves on the field: 'There's a lot we men could learn from the way women play cricket. They get on with the game, play it for the fun of it and can't be bothered with gamesmanship. I think they look fine in skirts and from a spectator's point of view are well worth watching.'

Inevitably, it was only a matter of time before apartheid in South African brought sporting isolation to the country. Legal racial segregation had been introduced in 1948 and banned all non-whites (defined as 'black', 'coloured' or 'Indian') from playing Test cricket for South Africa. Unbelievably, this 'legislation' also applied to all overseas teams wishing to tour South Africa. This whole sorry state of affairs blew up over the Basil D'Oliveira episode. D'Oliveira, a 'Cape Coloured', caused quite a stir when he emigrated to England in 1960. As a talented all-rounder who had captained South Africa's national non-white cricket team, he was selected to play for England's Test side to face the West Indies in 1966. A prolific run scorer, he was one of the *Wisden* Cricketers of the Year in 1967, and his call-up as a late replacement in the England team to tour South Africa in 1968/9 provided the spark that caused the fires of apartheid to rage in South Africa. There the Prime Minister, John Vorster, made his feelings quite clear, declaring: 'We are not prepared to receive a team thrust upon us by people whose interests are not in the game but to gain certain political objectives which they did not attempt to hide. The MCC team is not the team of the MCC but of the anti-apartheid protests.'

MCC cancelled the tour, in doing so helping to turn international opinion against the brutal apartheid system in South Africa. It was a turning point in South African history and the move provoked crucial changes in both sport and society.

This ostracism had a shattering effect on women's cricket in the country and in Britain the Labour government cancelled the England women's tour in 1968. The Dutch sent a team to replace them but they were no match for the South Africans and little was gained by the visit. Despite most of the world boycotting South African sport, the New Zealand women's cricket team toured South Africa in the 1971/2 season, much to the relief of the South African women's team desperate to play competitive and challenging international cricket.

Patricia McKelvey and her New Zealand team provided just the challenge that was needed with six tour matches and three Test matches. The South African team was full of fresh faces with only three of the old guard from 1960/61 remaining, namely Jennifer Gove and Lorna Ward, and Maureen Payne steering the ship as captain. New Zealand took the series 1–0 but there were some sterling performances by the new South African blood, the highlight of which was Brenda Williams' century in the third Test at The Wanderers. Lorna Ward's lethal right-arm-fast topped the South African bowling averages in this series and she closed her Test career as South Africa's leading wicket taker in women's Test cricket, taking 27 wickets in her seven Tests and bagging three five-wicket hauls.

In 1970, the International Cricket Council cut all ties with South Africa, announcing the suspension of all touring with the country until South African cricket lifted its apartheid ban, played the game on a multi-racial basis and selected international players purely on merit. Although the boycott was now official, this did not prevent some teams from touring in the 1970s and 1980s. In 1982 Geoffrey Boycott and Graham Gooch took an English XI to South Africa to play three Test matches and three ODIs. The 'rebels' were subsequently banned from international cricket for three years. Others were not deterred, however, and rebel tours from Sri Lanka, the West Indies, Australia and England continued until 1990.

These men's tours were the subject of intense international public attention but the women were at it, too. Rebel women's teams from England also toured, the pioneers of this controversial action first going abroad in the 1970s and 1980s.

Pam Crain, a Hertfordshire cricketer and a veteran of the 1960/61 England touring team to South Africa, was another bold lady who gathered a side of female rebels together, calling themselves the 'Unicorns'. They managed to tour South Africa twice in 1974/5 and 1975/6 and brought some of the joy of international sporting competition to the lives of the South African women.

That the ICC meant business in cutting off South Africa from the rest of the world was made clear when six South African women were forced to withdraw from the 1973 World Cup. They had been invited to compete in a combined International XI but their participation would have resulted in the withdrawal of the West Indian team since their government would not tolerate South African involvement.

The freeze on South Africa started to thaw with the advent of democracy and the end of apartheid, hastened by the release of Nelson Mandela and his fellow political prisoners in 1990 and the lifting of the ban on the ANC. At that point everything began to change.

In 1991, the two South African cricketing bodies, the SACB and SACU, merged after decades of strife. This union formed the United Cricket Board of South Africa (UCBSA), which went on to become Cricket South Africa. This was good news for women's cricket as, previously considered a disadvantaged group, they were now prioritised. The UCBSA's new constitution stipulated racial integration and equal opportunities across the board. It was a complete turnaround. This rejuvenation is explained in an article on the Cricket South Africa website: 'Due to the new nature of the UCBSA, certain areas of cricket were assembled in "target groups", this included women cricketers who were then selected for "accelerated advancement because of historical imbalances" along with black African and disabled cricketers.'

Women cricketers were now champing at the bit and had set their hearts on the 1997 World Cup. Preparation was the key and so the South African squad toured Ireland and England, playing their first international matches for twenty-five years. Their first ever ODI took place against Ireland, and the South Africans, playing like veterans of the format, whitewashed Ireland 3–0 in the series. England were tougher opponents, however, and South Africa lost the ODI series 2–1, an experience that put them on the right course as they reached the quarter-finals of the 1997 World Cup, where they were eventually knocked out by India. This arrangement of a warm-up tour to England followed by the World Cup was repeated in 2000 and reaped rewards when South Africa made it to the semis in the 2001 tournament.

Their success in the World Cup elevated the profile of the women's game in South Africa, which had previously been poor due to the absence of sponsorship and the difficulty in attracting touring sides. South African women's cricket was now in a healthy state and this renewed confidence and recognition led them to host the World Cup in 2005. India toured in 2001/2 and South Africa won the ODI series 2–1 but lost their first Test match by ten wickets – hardly surprising given that their last outing in Test cricket had been way back in 1972.

In the years leading up to the 2005 World Cup, South

Africa played three consecutive series against England with limited success in both their Test and ODI series. This poor form continued into the World Cup where they could only muster one win against the West Indies and finished seventh overall. Unfortunately, South Africa did not budge from seventh place in the 2009 World Cup. Something positive came out of this doomed period, however, when the first black African woman, Nolubabalo Ndzundzu, a batswoman from Border, was selected for the national side in 2000.

Other girls made dramatic breakthroughs in the men's game. Fifteen-year-old Tara Weinburg played for the boys' Western Province U-19 team in 2001. Staggeringly, her exclusive school, Westerford, in Cape Town, would not allow her to play in the school teams with the boys, their feeble argument being that she might deny a boy the opportunity to play. In KwaZulu-Natal, Johamari Logtenberg became the first girl to play for a boys' provincial team and six of her team-mates were black.

The South African women undertook their last Test match in 2007, having played just eleven Tests in their short international history. Twenty20 cricket is now dominating their game, as it is more lucrative, and Test cricket has taken a back seat. The first women's ICC World Twenty20 tournament was held in England in 2009 and this has not only given far more exposure to women's cricket but has raised the game of the top international teams.

The South African women cricketers have a positive outlook and are focused on the future, as this posting on their website indicates: 'We cannot undo the past, but we can shape the future. We do what we do today, for what will happen tomorrow!'

## Sri Lanka

The chaps started playing cricket in Ceylon, as it was known until 1972, around the time the island first became a British colony in 1815. Despite this early start, the women didn't show an interest in the game until very late in the day, in the 1990s, and, given that this is a country which has had two women presidents, it is difficult to understand why this should be the case. The women hit the international arena in 1997 when they played the Netherlands in a three-match ODI series, which they lost 2–1. This series served its purpose of preparation for the World Cup in India a month later, in which they fared well, making the quarter-finals, where they succumbed to the more experienced England team.

Their achievements continued with a 3–0 whitewash of Pakistan in an ODI series and then they won their first ever, and so far only, Test match to date. The Sri Lankan women are naturals at the one-day game, winning more matches than they have lost. They have reached the final of both the Asia Cup and the 2009 World Cup but have never been champions.

The year 2012 was a busy one for the Sri Lankans when they hosted both the men's and the women's ICC World Twenty20 tournaments. Sadly, the women didn't have much luck on their home turf in Colombo and Galle, winning only one match in the tournament.

Sri Lanka caused a major upset in the 2013 World Cup when they hunted down a huge total and beat the defending champions, England. Regarded as one of the minnows of the tournament, they stunned the crowds once again when they knocked the hosts, India, out of the competition, beating them by 138 runs. The Sri Lankan skipper, Siriwardene, put their success down to sheer hard work and their focus on yoga to increase psychological strength and physical agility.

## USA

If the American War of Independence (1775–83) saw 'the world turned upside down', it also struck a solid blow against cricket, as all things British were given the cold shoulder, and it only survived after the war with the help of international touring sides to the USA. The American Civil War (1861–5) put another spanner in the works because soldiers found they preferred the more rudimentary game of baseball, probably because it was slightly shorter and sweeter and always produced a winner.

American cricket had established itself on the East Coast, in New York and Philadelphia, by the late 1860s and 1870s, and by the 1890s women's cricket was being considered. The USA did not want to be left out of a growing phenomenon, and efforts were made to galvanise women's cricket. In 1888, the Seabright Lawn Tennis and Cricket Club in New Jersey had a crack at arranging a few cricket matches for its lady members, and in the 1890s women's clubs had sprung up in Philadelphia and on Staten Island. Two girls' private schools were particularly enamoured with the game; it was played at Mrs John Cunningham Hazen's School in Pelham Manor, New York, and at Rosemary Hall in Wallingford, Connecticut, as revealed in Tom Melville's *The Tented Field: A History of Cricket in America*: 'The cricket match these two schools played in late fall 1896 – a rather over-publicized and mildly sensationalized event – may very well have been the first interscholastic girls sporting event in American history.'

The *New York Times* of 14 November 1896 reported: 'Bareheaded and wearing sweaters and short skirts, daughters of some of the most prominent men in the country defied the cold, wintry wind. With enthusiasm and skill the twenty-two bowled, batted and fielded. A large crowd, chiefly composed of Pelham's most fashionable folk, witnessed the game.' The weather, at least, sounds English.

Alas, any success at trying to establish the game was short-lived as lawn tennis became the popular sport of the day for the more genteel classes and cricket faded into the background.

It has been a pretty barren time for women's cricket in the US for a good hundred years, although in her book *Fair Play* Rachael Heyhoe Flint does allude to pockets of activity there. The England WCA touring team dropped into San Francisco in April 1969 on their way back from a fruitful tour of Australia and New Zealand but they were in for a rude shock. The weather plummeted from the sweltering heat and rock-hard wickets of Australasia to a decidedly chilly California, with the snow-covered hills circling the San Jose cricket pitch. Dressed for a snowball fight, it is not surprising they lost their two matches against the Southern

Californian Cricket Association men's team. There is, however, no mention of any American women taking part.

Heyhoe Flint sought the expertise of John Marder, the USA cricket guru and an expat Englishman who had helped to establish the United States of America Cricket Association in 1961. He had some interesting observations to make on the absence of female involvement in the game in the US:

> A few lonely female participants come to mind ... In the 1950s a very fine opera singer, Patricia Westwood, was a keen cricketer. She appeared several times for the Harlequins of Los Angeles. There was opposition at first but the league rules made no mention of the sex of the players: she was confirmed in her membership.

The United States of America Women's Cricket Association was formed in 2003 to stimulate interest in cricket among American women and the Caribbean territories of St Thomas and St Croix. A few months later they combined with the Canadian women and sent a North American team to the West Indies to compete in their Cricket Championships in Grenada. They failed to win a match but put up a good fight all the same. The USACA website has a rather gloomy description of the state of women's cricket and the national team, the 'Lady Eagles', on their history page:

> Women's cricket in the United States is in its nascent stages. There is not a fixed domestic league or any organized clubs. Players are scattered throughout the US and largely consist

of ex-pats. At present, cricket is not a mainstream sport and is not very popular in the United States. Women's cricket globally suffers, more so in the United States. Funding for women's cricket is also non-existent.

Well, at least they're honest. Things have improved since then. In 2010 the Lady Eagles beat Canada to become eligible for the 2011 Women's World Cup qualifiers in Bangladesh. They returned home fairly quickly but now at least had international experience under their belts. They only just lost out on a place in the 2012 T20 World Cup when they took silver in the Americas T20 Championships.

As part of the 2012 national Five-Year Development Plan for cricket, the targets for the women are to establish a schools programme, a national tournament and a women's committee, to gain corporate sponsorship, increase the number of women's teams and have a minimum of one international tour per year. All of this is underway and Reebok has already come on board with the national team. Their ultimate goal is to get the US team to the 2017 World Cup.

**West Indies**

The staid Victorian view that cricket was a male preserve was one firmly held by the white cricket administrators of the late nineteenth century, and the white women of the Caribbean obediently accepted this well into the 1950s. In contrast to their sisters in England, Australia and New Zealand, women in the West Indies made no attempt to organise their own matches. Gender sensibility ruled for far too long.

So black women had to play a waiting game and it wasn't until individual islands got autonomy that women felt brave enough to formalise their own game. They had probably been playing casually with fathers and brothers for years but now was the time for recognition.

Jamaican women were the trailblazers, their courage and determination playing a huge part in the nationalist, anti-colonial movement, and their vitality shone through when they became the first to establish a women's cricket association in 1966. Monica Taylor, already a recognised cricketer, and a prominent upper-class 'coloured' businesswoman and aggressive campaigner, became the first president of the Jamaican Women's Cricket Association. The JWCA wasted no time in creating a league for the initial six teams and within a year, in 1967, they had selected a Jamaican touring team to visit Trinidad. Led by the vibrant Monica Taylor, they drew the three Test matches but, more importantly, provided the catalyst for the formation of the Trinidad and Tobago Women's Cricket Association in the same year.

Cricket blended in well with the dance, song, storytelling and street drama of the West Indian culture. You only have to see the current West Indian women celebrate on the pitch with their gyrating and copious nifty dance moves to get the picture.

Bursting with fresh confidence, Jamaica issued an invitation to an English representative XI to tour the island, and Rachael Heyhoe and her squad of international and senior representative players arrived in 1970. The tour was a raging success with thousands turning up to watch and the Jamaicans put on an entertaining show, despite their lack of international exposure. 'Strebor' Roberts, a sports writer for the *Sunday Gleaner,* reported:

> Some of the catching I have seen by the women of both sides should be an object lesson for the butter-fingered male cricketers. Another lesson for the men was the use of the feet in getting to the pitch of the ball. It was nice to watch the women as they danced down the wicket to make their shots.

Trinidad wanted to get in on the international act, too, and in 1971 boldly invited Jamaica and England to play in a triangular Test tournament. The hosts triumphed over a frustrated England and then a deflated Jamaica. By 1970, cricket was spreading like wildfire across the Caribbean with girls' cricket in schools and women's teams and leagues springing up in Barbados, Grenada, St Vincent, St Lucia and Guyana.

The then all-male West Indies Cricket Board (WICB) was worse than useless in supporting their cricketing women, and the Jamaican Cricket Club in Sabina Park and Queen's Park Cricket Club in Trinidad continued to bar women from much of their members' pavilions. The WICB further snubbed women by maintaining the ban on women at their prestigious annual dinner. Even when megastars of the men's game such as Michael Holding, Viv Richards and Gordon Greenidge took up the women's cause, it still proved difficult to storm the bastion of male power. Astonishingly, it wasn't until the 1990s that the WICB changed their tune and offered their backing to the women's game.

Despite such outrageous behaviour from the WICB, West

Indian women were hypnotised by the genius of the male cricket personalities; Grace Williams, a spectacular West Indian fast bowler of the 1970s, modelled herself on the great Wes Hall and Charlie Griffith. Like Griffith, she even gave her hair a middle parting.

Jamaica, hungry for match practice before the 1973 World Cup, hosted the Australian women's cricket team in a three-match tour while en route to England. Both Trinidad & Tobago and Jamaica took part in this World Cup and came fifth and sixth respectively out of seven entrants. Three other West Indian ladies played in the International XI that finished fourth in the competition.

In 1975 the islands united to form the Caribbean Women's Cricket Federation and a West Indian team was born. The Federation got off to a flying start with the inaugural annual Caribbean tournament in which the islands competed against each other. The West Indies played their first Test match series against Australia at home in 1975/6 and drew both matches. Next, having acquired an appetite for Test cricket, they jetted off to India in 1976/7 for a marathon six-match Test series, and showed guts and perseverance in winning the final Test by an innings to draw the series. Their last stab at Test cricket during that era was in 1979; this time they were thwarted by England and lost 2–0, but they did manage to draw the ODI series. They then abandoned the Test arena for twenty-four years, playing only Pakistan in a one-off Test in 2003/4, which ended in a draw.

Since 1993, the West Indies has played in the World Cup, but with mixed results, and their best-placed finish so far has been fifth place in 2005 and 2009. Currently, their real passion and expertise lie in Twenty20 cricket and they put on an outstanding performance when they knocked out the favourites, England, in the 2010 ICC World Twenty20 to reach the semi-finals on home turf. Under the captaincy of Merissa Aguilleira, and with the expert coaching of Sherwin Campbell, a swashbuckling former West Indian opening bat, the West Indies did it all over again when they beat South Africa to reach the semis in 2012.

Twenty20 cricket is clearly their thing and a handful of their players are ranked among the best in the world. Stafanie Taylor, the West Indies' number one all-rounder, won the prestigious ICC Women's Player of the Year award in 2011. Other hot names are Deandra Dottin, who holds the world record for the fastest century in a T20 international by a man or a woman, and all-rounder Shanel Daley and off-spinner Anisa Mohammed, who are ranked in the top ten.

The West Indies Cricket Board finally took over responsibility for the women's game in 2005 and since then the women's team has seen a marked improvement. Much-needed funding and support has been pumped into their game, as the CEO of the WICB, Michael Muirhead, recognised when he met the team for the first time: 'The WICB is in the forefront in offering Central Retainer Contracts to women cricketers and we are looking at ways to offer even more support to the players, who have done us proud. We see this as a truly worthwhile investment.'

All eyes were on the West Indies in the 2013 World Cup when they saw off the top teams, South Africa, New Zealand and Australia, in the heat and the dust of Mumbai and found themselves in the final, facing Australia once more. On that occasion, however, the clinical Australians were too much for them and sloppy fielding and ill-disciplined bowling hampered their game. All the same, it was a tremendous achievement to have got so far.

## Zimbabwe

When Zimbabwe gained independence in 1980, cricket was in a healthy position with superb facilities, professional coaches, an organised club structure and a strong cricket tradition in the leading private schools. However, there was still an urgent need to develop the game among the native Zimbabweans and to revive women's cricket after its almost complete decline. The women's game was in a dire state with very few players, no funding and a weak standard.

Concerns about financial corruption within the Zimbabwe Cricket Union (ZCU) led to its demise and it was replaced by a new organisation, Zimbabwe Cricket. Under ICC policy, Zimbabwe Cricket is responsible for the women's game, and attempts were made to breathe new life into it when the Zimbabwe women's team made their international debut at the African region tournament in 2006. They won the competition and qualified for the next stage in the Women's Cricket World Cup qualifier in Pakistan in 2007. Not much has happened since then, although the women's national team did take part in the World Cup qualifiers in Dhaka, Bangladesh, in November 2012 for a place in the 2013 World Cup in India. The tournament was a disaster for the team, as *The Zimbabwean* remarked in an article on its website: 'The team finished without even a single point after heavily losing their final match to neighbours South Africa on Sunday.'

Sadly, Mugabe and his thugs have mismanaged the economy and the country to such an appalling extent that Zimbabwean cricket, as with everything else, is in a state of crisis. This is unlikely to change in the foreseeable future.

'At country houses the ladies' cricket match is quite an institution. It is not harder work than lawn-tennis, it gives opportunity for the wearing of some very pretty costumes, and it amuses the other sex.' *The Graphic*, June 1890.

# FROM MAJOR TO MINOR

The more obscure cricketing nations deserve a mention, too, as some of them have plenty to say for themselves. I have tried to cherry-pick some of those countries that have particularly piqued my interest and added a bit of vibrancy to the story of women's cricket.

## Canada

Cricket for the chaps was first recorded in Canada in 1785 at Île-Ste-Hélène in Montreal, Quebec, and the country's oldest club, the Toronto Cricket Club, was founded in 1827. The ladies did not appear until much later when, in the late 1930s, the Overseas Educational League sponsored a team of schoolgirls from Harrogate Ladies' College, Roedean and Newcastle School to tour Canada in 1939. Sadly, the visit was cut short by the declaration of war. One Montreal newspaper encouraged the locals to go along and watch this novel match between the English and Canadian girls:

Attention cricketers, we suggest you wend your way to

McGill Campus tomorrow and take in the match which the English girls will play – they tell us bowlers Ann Grant and Leila White are tops in the school. They should start a new boom for cricket among the girls in the Dominion – this corner is converted already.

The late 1950s saw a flurry of activity in women's cricket in Vancouver, all thanks to a highly energetic and resourceful South African woman named Eileen Stevens. She obviously missed the cricket back home and so embarked on a publicity campaign, through the press and radio, to attract the sporty ladies of the city. It worked, and the Vancouver Vagabonds Women's Cricket Club was born. The leading cricket writer of the day, Donald King, commented: 'The Vagabonds played three matches against a men's team and one match was actually played against a scratch women's XI on Vancouver Island.'

When Eileen left Vancouver in 1959, cricket unfortunately went with her. The club promptly folded and women's cricket disappeared without a trace.

The Canadian Women's cricket team made a false start in July 2005 when their proposed debut in the international game was called off in Jamaica because of the threat of a hurricane. They had to wait until 2006 to face, and lose to, Bermuda, but success eventually came their way when they won the inaugural ICC Americas Championship in Toronto in 2007 and then again in Florida in 2009. They have also made an impression in Twenty20 cricket, winning the ICC Americas T20 Championship in 2012, overcoming Brazil, Bermuda, Cayman Islands and Argentina.

## China

The Chinese have rather poetically described cricket as 'shen shi yun dong', 'a noble game'. Cricket in China is a recent phenomenon and it will be quite a job to establish and develop the game there. The ICC Global Development Manager, Matthew Kennedy, recognised this in 2006 when he said: 'Developing cricket in China is a twenty-year project.'

One of the main problems is that in China cricket is classed as a non-professional sport and is therefore at a huge disadvantage as the youth will not play it. Parents and schools put enormous pressure on their teenagers to focus completely on their studies to the exclusion of everything else. Dr Liu Jingmin of Tsinghua University has summed up this single-mindedness very succinctly: 'No teenager in China plays sport for fun.' Chinese culture places high value on material wealth and as cricket in China does not currently promise any financial gain, it is not on the radar of the hard-working Chinese man and woman.

Dr Jingmin has tried to address this rather dismal situation by writing a textbook on cricket in Mandarin and has qualified as an umpire and Level 1 coach.

For the state of the game to advance in China, cricket needs to generate a serious income for those who play it. The ICC and the Asian Cricket Council recognise China's potential in increasing global revenues for cricket and have therefore allocated funds for development. Things are slowly moving in the right direction so fingers crossed for the future of cricket in China.

In modern China, football and basketball (both professional sports) seem to be the great loves of the Chinese men. Women, however, seem to have better taste altogether and are far more enthusiastic about cricket. The well-known Shanghai International Sixes competition, which was inaugurated in 2003, attracted the Hong Kong Ladies the following year and they played two matches against the Shanghai Pearls. These ladies, keen to better themselves on the cricket pitch, spent many hours with coaches, and by 2006 had formed a national team to represent the People's Republic of China in the Shanghai Sixes. Despite their sterling efforts, however, the Chinese Cricket Association refused to recognise them as the official team. But all was not lost as, in 2007, the official Chinese National Women's Team was at last created and a group of twenty-one girls from nineteen schools were sent off for vigorous central-ised training as part of the Chinese state sport machine. This produced some talented young women and they went on to reach the semi-finals of the Asian Cricket Council's Women's Tournament in 2007 in Bangkok.

Since then, China has embraced women's cricket and the ladies went on to be finalists in the ACC Twenty20 Championship. This competition was held in Guangzhou, China, in 2012 and the Chinese women, well ahead of the men by now, managed a solitary win against Nepal.

### France

The French National Archives reveal that 'criquet' was being played in northern France as early as 1478 and perhaps the most startling event of that year (in sport anyway) was the death of a batsman as a result of a violent pitch invasion. It may well be the first ever recorded.

France Cricket, the national cricket association, has 1,200 playing members, 40 per cent of whom are Frenchmen or women and the rest eccentric expats. They have even adopted their own vocabulary: 'un batteur' means 'a batsman', 'un lanceur' – literally 'a thrower' – means 'a bowler', and at the end of an over the umpire declares 'fin de série'.

Controversy dogged the French again in 1999 when they selected a girl, Cindy Paquin, a fifteen-year-old leg-spinner, in the French squad for the European Colts Championships. Rather preciously, the European Cricket Council banned her from the tournament on the grounds of possible risk of injury in an all-male tournament. Cricket is a non-contact sport and is an ideal game for boys and girls or men and women to play together. France, quite rightly, refused to budge and was consequently barred from the Championships. Cindy Paquin refused to go away and her innate talent eventually overcame the pettiness of the ECC when she represented France in the European Indoor and U-21 Championships. We have yet to see whether she will make it as far as the national side in an official ICC tournament, but it is clear that France was crying out for a ladies' international team. Laura Codrons, another bright young talent, was picked for France in 2002 for the European boys' U-13 tournament.

Currently, France's efforts to promote and play women's cricket are promising and girls are treated equally with boys in the schools cricket programme. It is now the norm to have mixed teams for teenagers and some women even play with the men at club level. The development of women's cricket is being taken seriously and women of all ages are encouraged to play. The Château de Thoiry Cricket Club showed their commitment by holding an 'Initiation Weekend' in 2010 and now have a flourishing women's section. The 'Coupe de France' has been held in France over the last couple of years with teams from Nantes, Saumur and St Aulaye taking part. The first women's France XI was born when they played Jersey in Saumur in 2011. *Encore du cricket feminin!*

## Italy

The British admiral Horatio, Lord Nelson, organised the first known cricket match in Italy, in Naples in 1793. Interestingly, Nelson's love of cricket, coupled with the loss of certain body parts, lent its name to the expression 'a Nelson', a score of 111. Although Nelson lost an eye (in 1794) and his right arm (in 1797), legend had it that he also lost a leg. This is untrue: he managed to hang on to both legs. 'Nelson' multiples are also thought to be unlucky, and doubly so if the number of wickets also matched – 111 for 1, 222 for 2, etc. The umpire David Shepherd even had a particular way of quashing this potential bad luck, by shuffling and jiggling about when the score reached a 'Nelson' multiple.

In Italy itself, with the advent of Mussolini and the National Fascist Party in the 1920s, cricket very wisely retreated and went into hiding, re-emerging after the Second World War. It was the foundation of the Associazione Italiana Cricket in 1980 that marked the beginning of proper Italian involvement in the game. The signoras of cricket at this time tended to be drawn into the official roles of umpires and scorers, and by the 1990s women umpires were dominating Italian domestic cricket and giving men the finger. More recently, women have abandoned umpiring duties for the field of play, and 2002 saw the inauguration of an Italian Women's Championship. This competition took place in Catania, Sicily, and it needed to spread on to the mainland if it was to catch on.

Most of those participating in cricket in Italy today are juniors involved in Kwik Cricket development programmes delivered to schools. In 2009, women and girls of Italian cricket were playing in Kwik Cricket, U-13s and senior tournaments. *Viva il cricket italiano!*

### New Caledonia

The New Caledonia tourism website describes this Eden as, 'Distant land, land of contrasts, pristine land ... New Caledonia is a diverse and unique destination. Bathed by clear waters at the heart of the Pacific Ocean, lulled year round by gentle trade winds, le Caillou (the Pebble) has more to offer than just its heavenly beaches and brilliant sunshine.'

I'm packing my bags and booking my flight. And, yes, it does have more to offer than just beaches – cricket is also on the menu.

This tropical paradise, discovered by Captain Cook in 1774, lies 1,150 miles north-east of Sydney. It became a French colony in 1853 and a French Overseas Territory in 1946. The locals hung on to the cricket brought to them by English missionaries in the nineteenth century and it evolved into their own bizarre version of the game, 'cricket traditionnel'. Astonishingly, this curious game has traditionally only been played by women. Despite being a French colony, it is a relief to see that 'cricket traditionnel' bears no semblance to the silly game of 'French Cricket' and parts of it are definitely recognisable as our very own MCC cricket.

The ladies run up and down a 62-foot pitch with 27½-inch-high stumps without bails. There is no bowling or popping crease but, instead, the batswoman, or 'joueuse', stands inside a 3¼-foot square marked out around the stumps. Baseball and football take up any grassy areas available so these cricket matches are mainly played on a slag pitch, and the ball, 'la boule', consisting of dried sap, bounces evenly on this type of surface. The bat is more like a baseball bat, 3 inches wide, up to 39 inches in length and can be any weight. The bowling is a mixed bag of obvious 'chucking' to a more orthodox lob and there is only one ball per over!

The players dress in brightly coloured floral frocks and don't bother wearing any protection. The lack of equipment is not surprising as the 'joueuse' has to run all her runs, or 'pines', as there are no boundaries. Once the bare-footed batter is on the verge of collapse she is allowed to call for a substitute runner or be replaced by the next 'joueuse' in the order. Phew! Runs are rewarded with a cacophony of whistles and clapping from the other players, which is all part of the colourful tapestry of this game. Teams are made up of fifteen players and two substitutes and there are approximately fourteen sides in the capital, Noumea, and three in the nearby islands of Mare and Lifou.

When Brian Johnston wrote about these extraordinary ladies, he was obviously tickled by their eccentric rules:

And now, just in case the whole thing smacks of women's lib, here comes the rub. Both the umpires and the off-pitch scorer must be male. They are considered fairer and have authority in a dispute and are capable of breaking up a scrap if the women get excited and fight – as they often do. Here are some of the general rules these umpires must enforce: It is forbidden for players to throw insults (modern Test players please note!), nor must any player enter the field in a state of drunkenness. And here is something that might well be introduced into Test cricket – the umpire has the right to expel a player from the field after a warning. Finally, further proof that the umpires are in complete charge of the game – neither the players nor the public are allowed to look at the score!

The game only ends once the umpire declares one team the winner and, often, the losers have to cough up some money to hand over to the winning side.

More recently, the men have started to play this unusual take on the game and there are now roughly 4,000 men and women involved. To give the game an official status, the Comité National de Cricket de Nouvelle Calédonie has taken over the organisation.

The New Caledonian men also play the standard version of the game with catastrophic results: so far they have lost every single match they have played. They made history in the South Pacific Games in 2003 when they lost to Papua

New Guinea by nearly 500 runs in a 50-over match, which has to be one of the biggest defeats in one-day cricket. Their dire performances have continued and, true to form, they have been dismissed for under 50 runs on six occasions in fourteen matches. Perhaps they should take up French Cricket...

## Rwanda

Rwanda is a late developer in the game with cricket only starting to be played after the 1994 genocide. Thousands of exiled Rwandans who had sought refuge in Kenya, Uganda and Tanzania had grown up playing cricket in these countries, and when they returned to Rwanda they took cricket with them. The Rwanda Cricket Association was formed in 1999 by just such a group of returning Rwandans and they built their first cricket ground in 2002 on the site of a genocide massacre.

To begin with, the Rwandan women struggled to find funding and had to withdraw from the East Africa Women's Championships in Nairobi in 2006. Since then, however, they have recovered well and in 2010 the Rwanda U-19 Girls' team beat the mighty Kenyans. In January 2012, two talented Rwandan female cricketers were chosen by the ICC to take part in a training clinic in South Africa. This event made it into the *New Times* of Rwanda, and General Emmanuel Byiringiro, Secretary of the RCA, commented: 'One of our objectives this year is to develop women's cricket in the country and we hope that these two cricketers will share their experience with the rest of the team.'

As an aside, Rwandan women generally have been doing

a lot better in the gender equality department, for in 2008 Rwanda became the first country in the world to elect a majority of women MPs, with forty-five females to forty male. This is reflected in their attitude to women's cricket and can be illustrated by a *New Times Society* magazine interview with the new Rwanda captain, Rina Ntagonzera, in March 2011:

> Most people perceive Cricket as a man's sport, however Rwanda's women are levelling playing grounds at all fields in their quest to make gender equality a success story. Rina Ntagonzera has risen up to the occasion and managed to become a leader in Cricket, a sport mainly dominated by men in the country.

Rwanda joined the Commonwealth in 2009 and it is now an English-speaking country. This has accelerated the spread of cricket throughout Rwanda and both men and women are involved in the game in schools, universities, orphanages and cricket clubs.

On the sports front, the MCC Foundation has clubbed together with the Rwanda Cricket Association to raise funds for 'The Rwanda Cricket Stadium Foundation Appeal', to build an international cricket and sports centre in Kigali, Rwanda. The emphasis is on a 'sport for all' policy to benefit children from all over the country in addition to Rwanda's elite cricketers. This proposed ground will be the home of the Rwanda national cricket teams for all age groups and aims to be completed by April 2014, the twentieth anniversary of the 1994 Rwandan genocide.

## Samoa

Samoa has a colourful cricket history and the game was introduced by William Churchward, the British Consul from 1881 to 1885. Initially, Samoans were unmoved by this peculiar English game and much preferred to wave-ride and hunt pigs, but in 1884 they apparently had a dramatic change of heart when the crew of HMS *Diamond* provided the opposition for the first match. As is the habit of the South Pacific islands, the locals soon became devoted to the game and adapted it into their own wacky version which they called kilikiti, with entire villages making up teams of 200 to 300 players with whip-wielding coaches. Matches would last for days or even weeks. Not surprisingly, the economy ground to a halt since not a jot of work was done during these endless matches and in 1890 the King of Samoa had no choice but to ban the game.

In Robert Gibbings' book *Over the Reefs* he tells the story of a shipwreck in the late nineteenth century on a nearby island: 'It is told when a schooner was wrecked on Palmerston atoll the crew clambered ashore, expecting to have to fight "the savages" for their lives. But, instead, they were challenged to a cricket match by the women of the island – and beaten.'

Once the German colonists had been booted out in 1914, New Zealand assumed administration of the island and cricket was revived. This time, both the quirky local version and the conventional MCC game were played, and the local version was watered down to teams of twenty-a-side in which men and women still played together amid scenes of general revelry. These people know how to have fun.

In January 2010 the Samoan International Cricket Association (SICA) selected its first ever all-women squad to play the conventional game and it is all thanks to Auckland Cricket, who galvanised the women into action.

Only ten days after the national squad had been selected, the Samoan women beat Fiji to qualify for a tournament in Japan. They lost to the host country but this invaluable experience fed their ambition to train hard and compete well against other teams.

The squad are now focusing on qualifying for the Women's T20 World Cup in 2014 and feel confident they will present a real challenge in Vanuatu where they will face Fiji, Papua New Guinea, Japan and the Cook Islands.

Domestic cricket in Samoa has blossomed into a full league competition with matches being played every week-end, and, together with regular training sessions, some real talent has been unearthed. Capable players such as Regina Lilii, Fou Charteris, Lily Mulivai and Maddy Chapman will give the team the best chance of succeeding.

**Scotland**

It seems to have taken an eternity for Scottish women to appear on the international cricket scene. This is surprising as women have probably been playing the game for as long as their sisters in England and Ireland. Rain may have had something to do with it as the men have suffered countless wash-outs in international matches through the years. In addition, cricket had never been a part of the sports curriculum in the state sector and girls' schools in Scotland, so very few women came across the game at an early stage. Those who did play for local clubs seem to have had no ambition to take the game to a national level. Understandably, therefore, the standard was poor and in 1978 a women's team touring Ireland were slaughtered by the women's clubs in South and North Leinster.

Scottish Cricket eventually took over the development of women's cricket and in 2001, when it was restructured, a Scotland women's side was born which promptly entered the Women's European Championships. Unsurprisingly, success was hard to come by, with no experience at international level and very few women to select from. Since then, however, the standard has rocketed and in 2008 the Scottish team, known as the 'Scotland Wildcats', was entered into the ECB county competition. They had immediate success and finished top of the table in the lower division. There is now a dedicated women's cricket academy, sponsored by Lloyds TSB Scotland, where talented female players are trained and play in high-standard competitive matches.

The Scotland women's national team now has a busy fixture card, competing in both 50-over and Twenty20 matches against the counties, MCC and internationally. They are certainly making up for lost time. This renaissance is backed up domestically in the shape of the Women's National League and the Women's Scottish Cup. Fingers crossed for an end to 'rain stopped play' next season.

## Singapore

The earliest evidence of cricket in Singapore is found in a letter to the *Singapore Free Press*, dated 1837, from a Mr 'Z' who was most probably a Scottish Presbyterian. He was having a moan about Europeans playing cricket on the Sabbath near the New Church, on the site of the present cathedral.

Despite cricket having been around for a good 170 years or so, the women did not don their whites until 2004 when the Singapore Cricket Association (SCA) organised a women's cricket carnival. Three local teams took part and one team with a risqué sense of humour called themselves 'No Balls'! In 2006 the Singapore women's national team played their first international against Malaysia and, according to the SCA website, they had a 'nail-biting encounter with just a one-run victory to Malaysia!' They have their own spirited cricket publication called *Sportmag* and this magazine takes pains to point out that women no longer play just a supporting role to their cricket-playing men: 'Well those days are gone mate, whether you like it or not! The girls are here and they've got the bowls to prove it.'

These feisty women held the inaugural SCA International Women's T20 challenge in 2012 with five teams taking part: Cricket without Borders (Australia), Hong Kong, Japan, Singapore and Thailand. Despite the tropical rain that plagued the tournament, Thailand came out top in the end. Singapore's domestic game is also in a healthy state: there are four teams playing in a women's league and some women have even opted to play in division six of the men's competition in order to experience a higher standard of cricket.

## Spain
An article titled 'Costa del Sol Lady Cricketers make history and produce quality display' claims to have reported on

'The first ever "All Ladies" Cricket match to be held in the Kingdom of Spain.'

This was played between the provinces of Malaga and Cádiz at the Grasseuropa cricket ground in Cártama in November 2004. The teams were made up of the yummy mummies among the junior players who were itching to play the game, having spent many hours roaming the boundary watching their little niños perform. It was a raging success and so over-subscribed that they had to field 14-a-side teams. Ladies' matches of this kind had been played on Ibiza in the 1980s between the towns of San Antonio and Santa Eulalia but it is likely that this was the first ever women's cricket match on the mainland.

Spain now has a thriving youth development cricket scheme with the Cricket España schools programme which is involved in the cricket-playing regions of Spain. Both boys and girls are targeted in the hope that they will catch the cricket bug and the game will stay with them for life.

## Wales

As with the men's national team, the status of the Welsh women's cricket matches is confusing because they do not play official international fixtures. They fall under the umbrella of the Cricket Board of Wales (Bwrdd Cricet Cymru) which represents the recreational game and is affiliated to the England Cricket Board. Women in Wales have played club cricket for at least sixty years but it was not until recently that they organised themselves into an unofficial national team.

In 2005, they made their international debut and played

in the ECB County Championship Division 3, against Worcestershire, Warwickshire and Northamptonshire. They are currently in Division 2, which also includes the Netherlands, and have avoided relegation to hang on in there for the 2013 season.

Their debut year, 2005, saw them host the European Women's Championships with defeats against England and the Netherlands and wins over Ireland and Scotland. This is their only appearance in the tournament to date. They really need to sort out their administrative structure in order to field official national sides, as the women are currently good enough to rank in the top five countries in Europe. They would then be given proper recognition on the international circuit. *Ddod me heulwea!*

Rachael Heyhoe at The Oval.

# SUPERSTARS

## Myrtle Ethel Maclagan, MBE (1911–93)

'No matter that we lost, mere nervy men,
Since England's women now play England's game,
Wherefore Immortal Wisden take your pen
And write MACLAGAN on the scroll of fame'
– *Morning Post*, 1934

The England men having lost the Ashes in the summer of 1934, the 23-year-old Myrtle Maclagan's 'tour de force' against the Australians the following winter was sung from the rooftops back home. Hers was quite a performance. This talented all-round sportswoman and self-taught cricketer took 7 wickets for 10 runs in the first ever women's Test match, skittling the quivering Australians for 47 in their first innings in Brisbane in December 1934. There was even blood on the pitch when Australia's wicketkeeper retired hurt with a broken nose. England's nerves proved to be equally frail when Australia's left-arm-over bowler

Ann Palmer replied with 7 for 18, and it was down to our heroine to come to the rescue with a punchy 72, aided by her captain Betty Archdale with a responsible 32 not out. England went on to win the Test with ease.

With Australia on the back foot in the second Test at Sydney, they put on a colourless performance with the bat, and one Australian batswoman, Essie Shevill of New South Wales, was rooted on nought for forty-seven minutes before falling to Molly Hide. Maclagan took 4 for 33 with her devilish off-spin and she then swung the willow for a blistering 119. Her hard hitting as an opening bat earned her a place in the record books as the first woman to score a Test century. England walked to victory, winning by 8 wickets.

The Australians were improving fast, however, and managed a well-earned draw in the final Test at Melbourne. England went home with a 2–0 win in the series and Maclagan did the same with a series record of 253 runs at 50.60, as well as a haul of 20 wickets.

This extraordinary cricketer is regarded as the W. G. or Wally Hammond of women's cricket between the wars. She opened the women's Test account with Betty Snowball and the pair were considered the Hobbs and Sutcliffe of the women's game. They opened the batting together for many years, with great success.

Myrtle began playing cricket at a young age with her two brothers and sister and represented the Royal School, Bath, in the 1st XI from the age of twelve. Her school diary is full of cricket chat and one entry reads: 'Freeman [the Kent and England bowler] came and coached us and taught me to bowl so that the ball curled in the air.'

Myrtle came from distinguished military stock, both of her grandfathers being generals and her father an officer in the Royal Engineers. This pedigree seems to have shown itself in the meticulous, almost military precision with which she planned her bowling attacks and few batsmen lasted long against her flight and guile. With the bat she kept a cool head out in the middle and her powers of concentration were unshakable, making her extremely difficult to dismiss. Her talent, determination, perseverance and deep knowledge of the game made her a formidable opponent.

The Australians proved themselves worthy adversaries when they toured England in 1937. As expected, their biggest problem was Myrtle Maclagan and her best was yet to come. Australia won their first ever Test match at Northampton by 31 runs – even Maclagan's 89 not out could not thwart the Aussies this time. It turned out she was saving herself for the Blackpool Test, when she managed an aggressive 115 in the first innings, including fifteen fours, and 49 in the second. In addition, she bagged 5 wickets in the match with her fizzing attack, and steered England to victory. With the final Test ending in a draw, the vastly improved Australians had managed to draw the series. Myrtle was still at the top of her game as England's most penetrating bowler and leading batswoman, but this time the accolade of bowler of the series went to an outstanding Australian bowler, Peggy Antonio, who took 25 wickets for the tourists in three Tests. Myrtle improved on her figures from her last Test series with 315 runs at an average of 63 and bowled more overs than any other England bowler.

After the war, Myrtle embarked on her second tour of Australia and New Zealand in 1948/9. Her personal high point in this series was described by Nancy Joy in her *Diary of the 1948–49 Test Tour to Australia* and offers a good example of Maclagan's perfect temperament which enabled her to save the match: 'Hers has been an innings of Churchillian determination; she is seventh out for 77, scored in just under four-and-a-half hours.'

She justified her status as number-one all-rounder when she was, once again, England's leading wicket taker in the series. This time, though, she couldn't prevent her team losing the Ashes to the Australians for the first time in a 1–0 series defeat. The imposing Myrtle Maclagan made her final appearance in Test cricket against Australia in England in 1951. She went out with a bang, scoring two half-centuries and taking 11 wickets in the series, but Australia hung on to the Ashes when the series was drawn. Her last official innings came in 1963 at the grand old age of fifty-two when she played for the Combined Services against her old foes, the Australians, and scored an effortless 81 not out in the presence of HRH Mary, the Princess Royal, a mere twenty-nine years since she had made her Test debut in Australia. She had lost none of her class.

Myrtle Maclagan was more than a cricketer, however, and Rachael Heyhoe Flint, writing her obituary for *The Independent* in March 1993, paid due attention to her distinguished military career:

Myrtle Maclagan qualified for the Combined Services when she joined the Army in 1951 (having also served in the

Second World War as a senior ATS officer in the anti-aircraft regiment in Dover in 1944 during the flying-bomb raids). She was an Inspector PT, WRAC, but rose to the rank of Major and was appointed MBE for Army services in 1966 – which would have greatly pleased her military antecedents.

Some of Myrtle Maclagan's Test feats are worthy of further scrutiny:

- 119 runs versus Australia at Sydney 1934/5 – first ever female Test match century
- 300 or more runs in a series (a series consisted of three matches of three days each in length): 315 runs at an average of 78.75 in 1937
- 500 or more runs in a career: 1,007 runs in 14 matches at an average of 41.95
- 5 or more wickets in an innings:
  - 7 for 10 versus Australia at Brisbane 1934/5
  - 5 for 22 versus New Zealand at Christchurch 1934/5
  - 5 for 43 versus Australia at Scarborough 1951
- 20 or more wickets in a career: 60 wickets in fourteen matches at an average of 15.58
- 15 or more wickets in a series: 20 wickets versus Australia 1934/5
- 100 runs and 10 wickets in a series:
  - 253 runs and 20 wickets versus Australia 1934/5
  - 315 runs and 11 wickets versus Australia 1937
  - 198 runs and 11 wickets versus Australia 1951
- 10 or more catches by a fielder in a career: 12 catches in fourteen matches

## Elizabeth 'Betty' Alexandra Snowball (1908–88)

Our next superstar is Betty Snowball, 'Sutcliffe' to Myrtle Maclagan's 'Hobbs' in a perfect opening partnership in which Betty's dexterous and tidy batting complemented Myrtle's sound and dependable style. On the field, this harmonious duo worked perfectly in tune, with Betty behind the stumps apparently able to read every line of attack that Myrtle sent down to her.

Her cricket was transformed when she was coached by the West Indian cricket genius Learie Constantine, and, by her own admission, Constantine turned her from a mere cricket enthusiast into a cricket 'maniac' for life. He was impressed by her boldness when standing up to the wicket to his fast bowling and considered some of her 'takes' to be on a par with almost any international keeper. In his book *Cricket Crackers*, he comments on her courageous work with the gloves: 'She was never at all afraid of the speed and bounce, and in the end I had to advise her to use more caution...'

When she toured Australia in 1934/5, the Australian press likened her to the great Australian wicketkeeper Bert Oldfield – praise indeed. Her magic moment came when she was introduced to Bert in Sydney and she later recalled: 'I bounced all the way back to our hotel after shaking hands with him.'

Her stats say it all: 21 scalps to her name, 13 caught and 8 stumped in a career of ten Test matches. She still holds the record for the most stumpings in a Test-match innings when she took four at Sydney in 1935.

One of Betty's signature strokes was a very fine cut shot which very few women had in their armoury at that time. Once the supreme Constantine had sorted out her footwork, she was able to execute the shot to great effect and it made her a joy to watch. Major C. H. B. Pridham, a prolific writer on cricket at the time, was full of praise for her regarding her favourite shot. In *The Charm of Cricket Past and Present* he wrote:

> Her most telling stroke is the square-cut, which she uses with delightful certainty – even to slow bowling. Once she chased a very wide ball and cut it past point to the boundary. Any amount of wrist goes into her cutting, and she can pull a full-pitch to the ropes with the facile timing of a Hammond.

The diminutive Betty Snowball was only five feet tall, but with this came a perfect stance and impeccable timing. Once again, Major Pridham is found singing her praises:

> With the bat she faces the bowling with her left shoulder and elbow pointing straight down the line between wicket and wicket; yet she manages – without restraint – to get both eyes square to the line of flight of the ball. Owing to her rather short reach she cannot drive powerfully, like Miss [Molly] Hide; but her cutting and pulling leave nothing to be desired.

Betty revealed her talent to the world in the second Test match at Sydney in 1935 when, together with her partner in crime Myrtle Maclagan, she participated in the first ever century stand in women's cricket, as they put on 145 and sealed victory for England. It was in Australia's second innings that she made history and made four fine stumpings. Her form with the bat continued in Melbourne where she notched up 83 not out, and *Wisden* singled out this innings as her best in the series, 'her leg-glides off the fast bowling being delightful'.

She saved the best till last when she stunned New Zealand in February 1935 with a staggering 189 in 222 minutes, including 23 boundaries; together with Molly Hide (110), she destroyed the hosts by an innings and 337 runs. Two more Test records were set with the world-record second-wicket stand of 235 and the highest score by a woman, which she held for a further fifty-one years.

Australia visited England for the Ashes in 1937 and Betty played a large part in keeping the series level in the third Test at The Oval with an exciting 99, before she was run out by a razor-sharp throw from Mollie Flaherty from 30 yards. Mollie was the first genuinely fast female bowler and she had an uncanny ability to throw down a batsman's wicket with her powerful throws from the outfield.

Betty's tally of dismissals with the gloves in the 1937 series was 8, with 6 caught and 2 stumped, and this kept her in the number one spot as wicketkeeper for the 1948/9 tour to Australia. This was to be her last international airing and she finished her Test career with an impressive average of 40.86 in just 18 innings from 1934 to 1948.

Betty was fastidious in her appearance and this was

reflected in her economy of movement and neatness of technique behind the stumps. Her gloves and pads were tailor-made to her specifications and her bats, too, were specially made for her by Lambert's at Nelson in Lancashire, her home county. She insisted on her shoes having rubber soles, unless, that is, the ground was wet and slippery. 'Immaculate' was her middle name and she never had a hair or a crease out of place.

As well as being a fine cricketer, she had other feathers in her all-round sports cap, playing hockey for Hampshire and international squash and lacrosse for Scotland.

## Mary 'Molly' Edith Hide (1913–95)

Three names were dead certs for selection in those early Tests: the first two were the aforementioned Betty Snowball and Myrtle Maclagan, and the third was Molly Hide. As one of the pioneers of women's cricket, Molly played in the first ever women's Test in Brisbane in December 1934, and was England's captain from 1937 to 1954. Once her playing days were over she gave her all to the WCA as a selector for county and country and occasional team manager, and then took over the presidency of the Association after the death of Mary Duggan in 1973. As this was also the year of the first Women's World Cup she had a great deal on her plate.

Molly Hide was born in Shanghai, China, and moved to Haslemere, in Surrey, at the age of six. She was introduced to cricket at Wycombe Abbey and developed a passion for the game. She was even known to help the groundsman prepare the pitch before a match so that she could weigh up the pros and cons of the playing surface.

At the age of twenty-one, Molly batted number three for England during the 1934/5 tour of Australia and New Zealand, and her signature cover drive, executed with style and strength, provoked astonishment among the many male cynics in the crowd. She further wowed spectators in New Zealand when she scored a century in the Christchurch Test and built a record partnership of 235 with Betty Snowball.

Molly was the natural choice for the England captaincy in 1937 when Australia made a return visit for the Ashes. She set high standards, expecting only the best from her team and so took a tough approach to captaincy. Most players found her inspiring but some found her somewhat masculine manner difficult to handle. The prolific cricket writer G. D. Martineau was a genuine fan, and wrote in his book *They Made Cricket*:

The chief characteristic of Molly Hide on the cricket field was a very positive attitude that asserted what a game of cricket should be like. She put her ideas into practice, making great declarations, trusting her keen eyes, ready to hit the first ball for four, and always on the attack. There have been less chancy batsmen but her aim was ever to get on top of the bowling, so that the rate of scoring almost always quickened on her arrival. With a particularly strong on-drive 'off her toes', she put character into her strokes, and there has been no better batsman.

Her off-spinners proved lethal in the second Test at Blackpool in 1937 when the Australians found themselves on a spinner's wicket in the fourth innings of the match. She ended up with outstanding match figures of 8 wickets for 58 runs with England winning by 25 runs. Her batting has attracted more attention than her bowling but she was a reliable change bowler who only ever accepted the ball rather reluctantly.

The third Test at The Oval marked another milestone in her career, when she scored her first fifty against Australia to help England draw the series. She exhibited many of her classic cover drives during this innings, as described by Major Pridham in *The Charm of Cricket Past and Present*: 'One of these – during her innings of 64 in The Oval Test – flew with the speed of lightning over cover-point's head. Usually, however, her drives skim the grass; for it should be noted that, like the best of these batswomen, she seldom lifts the ball.'

Another remarkable innings in that summer of 1937 saw Hide score a century at Hove before lunch during the South of England v. Australia match. This was one of the rarest feats in first-class cricket and she blasted her way to 145 in ninety minutes with eighteen fours.

With a diploma in agriculture from Reading University, Molly Hide spent the war years working on her father's farm in Haslemere, much to the delight of her parents who were less than enthusiastic at her gallivanting around the world playing cricket. It would be another eleven years before the next Test series and by 1948 Molly was more than ready to take on the captaincy again for the 1948/9 tour to Australia. She was in superb form and accumulated over a thousand runs with five centuries to her name, including one in Colombo en route to Australia. One of these centuries, 124 not out, was made in the third Test at Sydney to draw the match and this was to be England's only Test century in the series. Australia took the Ashes 1–0.

Despite the loss of the Ashes, Molly's contribution to this series was flawless and she finished at the top of the Test batting and bowling averages with enviable figures: 285 runs with one century and one fifty at an average of 57.00; six wickets for 132 runs at an average of 22.00.

Molly was dogged by injury in the 1951 Ashes series at home and had to relinquish her captaincy to her vice-captain, Myrtle Maclagan, for the first two Tests. With the Aussies one up and England desperate for a win in the last Test at The Oval, although not 100 per cent fit, Molly took the helm once again and made an astonishing comeback. She led England to victory by 137 runs and personally knocked up the most runs with a 65 (her fourth fifty in twelve Tests) and 42, and 3 wickets to boot.

Molly announced her last season in first-class cricket in 1954 when she captained England against the touring New Zealand team. She ended on a high note with England taking the series 1–0 and excelled with both bat and ball. Her international career lasted from 1934 to 1954, and in those twenty years she played in fifteen Test matches and scored 872 runs with a batting average of 36.33. She worked wonders with her potent spin, collecting 36 wickets at 15.25 apiece.

Her work in cricket was ongoing and took on various forms. She and Netta Rheinberg engineered the first ever exhibition dedicated to women's cricket at the Qantas Airways Gallery in Piccadilly, London, during the 1963 Australia visit. Sponsorship was unheard of in women's cricket at that time but they managed to squeeze some loot out of Rothmans of Pall Mall to help finance the enterprise. Among other things, on exhibit was the Blue Cricket Ball made by Alfred Reader in 1897 for the 'delicate' lady cricketers of the day, designed to prevent these ladies expiring at the crease when facing an angry red cricket ball...

Molly also added the art of commentary to her CV when she assisted Robert Hudson on TV for the final afternoon's play of the third Ashes Test at The Oval in 1963 when Australia were set a tantalising 210 to win in 255 minutes. Luckily, it went England's way and they won the Ashes.

To add another feather to her cap, Molly Hide also played lacrosse for England.

### Mary Beatrice Duggan (1925–73)

'Big in build, big in heart, kind, generous and gentle, Mary led her team in maternal fashion and was England captain from 1957 to 1963.'

These are the words of Netta Rheinberg in *Fair Play*, describing the fine all-rounder Mary Duggan. By the time she was captain, Mary's bowling had changed from a medium-fast opening bowler to orthodox left-arm spin. This was a shrewd move as this gifted spinner went on to bag even more Australian and New Zealand scalps for her country.

Mary had moderate success with bat and ball on her debut tour of Australia and New Zealand in 1948/9 but showed real promise for the future. Her cricket really took off, however, in the second Test at Worcester against Australia in 1951. With her lethal left-arm seam zipping across the batswoman on a good length, she took 5 wickets in an innings for the first time in her career and reaped 9 match wickets altogether for very few runs. The Aussies snatched a victory at Worcester but were not so fortunate at The Oval. All praise to Duggan for her bowling in this Test as she turned in a match-winning performance of 5 for 5 in just seven overs in Australia's second innings. She dazzled the crowd and a packed press box and impressed the likes of Sir Jack Hobbs, Percy Chapman and Neville Cardus, all of whom witnessed this crushing of the Australians. She finished with match bowling figures of 9 for 104 and she was splashed all over the front pages of the national papers. England won the game with only fifteen minutes to spare.

New Zealand were her next victims when they arrived on English shores in the summer of 1954. Hide and Duggan worked their way through the Kiwi batting order with ease in the first Test at Headingley, each collecting 5 wickets in the match as England cruised to a win. Duggan was without doubt the pick of the England bowlers in this three-match Test series, finishing with 13 wickets off 126 overs.

When Duggan took over the captaincy from the tough and experienced Molly Hide for the 1957/8 tour of New

Zealand and Australia, she had difficult shoes to fill. Her first real challenge as skipper loomed at Christchurch in the first Test, a match that turned into a huge personal triumph for Mary as she smeared the ball all over Lancaster Park with well-placed drives and scored 108 in 135 minutes, the second-fastest century on record. Unfortunately, at the other end Cecilia Robinson (known as Robbie) seemed particularly bogged down, and, in stark contrast to Mary's lightning innings, she registered one of the slowest fifties on record, and poor old England ran out of time. Duggan added to her scorching century by taking 6 for 55 in New Zealand's first innings when she employed her devilish spin for the first time in an international match. The match ended in a frustrating draw.

Mary's glorious form continued into the second Test in Auckland when she notched up 85 runs and set a new record with her fifth-wicket partnership of 104 with Shirley Driscoll. Her flight and guile produced a premiere show with the ball with 7 wickets, including 5 for 46 in the second innings. Only two Tests were played and both were drawn: an honourable result for New Zealand.

On to Australia, where appalling weather completely washed out the first Test at North Sydney Oval. To compensate for this, it was decided that this series should be played over four matches rather than the usual three. The wicket at Melbourne caused all sorts of trouble, with the batswomen of both countries recording their lowest ever total in an innings. Australia scratched a miserable 38, with Duggan taking an extraordinary 7 for 6 for a new Test best, overtaking Maclagan's previous height of 7 for 10. She held on to this record for thirty-eight years. Australia's batting debacle was soon to be outdone by England who were all out for 35, Betty Wilson taking 7 for 7, including a hat-trick. Between these two bowlers, 14 wickets fell for just under a run apiece.

Flash forward to the 1963 Ashes Test at The Oval in south London for Mary Duggan's last international appearance. She is still captain for this series and her side has so far drawn the first and second Tests. Both sides have everything to play for. Mary will go down in history as the first woman to score a century at The Oval, with 101 not out in the first innings, joining Myrtle Maclagan, Molly Hide and Cecilia Robinson as the only women to score centuries against Australia. Duggan makes a sporting declaration on 160 for 7 in their second innings to set Australia 210 to win in 255 minutes. Duggan and Sanders then proceed to destroy the Australian middle order to win back the Ashes – a perfect ending to Duggan's international career.

Her distinguished career stretched over fifteen years and seventeen Tests, during which she took a total of 77 wickets, alternating between her medium pace and spin, and took more than five wickets in a match nine times. Another feather in her cap came when she and wicketkeeper Ruth Westbrook became the first women to be awarded the MCC Advanced Coaching certificate in 1962. They passed with flying colours and rattled more than a few cages when many of the men (all of at least first-class county standard) failed the course. Duggan capped this with an unofficial record when she hit a target on the wall thirty-six times in succession with her lofted straight drive!

When Mary Duggan died at the age of forty-eight, she

was deeply mourned by the world of women's cricket. It had lost a warm-hearted and much revered figure. An upbeat G. D. Martineau wrote a poem about the last Test against Australia in 1963 and his opening lines sang the praises of England's victorious captain:

> Praise be to Miss Duggan – her smiting and spinning,
> Her daring declaring, and ways that proved winning.

### Elizabeth Rebecca 'Betty' Wilson (1921–2010)

Here is a question for you cricket nerds out there: who was the first player to score a century and take ten wickets in a Test match? Gary Sobers? Keith Miller? Ian Botham? All decent guesses but all wrong. Try Betty Wilson.

She was Australia's greatest all-rounder and undoubtedly the finest woman cricketer of all time. She had to be seen to be believed. Labelled the 'female Bradman' for her exquisite stroke play and prolific run scoring from a considerable repertoire of shots, Betty was also a versatile and deadly off-spinner who took countless victims and bowled her way into the record books on many occasions. Practice with precision was her discipline and her self-imposed training regime saw her out every day working on her technique with bat and ball. Just as 'The Don' spent hours practising with a stump and golf ball in his backyard to perfect his timing, so Betty would spend every spare moment in the nets bowling at carefully laid markers arranged to represent the reach of certain batswomen of different heights. Once she had lured her real victims into reaching just that little bit too far, she went for the kill.

Growing up in Collingwood, Melbourne, she invented her own backyard training device by placing a cricket ball in one of her mother's stockings and suspending it from a clothes line. With the ball coming down at her from all directions she was forced to focus on her footwork and to play every shot. She believed in the merits of endlessly practising the shots with which she had difficulty: 'There's no use standing there all day waiting for the ball you want to hit. There are a lot of other balls that are going to come your way. So you need to learn how to hit them all.'

A natural athlete, this talented player could 'run like a hare' and her fielding was breathtaking, notably the pinpoint accuracy with which she threw from the boundary into the keeper's gloves, on a par with any man.

Betty had a happy childhood with her three siblings, mother and father, a boot-maker, in Collingwood in the 1920s and 1930s, and spent most of her time playing cricket in the streets, using the lampposts as wickets. She was soon spotted and played for the Collingwood Ladies Cricket Club at the local oval at the age of ten and a half. Three years later she moved to Clarendon Women's Cricket Club in Middle Park and, at sixteen, this unbelievably gifted child was selected for the senior Victoria state squad.

Ultimately Betty had to choose between cricket and love, and her fiancé's patience finally ran out when she asked him to postpone their wedding for a third time so that she could tour England in 1951. The two previous occasions had been the tour of New Zealand in 1948 and England's visit of 1948/9. In those days it was impossible for a woman to combine international sport with marriage and, in Betty's case, cricket had to come first. She remained single for the rest of her life and always maintained that no one who came after him could ever match her first love.

Betty took the cricket world by storm when she made her debut in the first international between Australia and New Zealand in 1948 at the Basin Reserve, Wellington. Aged twenty-six, she made a quick-fire 90 and took 10 wickets in the match with 4 for 37 and 6 for 28. Australia annihilated New Zealand by an innings and 102 runs.

England felt the full force of Betty Wilson in their first encounter with her at Adelaide in the first Test in 1949. Wilson's 111 set a new record, the first century in a Test against England, and her 6 for 23 were the best bowling figures for the Adelaide Oval. Her overall match analysis of 9 for 62 was crucial in Australia dismissing England to win by 186 runs. Mention in dispatches also goes to the partnership of 115 between Wilson and Una Paisley in a mere 129 minutes. Clarrie Grimmett, the former Australian wizard of spin, was among the spectators at the game and declared that he wanted to see the exceptional Betty Wilson perform against men. Australia's domination of England continued to Melbourne for the second Test when Wilson (74) set a new Australian record with her captain, Molly Dive (51), with their third-wicket partnership of 123. Throw in her match figures of 6 for 62 and we have another fabulous all-round performance from the lady Don. Wilson was voted woman-of-the-match in both of these Test matches. When writing up his report for the *Sunday Herald* on the third Test of this series, Bill O'Reilly expressed his admiration for these extraordinary women: 'When Betty Wilson and Una Paisley were entrusted with the spin attack, I realised that if we men have any laurels we had better set about their defence immediately', adding, 'from this time onward I shall steadfastly refrain from saying that "so and so" batted or bowled "like a woman".'

A mighty Australian team boarded HMS *Mooltan* at the Melbourne dock and sailed for England in 1951 for their second tour of the British Isles. Betty was quick off the mark in the first Test at Scarborough, scoring 81 runs in her first and only innings. Her most sublime performance on this tour, however, took place when Australia played Yorkshire at Headingley, which she described in her own words:

> I was told it was a ground where Bradman always made a century whenever he took guard. I thought, 'If Don can do it, I can do it.' And I happened to crack the ton in 75 minutes. It was the last ball of the day I hit for a boundary that won us the match.

Bill Bowes, former England bowler and latterly a cricket correspondent, was so roused by this century that he wrote an article on the game proclaiming it to be the most impressive innings he'd ever seen by a woman.

Coming in at number seven in the second Test at Worcester, Betty scored a gritty 41 not out on a dreadful wicket and saved Australia from a first-innings collapse. With her match bowling figures of 7 for 82 off 35.3 overs, she almost single-handedly won the Test for the Australians.

Yet again, her terrific skill and shrewd knowledge of the game resulted in her topping the batting averages with 43.75 and the bowling with 16 wickets for the three-match series. For some reason, England agreed with Betty and after the tour she stayed on to live there for two and a half years.

Betty certainly made an entrance on her return to Australia in 1953, scoring her thirty-second century when she represented Victoria in an inter-state match. She attracted universal admiration and at one point during a lull in batting in the men's Test match against England at Melbourne there were even calls for her to liven things up, with shouts of 'Send Betty Wilson in!' rolling around the ground.

As Betty matured she simply got better and better and by 1957/8 she was still Australia's leading run scorer when she knocked up two centuries in the series against England. Her glory of glories arrived in 1958 at the age of thirty-seven when she celebrated the dizzying heights of her career with two phenomenal records. As mentioned above in relation to Betty Duggan, in the second Test at the St Kilda Oval, Melbourne, on a soggy wicket Australia were bowled out for a paltry 38, the lowest score ever recorded by an Australian team anywhere in the world, with Betty Wilson top scorer with 12. England, apparently, were 'killing themselves laughing', only to endure the ultimate humiliation when they seized the wooden spoon and were all out for 35. This remains the lowest score ever recorded in a women's Test match. With Australia taking a lead of 3 runs into the second innings, Betty's devastating spin saw her take 7 for 7 in 63 balls, including that remarkable first Test hat-trick by a woman, a feat that would not be repeated until 2004 when Shaiza Khan of Pakistan took 13 for 26 against the West Indies in Karachi. Wilson went on to score a swashbuckling century and enjoyed a record stand of 136 with Val Batty in the second innings out of Australia's 202 for 9 declared. This superwoman had achieved what no man or woman had done before by being the first person to complete a hat-trick, a century and take 10 wickets in the same Test. Her startling match figures read: 11 wickets at 1.45 runs and 18 maidens in 29.3 overs. Unbeatable!

Her great final flourish in international cricket took place at the Adelaide Oval in the third Test where her century and 6 for 71 in England's only innings secured the draw for Australia. She hung up her boots for good in 1960 and eventually became the first woman cricketer to be inducted into the Australian Sports Hall of Fame in 1985, a recognition of her consummate skill that should have happened much earlier. More recently, she was awarded honorary membership of the Melbourne Cricket Club and again this was a first for a woman cricketer. She appeared most thrilled when she received the Australian baggy green cap in 2005, bearing the number twenty-five: 'I would have been so proud to have worn that while I was playing, but better late than never.'

Betty never made a penny out of cricket, always playing for the love of the game, and earned her living as a secretary. She continued to show a strong interest in women's cricket in her twilight years and kept fit down at the bowls club.

Her comparatively short international career, interrupted, like so many others, by the Second World War, spanned a decade and she only had the opportunity to play in eleven Test matches. But, boy, did she make the most of it, scoring 862 runs at an average of 57.46 and taking 68 wickets at 11.80, with three centuries and three half-centuries to her name. Words alone cannot do her justice.

## Rachael Heyhoe Flint OBE, DL (b. 1939)

Heyhoe for Cricket
The frolic and fun – that were cheered to high Heaven –
Of Miss Rachael Heyhoe's (not out) thirty-seven;
She flirted with Fortune; she courted disaster –
And never stopped laughing as runs came the faster;
She struck a long sixer that staggered the bowler,
And only retired to make way for the roller –
So thanks, above all, for such joy at the wicket:
Sing Heyhoe for laughter, and Heyhoe for Cricket!
– G. D. Martineau

For anybody who knows anything about cricket Rachael Heyhoe Flint is a household name. Her exuberance and sense of fun have served her well in the world of cricket over the past half a century and her sheer force of personality and innate talent have thrust women's cricket on to centre stage on many occasions, giving its participants the respect and exposure they deserve.

Born on 11 June 1939, Rachael is a Wolverhampton girl through and through. As a fourteen-year-old schoolgirl she was so inspired by watching the Midlands versus New Zealand women at Birmingham that she immediately took up the game, and from then on she never looked back. Her progress was rapid and five years later she was selected for the Young England team and toured Holland in 1959 with manager Molly Hide. Her Test debut soon followed when she toured South Africa in 1961 and she played in all four Test matches, ending the eleven-match tour with a respectable batting average of 31.7. Her aggressive style did not yield a great average in the Tests, at 17.00, but she did score the fastest fifty on tour in only sixty-six minutes, giving us a glimpse of what was to come.

Rachael brought much needed hilarity to a day swathed in mist and a dour England defence in the second Test at Scarborough against Australia in 1963, when she scampered a quick single and left her shoe in the middle of the wicket. A. A. Thomson of *The Times* pounced on this delightful interruption, describing it as 'stealing a run like Cinderella'.

She was responsible for another flamboyant diversion at The Oval when she walloped the first six in a women's Test match, as witnessed by Netta Rheinberg: 'a beautifully timed shot over long-on, the ball travelling with surprising power for a slightly built person of short stature'. The press loved it and referred to it as a classic low-trajectory drive over mid-on, even though the self-deprecating Rachael described it more prosaically as a 'hoick to leg'.

Rachael Heyhoe exploded on to the scene as captain in 1966, despite some rumblings of opposition in the ranks. She couldn't have been more different from her predecessor, Mary Duggan, either in character, temperament or attitude, and her bushy-tailed and unique approach to captaincy would inject new life into the England team. Those who were miffed by her appointment liked to label her flippant and cavalier but she proved herself immediately with a majestic 113 in the first innings against New Zealand at Scarborough, and produced a record third-wicket partnership of 121 with Edna Barker, her vice-captain. Her lioness status came to the fore when she not only hit an unbeaten 59 in the second innings, but threw in some bowling and wicketkeeping to boot, and took a catch behind the pegs. This first Test is unique for the fact that every player on the England side bowled, with the exception of Sheila Plant, the injured wicketkeeper. Rachael did not let up with the bat and finished with a staggering average of 71.2 in the three Tests. Her critics were finally silenced.

In 1968/9, Rachael led a united and jubilant England team on a tour of Australia and New Zealand. England, however, were cursed with injuries and this gave Rachael another chance with the gloves on a couple of occasions and she snaffled two catches. Her consistency with the bat gave her four half-centuries in the series, with a top score of 76. Another world-record third-wicket partnership of 137 was set by the invincible duo, Heyhoe 54 and Barker 100, in 117 minutes in the second Test at St Kilda, Melbourne. Injuries prevented them from winning a game and all three Tests were drawn.

In New Zealand, Rachael was at last blessed with a fully fit team and England returned home with a convincing 2–0 series win. As she grew in stature as a player, so her captaincy matured and she revealed her artfulness in this role on many occasions. An example of such cunning took place in the second Test at the Hagley Oval, Christchurch, when she lured New Zealand into going for the win. She cleverly persevered with her pace bowler Moorhouse, who was not getting anywhere at all, having been hit for 35 in 8 overs with no wickets. She explained, 'I knew that if they got within sight of victory, they'd have a go at the other bowling.'

The 'other bowling' came in the form of Enid Bakewell and she laid waste with her devilish leg-spin for England to win the match by 37 runs. Another Heyhoe milestone was achieved when her three half-centuries in this series carried her to a thousand runs in Test cricket.

The year 1969 was a golden one for Rachael when she featured in the top ten of the Sportswriters' Association 'Sportswoman of the Year' as the first woman cricketer. Another highlight was the invitation to tour Australia as a coach, with fellow coach Anne Sanders, spreading the gospel of cricket to young players. Rachael had passed her MCC Advanced Coaching course with flying colours and was top of the class.

In her quest to encourage Caribbean women to play inter-national cricket, Rachael spearheaded an unofficial tour of the West Indies in 1970, followed by an official outing in 1971 to play against the recently established Jamaican Women's Cricket Association. Her trailblazing did wonders for women's cricket there. In 1972 she was awarded the MBE in recognition of her services to women's cricket, becoming the first woman to gain such an honour in the cricket world.

The 1970s were punctuated by all manner of remarkable moments in Heyhoe's career, one of which saw her achieve her highest ever score of 144 in a first-class game at Hove in 1971, which also saw a stand of 207 with Lynne Thomas. However, the ultimate coup was the first ever Women's World Cup. Rachael Heyhoe Flint (she was married in 1971) and Jack Hayward put their heads together and came up with this stroke of genius in 1973, two years before the first Men's World Cup was played. Like Rachael, Jack was Wolverhampton born and bred and was also a successful businessman, property developer and philanthropist. His unbelievable contribution of £40,000 financed the entire competition, and he is quoted as saying that he loved women and he loved cricket so what better than to support something that combined both.

Rachael captained the England side in the World Cup and took them to the final against Australia at Edgbaston, where they beat the Aussies, with surprising ease, by 92 runs. Enid Bakewell played a match-winning innings of 118, ably supported by Rachael's 64. And this all took place in front of HRH Princess Anne, who presented them with the cup to the delight of a packed grandstand. The Prime Minister, Edward Heath, then hosted a reception for the victorious England team at 10 Downing Street. Life didn't get any better. The press couldn't get enough of them, and Brian Marshall of the *Sunday Telegraph* reported:

> They put on 101 for the first wicket and following the dismissal of Thomas for 40 she [Bakewell] found an admirable partner in her captain Flint. Scoring almost at will for a spell Enid

Bakewell failed by only two runs to obtain her century before lunch. The feature of the second wicket partnership of 117 was Heyhoe Flint's aggressive 64. She made a hesitant start but later made amends with powerful leg shots as Australia began to wilt in the face of such belligerent opposition.

During the 1976 series in England, Rachael was a thorn in Australia's side. She scored her third Test century in England's only innings in the first Test at Old Trafford and, remarkably, it was her maiden century against the Australians. Since the first two Tests were drawn it was decided that the final Test at The Oval would be played over four days. This was uncharted territory as all previous women's Tests had been a maximum of three days. This first-ever four-day Test turned out to be an astonishing act of endurance. The whole match was littered with records and the most mind-blowing statistics to emerge were those of England's second innings. By day three the Australians were in command, with a day and a half to bowl England out, and England needing 254 runs to avoid an innings defeat. Astonishingly, England's second innings lasted almost eleven hours. They scored 326 runs with 264 overs being bowled, 157 of which were maidens. Rachael subdued her natural attacking instincts and saved the match, and the series, with the longest individual innings on record of more than eight and a half hours for her fourth Test century of 179 runs, a new personal best. All in all, it was a storming series for Heyhoe Flint who notched up scores of 110, 49, 12 and 179 and a series average of 87.5 in the three Tests.

BACHELOR GIRL'S CLUB

LEFT A maid all dressed in white… Idyllic lady cricketer from about 1905.
© The Roger Mann Collection

BELOW Schoolgirls take over the Harrow School ground in 1885.
© The Roger Mann Collection

The OELC Red v. Blue XIs 1888. The short-lived attempt to produce the first professional female cricketers. © Women's Cricket Association

ABOVE The smart set at a country house mixed cricket party, c. 1890. © Women's Cricket Association

LEFT Bessie Grace, daughter of W. G., who played for the Clifton Ladies Club 1878–99. © Women's Cricket Association

ABOVE The star bat of Noumea women's cricket team all set for a swipe to the boundary in the 1920s. © Women's Cricket Association

LEFT Lucia Nichols, nineteen-year-old member of Birmingham Women's Cricket Club, being coached by a fellow West Indian, Derief Taylor, at Edgbaston. Nichols was a promising right-hand bat of the 1960s who learned her cricket in her home town of St Lucia. © Women's Cricket Association

BELOW A country house cricket group in the 1920s including members of The White Heather Club. © Women's Cricket Association

LEFT Betty Belton played in the first Test series on English soil against Australia in 1937. © Women's Cricket Association

RIGHT 1958. Ruth Westbrook played eleven Test matches for England and married Test cricketer Roger Prideaux, producing the only married couple to have both played Test cricket. © Women's Cricket Association

Straight out of the MCC handbook: Harry Crabtree showing the ladies the forward defensive in the 1960s. © Women's Cricket Association

LEFT Enid Bakewell, possibly the best female all-rounder England has ever produced, in the 1970s. © Women's Cricket Association

RIGHT Rachael Heyhoe Flint leading the England women's team out on to the hallowed turf at Lord's for the first time in 1976. © The Roger Mann Collection

LEFT Janette Brittin, 1986. Her total of 1,935 runs is a Test record, and so are her five Test centuries. © Women's Cricket Association

RIGHT Denise Annetts, 1987. This prolific Australian bat caused controversy in 1994 when she claimed her omission from the Australian team was because she was not a lesbian. Her appeal fell on deaf ears as the Australian discrimination law only protected homosexuals. © Women's Cricket Association

LEFT The author on the front cover of *Wisden Cricket Monthly* in their October 1998 issue, attempting to draw attention to the women's struggle to become members of MCC.

BELOW Clare Connor ended her six-year reign as England captain on a high by winning the Ashes in 2005. © Don Miles

Skipper Charlotte Edwards retains the Ashes for England at Worcester in 2009 after a gritty fightback for a draw. © Don Miles

Charlotte Edwards celebrates her century against India in the 2013 World Cup by cradling her bat to mark the birth of her niece.
© ICC/Solaris

Sarah Taylor, a ferocious talent on the brink of playing men's county cricket.
© Don Miles

LEFT Ellyse Perry, a current double international for Australia in cricket and football. Perry played a vital role in World Cups for both sports. © Don Miles

RIGHT Pin-up Aussie pup Holly Ferling. © Getty Images

LEFT Holly Colvin delivers. She made her debut at the age of fifteen, the youngest Test cricketer of either sex to play for England. © Don Miles

RIGHT Eileen Ash, 101 not out and still counting. She is the sole surviving member of the side that played the inaugural Test on English soil in 1937. © Victoria Carew Hunt

Rachael was replaced as captain in 1978 for the 1979 series against the West Indies. This was to be her last Test series but not her final international outing, since she went on to play in the 1982 Women's Cricket World Cup.

The facts and figures of her career make interesting reading. She did not lose a Test during her eleven-year reign as captain; she made a record fifty-one appearances for her country spanning twenty-two years; her Test batting average was 45.54 in 38 innings; she captained the first England women's team to play on the hallowed turf at Lord's as part of the Ashes series in 1976; she hit the first six in a women's Test match in 1963; her one-day international batting average was 58.45 in twenty-three matches. I could go on.

Rachael had battled hard since 1971 to get her England team to Lord's. It took a few years, but, aided by victory in the first ever Women's World Cup in 1973 and the threat to take their case to the Equal Opportunities Commission, they finally got there. Aidan Crawley, MCC president, more or less gave them the green light when he congratulated the England women after they lifted the World Cup in 1973: 'You have done enough to deserve a game at cricket's headquarters.'

There was still a fly in the ointment, however. The availability of the ground depended on Middlesex's progress in the Gillette Cup (Lord's being their home) but fortunately for the ladies the men were beaten by Lancashire, failed to make the quarter-finals and so Lord's was available for the England women. The 60-over clash against Australia was an emotional occasion for Rachael and her team; for the first time in 171 years women would finally play at the home of cricket and Rachael was quite overawed by her surroundings: 'I've got those old butterflies,' she said. 'It's so exciting to be here at last.'

Not all was plain sailing, however, and some disgruntled elderly members shook their silver heads at the news of these women being allowed into the male-only Pavilion. The *Daily Mail* reported one MCC member as saying: 'I was praying for rain. I couldn't believe this would happen in my lifetime,' while another man declared, aghast: 'I was quite shocked when I saw the women playing. Cricket is a game where concentration is very important and women are the greatest distraction a man can have around.'

The players were given permission to use the England dressing room (an added touch was red roses) and they were allowed to enter the Long Room, but this applied to the players only – female spectators were still banned from the Pavilion and had to be accompanied by a member if they wanted to enter the Tavern or Warner stands.

Rachael astutely put the Australians in to bat. Clearly overwhelmed by the surroundings, the Aussies dropped like flies to 41 for 5 and only managed a total of 162. The England women, by now more relaxed, batted to victory with a comfortable 8-wicket win. Despite the success of the day it would be another eleven years before England's women played at Lord's again and more than twenty years before MCC opened the Pavilion doors to women members.

Rachael also achieved success outside the game. She has

always had a strong media presence and since the mid-sixties has pursued a career in journalism and broadcasting. She wrote a monthly column for *The Cricketer* from 1969 and at around the same time was appointed Sports Editor of the *Wolverhampton Chronicle*. Later she went freelance as sports writer for the *Daily Telegraph* and *Sunday Telegraph*, and she made her TV debut in 1973 when she became the first woman sports presenter on ITV's *World of Sport*. She has written four books: *Fair Play*, in collaboration with Netta Rheinberg, her autobiography *Heyhoe*, and two books on hockey.

Hockey is another great passion, and she represented England as goalkeeper in 1964, and played for Staffordshire for a record twenty-five years. Staffordshire also had the pleasure of her company in squash and golf, with a lowest handicap of 5. Is there anything this woman hasn't done?

Wearing her business hat, she is a Public Relations Sports Marketing consultant in Wolverhampton, and has been a director of Wolverhampton Wanderers Football Club, of which she was made Vice-President in 2005. On the cricket front she was chosen as one of the first female honorary life members of MCC in 1999, after 217 years of men only, and in 2004 she was the first woman to be voted onto the MCC main Committee. She has worked tirelessly for the Lady Taverners, and was made president in 2001.

To top her MBE, she was made an OBE in 2008, and in 2010 she took her seat in the House of Lords to become Baroness Heyhoe Flint.

## Enid Bakewell (b. 1940)

Petite in stature but a giant of the women's game, Mrs Enid Bakewell (née Turton) was a whirlwind of talent with bat and ball. From the age of nine she was already mucking in with the local boys in their impromptu games of cricket. She was soon streets ahead of the boys at Brincliffe County Grammar School, Nottingham, and the lads would often borrow her kit. An only child from a non-cricketing family, her parents were nonetheless thrilled by her talent and gave her all the encouragement and support she needed.

At fourteen, she made her debut for her county side, Nottinghamshire, as a steady right-handed opening bat. All those years of playing with the boys had ingrained in her the concentration and keen eye required to stay at the crease for long periods and to score freely. By 1959, Enid had been spotted by the powers that be at the WCA and was invited to tour Holland with the WCA team of young and promising players. At this stage she considered herself a batsman and didn't take her bowling too seriously. Once the county got hold of her she was coached in left-arm spin, and she modelled her action on the Surrey and England great Tony Lock, even taking the same number of paces and run-up around the umpire. She later commented: 'As a Nottingham girl I was torn two ways. When I went to watch Nottingham v. Surrey I admired Tony Lock's bowling and delighted in Peter May's batting, so I sometimes hoped Surrey might win.'

Her slow left-arm was lethal on the softer wickets, particularly in New Zealand, and she drifted the ball across the wicket with the breeze and it gripped and straightened sharply off the pitch.

In 1959, she graduated from Dartford College of Physical Education where she had played in the 1st XI with fellow students and future England stars Rachael Heyhoe, Mary Pilling, Sandra Brown and Ann Jago – a superb foundation from which to launch a career in cricket. It was relatively late in the day when she got the call and finally played for her country in the 1968/9 tour of Australia and New Zealand. By 1966 she had sidelined her career as a PE teacher, was married and expecting her first baby, which meant she could not be considered for selection for the New Zealand tour of England. It was a difficult decision for her to join the 1968/9 tour because it meant a long separation from her two-year-old daughter and finances were tight. Fortunately for England she had an understanding family and husband who offered her every support, and there would be no regrets as the triumphs that lay ahead would more than compensate for the cost of leaving her family behind. Her husband's patience, however, did wear thin at one stage. In a recent interview for the Sri Lankan newspaper *The Nation* in 2012, she was frank about the strain the love of her life, cricket, put on her marriage:

He [her husband Colin, then an electrical engineer with Rolls-Royce] was very happy at the beginning that I was playing cricket but then it got too much and at one stage I was asked to play at The Oval for a men's team because they were one short in a village game. My husband said 'if you are going to play for the men I am leaving.' He packed his bag and he actually left one night but he came back for a

Sunday lunch on the Sunday afternoon. He didn't stay away for long.

Enid wasted no time in revealing her master strokes to the world and hit a maiden century in her first ever Test innings against Australia in Adelaide. Her exquisite footwork and range of shots set the tone for the rest of her international career. A practice match versus the Victorian State XI was played in between the first and second Tests. With seven Test players in the side, Victoria were at the time a force to be reckoned with but the unflappable Bakewell made short work of them, top-scoring with 59, and then tearing them apart with figures of 7 for 28 when she was brought on as first-change bowler after only seven overs – an unusual but shrewd move by her captain, Heyhoe, who had unshakeable faith in her slow left-arm spin. Even the press were blown away by her performance, with headlines such as 'English girl does a Sobers' and 'Bakewell routs Vic'.

This was no one-off with the ball as she went on to take more than five wickets in an innings no fewer than twelve times on this tour.

She opened her account against New Zealand at Wellington in 1969 with her second Test century, 124, and followed up with 5 for 40 in this first drawn Test. Her relentless steamrolling of New Zealand produced 114 in the first innings and 66 not out in the second innings at Christchurch, and she once again swept through the Kiwi batting order with 8 wickets in the match, including a 5 for 56 that clinched the victory. She lived up to her reputation as a dynamo, tormenting batsman and bowler alike. Her vice-captain, Edna Barker, engineered things so that Enid hit the winning run to give England their first victory against New Zealand since 1954.

Next, in a warm-up match before the third Test, Enid took her hundredth wicket of the tour against a strong North Shore team in another epic England performance. She then achieved the 'double' in the third Test at Auckland when she passed a thousand runs for the tour, a unique feat in women's cricket. The record books were bursting with her statistics: in the entire tour she produced 1,031 runs at an average of 39.6 and 118 wickets at 9.7 apiece. These extraordinary statistics are worth recording – she topped both batting and bowling averages against New Zealand with 103.00 and 19 wickets at 12.73 apiece.

Enid's status in world cricket now rocketed and she was heralded as the world's best woman all-rounder, receiving endless plaudits from newspapers apparently bent on eclipsing each other in their praise of her:

'Mainstay of an aggressive English knock was Enid Bakewell who played as correctly as any male Test player might have as she moved relentlessly towards her century.'

'An audacious batsman, fast between wickets, who uses her feet better than many Plunkett Shield cricketers.'

If that first comment seems slightly condescending, most of the headlines and reports expressed genuine admiration for and wonder at her exceptional talent. Following this phenomenal tour, Enid was given almost unprecedented exposure in the 1970 edition of *Wisden*. She was the first woman cricketer to whom a full-page feature and photograph were devoted – up to that point, women were usually squeezed into the back of the book, somewhere near the obituaries.

Enid is always quick to recognise the contribution of her team-mates, notably that of wicketkeeper Shirley Hodges, who made 13 stumpings and took 3 catches off her commanding left-arm spin: 'I couldn't have done it without our brilliant wicketkeeper.' Her unassuming character masked an understanding of the paramount importance of the success of the team above her personal achievements.

Enid's cool and composed technique remained perfectly intact during the first Women's World Cup in 1973. At the opening match at Hove against an International XI, she and her fellow opener, Lynne Thomas, put on a world-record stand of 246 which would remain in the record books for another twenty-five years. Both scored unbeaten centuries. She was the match-winner in the final at Edgbaston against the Aussies when she calmly knocked up 118, prompting *Wisden* to remark that she 'looked as relaxed as if she had been on the beach'.

Vivian Jenkins of the *Sunday Times* joined in the praise: 'Enid Bakewell, the Nottinghamshire mother of three, was England's prop and stay in the final and decisive match … she scored a splendid 118 out of her side's 279–3 in the allotted 60 overs…'

Even at the age of forty-one Enid was still hot property in the cricket world and played in the 1982 Women's World Cup, claiming many victims with her crafty spin. Her one-day career was almost as glittering as her Test career – 500 runs (including two hundreds) scored in 23 matches at an average of 35.71, and 25 wickets at 21.12.

When the Australians toured England in 1976 Enid inflicted serious damage on them with her old partner in crime, Lynne Thomas. They managed a century partnership in both innings at the second Test at Edgbaston – yet another unique record – although unfortunately the magic century forever eluded Lynne Thomas, although she did accumulate a healthy number of half-centuries. Touchingly, Enid named her youngest daughter Lynne after her opening partner.

## Claire Taylor (b. 1975)

My grandfather was a firm believer in the adage that you could achieve anything if you wanted it badly enough. Claire Taylor has proved the truth of that sentiment. On her retirement in 2011, Clare Connor, ECB head of women's cricket and former England captain, spoke glowingly of her former team-mate: 'Her incomparable hunger to always improve, hard work, focus and mental toughness have combined to make her the best batter in the women's game. Claire has earned the respect of all who have played with her, against her, or who have had the pleasure of watching her.'

Claire possesses the drive, energy and conviction of good old-fashioned hard work needed to soar to the top of her game. She is an example to everyone. The most important man in her life is her long-term coach, Mark Lane, who puts her success down to her doggedness and determination. Over years of hard graft, Lane conditioned in Claire both a technical and mental approach to her game. As a high-flying Oxford maths graduate, Claire is a bit of an egghead, and has applied her intellect to her advantage when batting:

> I don't know if other people do it, but when I'm batting at my best I have a 3D awareness of the shape of the field and where the spaces are – I used to play chess at Montessori school. Maths, I think, has given me more control and confidence when I'm calculating the runs per over we have to score.

Taylor may have been the most single-minded player in women's cricket but she started out in life as a hockey-playing forward, representing her country at U-17 and U-19 levels. She discovered cricket at the age of thirteen and made her county debut at seventeen, though hockey was her number one sport in those early years. At Oxford, she won three Blues for hockey and three half-Blues for cricket and in the England camp she was considered to be a wicketkeeper with only limited batting ability. She finally made her international debut at twenty-three and it didn't take her long to impress the waiting world.

Her career reached fever pitch in 2009 and her mission was well and truly accomplished when England did the double, lifting the trophy in the World Cup and the inaugural World Twenty20 tournament. Claire was named Player of the Tournament in the World Cup as the leading run scorer with 324 runs at an average of 64.80, and claimed the same title in the Twenty20 competition. In the circus that is Twenty20 cricket she creamed the ball all over the park and, remarkably, was dismissed only once, finishing with a batting average of 199.00. In a bumper year she also hit the winning runs at Lord's in the T20 final and capped it all by playing a key role in helping England retain the Ashes.

Taylor was showered with accolades following a sensational 2009 and was, unexpectedly, named one of *Wisden*'s five Cricketers of the Year – a first for an Englishwoman in a usually all-male preserve. Belinda Clark had been honoured as Australia Cricketer of the Year in the first edition of the Australian version of *Wisden* in 1998. Peter Roebuck, formerly of Somerset and England, was editor at the time and he was a brave man. The male Australian cricket world was predictably horrified and he was, equally predictably, vilified. Scyld Berry, *Wisden* editor in 2009, risked a similar fate in England, but he stood firm, explaining that not to acknowledge Taylor's achievements would have been a crime, 'a sin of omission, an act of prejudice'. He went on to say: 'there is no element of political correctness or publicity seeking about her selection' and that she was 'chosen on merit, for being pre-eminent in her form of the game'.

Thanks to Berry, the profile of women's cricket reached new heights and quite rightly so.

The avalanche had been triggered and Taylor went on to win the ICC Women's Cricketer of the Year and was named as ECB Women's Player of the Year. The 2010 New Year Honours list wanted a piece of her, too, and in it she was awarded an MBE.

Statistics are everything and Taylor's stats say it all: in 15

Tests, 1,030 runs and 4 centuries at an average of 41.20; in 126 ODIs, 4,101 runs and 8 centuries at 40.20; in 27 International Twenty20s, 615 runs. Her most distinguished century, 156 not out against India, is still the record for the highest ODI score made at Lord's by a man or a woman, beating Viv Richards' 138 in 1979.

### Charlotte Edwards (b. 1979)

Charlotte Edwards was the baby of the cricket world when, at the age of sixteen, she became the youngest player ever to represent England, a record subsequently broken by her team-mate Holly Colvin when she turned out for England at the even more tender age of fifteen in the first 2005 Ashes Test. Teenage angst was never a problem for Edwards and in 1997, in the season following her debut, she smashed a ton off only 118 balls against the touring South Africans. On the eve of her eighteenth birthday she hit a then-record ODI score of 173 in the 1997 World Cup against Ireland. She was scoring prolifically in all formats of the game and by 1999 she had nailed her maiden Test hundred against India.

After sporadic periods out of the game with a nagging injury, Edwards re-entered the fold to take part in the 2005 World Cup in South Africa. Showing no signs of rustiness, she breezed past Jan Brittin's record of 2,121 ODI runs for England and, soon after, scooped the highly coveted Vodafone Player of the Year award for the second consecutive year. The best of 2005 was yet to come, however, when England won back the Ashes after a twenty-year drought. When England's captain, Clare Connor, suffered a foot injury, Charlotte was handed the captaincy for the 2005 tour of Sri Lanka and India. She took over permanently when Connor retired in 2006, and led her team through possibly its most triumphant period in the history of the women's game.

England comprehensively beat Australia in the solitary Test at Bowral in 2008 to retain the Ashes, and their steam-roller of victories continued into the ODI series against New Zealand, West Indies, South Africa and India. In the same year, Edwards picked up the ICC Women's Cricketer of the Year award to add to her other gongs.

A glorious 2009 saw Edwards and her girls sitting on top of the world. First they disposed of New Zealand in the World Cup final in Australia and then lifted the silver at Lord's to win the World Twenty20 championship. A well-earned MBE came her way that summer and, soon after, she hit an unbeaten half-century against the Aussies in a one-off Test to help England to a draw, and to hold onto the Ashes.

The months following the World Cup win were a highly charged time for Edwards:

The fact we won the World Cup away from home, in Sydney, made it extra special too. You experience a whole load of emotions. I was just so overwhelmed by it all. I couldn't stop crying, which, when you look back on it and see the pictures, is actually a bit embarrassing.

Another landmark on her map of success came when she won her 142nd ODI cap for England in 2010, making her the most capped female cricketer in the world. Two months later she hit her first Ashes century, 114 not out in England's first innings of 207 all out. Unfortunately, on this occasion her fine performance could not prevent an Australian win.

Charlotte and the England team sweated it out in India at the 2013 Women's World Cup. She was confident England had a good chance but, wisely, was wary of their opponents:

> India are a real threat at home, the West Indies over here are going to be equally as hard and Pakistan and Sri Lanka are used to these conditions. I would imagine people will think England, Australia and New Zealand are still the top three teams but I don't think anyone can write India off in India.

England could not hold on to the number one spot this time around as Australia overcame the West Indies in the final.

Edwards' services to cricket are immeasurable and in 2012 she became the first woman to join the MCC World Cricket Committee, where she will mix with the likes of Michael Atherton and Kumar Sangakkara. She captains Kent when she is not busy on the international circuit, is employed by Hunts County bats, and, most important of all, she is an ambassador for the charity Chance to Shine, campaigning to bring cricket into state schools all over the country. Charlotte is an inspiration for all girls and boys, and Clare Connor's words of praise for her come from the heart: '[she is] a credit to women's cricket globally, a superb role model for girls who aspire to play for their country'.

Finally, it should not be forgotten that Edwards is also a useful leg-spin bowler and her international stats with both bat and ball are impressive: in 19 Tests, 1,522 runs, 49.09 average, 4 centuries and 12 wickets; in 160 ODIs, 4,783 runs, 36.51 average, 6 centuries and 54 wickets; in 61 T20s, 1,599 runs, 31.98 average and 9 wickets.

Myrtle MacLagan, 1935.

# ENGLAND: HOME AND AWAY

## The First Tests

By 1934, Australian women's cricket had got its act together and had organised itself nationally. Both Australia and England were itching to play each other, and the Australian Women's Cricket Council invitation to the Women's Cricket Association to send a touring team to Australia was accepted with alacrity. It was a hell of a long way to go so, to make it more worthwhile, England wanted to take on New Zealand as well on this courageous tour. The New Zealand Women's Cricket Council was in its infancy at that stage but bravely accepted the challenge and cabled back: 'Delighted at prospect of English visit. Can guarantee billets, entertainments, matches, but regret no travelling expenses.'

Money was tight all round and the Australians were far from rolling in it with only four pounds and seven shillings in the bank! These were industrious and pro-active women, however, and the England players set about raising the £80 each needed for personal expenses well in advance of the departure date. The team that eventually sailed from Tilbury on the SS *Cathay* was made up largely of England's best players, with only one or two of the original selection unable to finance themselves or take time off work. These promising women were: Betty Archdale, captain (Kent), Betty Snowball, vice-captain (St Swithin's, Winchester), Betty Green, manager (Northwood), Molly Hide (Reading University), Myrtle Maclagan (Minley Manor), Joy Partridge (Wycombe Abbey), Mary 'Peter' Taylor (Gunnersbury), Doris Turner (Gunnersbury), Joy Liebert (Bushey), Carol Valentine (Cuckoos Club), Mary Spear (Dartford College of Physical Education), Grace Morgan (Ministry of Health, Civil Service), Mary Burletson (Anstey College of Physical Training), Molly Child (Harrogate) and Mary 'Dick' Richards (Dublin).

With an average age of twenty-four, these young women had, by all accounts, a fabulous – and enviable – time making their way to Australia across the oceans of the world. What a perfect way to travel and so much more civilised and pleasurable than the cattle class of today's air travel. The diaries of Grace Morgan, reserve wicketkeeper for the tour, bring to life the absolute thrill and elation felt by these unworldly and innocent women. Amid frenetic rounds of shopping, packing, dinners, receptions and team meetings prior to departure for the Antipodes, the 21-year-old Grace summed up her utter feverishness in her tour diary:

'We had a splendid dinner and then proceeded together to Caxton Hall in taxis. Crowds of people came there to give us a good send off and these included press photographers.

Excitement however got the better of me and I was sick on reaching home.'

These fortunate women spent what sounds like an idyllic time playing deck tennis, table tennis, quoits, lazing in the sun on the poop deck, and knitted and danced till bedtime. These hours of leisure were punctuated by cricket practice in their own deck 'nets' and cricket matches against the ship's officers and first- or second-class men, as further revealed by Grace: 'Knitted then played one game of table tennis. After lunch Doris and I wrote to Miss Cox and then I watched the deck cricket match against the 1st class men. WCA won 70–46. Helped choose prizes for fancy dress parade. Wrote up my diary and then changed for dinner.'

For many of the team embarking on their first trip abroad there must have been any number of overwhelming sights and sensations. They explored foreign soil on the isle of Château d'If off Marseilles, at Valletta and Sliema in Malta, Port Said in Egypt, Aden (in those days a British colony but today part of the Yemen), Bombay, and had a practice match in Colombo, Ceylon: 'Natives absolutely packed the ground. I have never seen so many spectators at a women's match before. Every possible vantage point was taken, including the trees. The Asst. Purser, First officer, and also a bishop from our ship were among the spectators.'

Invitations from all corners of the world came pouring in, including requests from men's teams in Aden and Colombo who were keen to challenge this historic team of ladies. Such requests were turned down as it was against the principles of the WCA to play against men. More's the pity. It would have provided invaluable practice for them to face experienced men's sides en route to Australia, not to mention a bit of a social romp.

The packed tour itinerary took them across the entire width of the Australian continent with fourteen matches played and six more in New Zealand. The England team were embraced by the Australian crowd wherever they went. They swept through the country with relative ease but it was the state matches that caused them to stop in their tracks. The state players showed more class and England had to settle for a draw against West Australia in Perth and Victoria in Melbourne. This first trip to Melbourne was something of an eye-opener for the women: they were placed on an equal footing with their male counterparts and given a slap-up lunch at the Melbourne Cricket Ground (MCG) and a grand tour. They were also introduced to some first-rate former cricketers, among them Bill Ponsford, Jim Kelly, Keith Rigg, Leslie Fleetwood-Smith, Hans Ebeling and Hugh Trumble, who passed on invaluable inside information about the state of the wickets around the country. They got a kick out of roaming the 'men-only' pavilion, as our indefatigable diarist records: 'Our dressing-room is the same one that Hobbs, Sutcliffe and Co. used when they were over here and we felt honoured in that we were the first women to be allowed in certain parts of the pavilion which are regarded practically as "hallowed ground".'

The England girls were learning fast on quality hard wickets and gaining vital experience against spin. They beat New South Wales by 7 wickets, following a 'very sporting' declaration by their captain, and then destroyed Queensland by an innings and 41 runs.

As an aside, not only do we have convincing evidence that women invented overarm bowling (see above) but one of the Australian Shevill sisters may have been the designer of the first (albeit cobbled together) 'helmet'. Essie Shevill, a wicketkeeper, had been bashed on the hooter a few years earlier, and so turned out behind the stumps for NSW against England wearing a wire mask. Admittedly it was homemade and uncomfortable and was abandoned after a few overs, but who knows? It may have been a first.

Oozing with confidence after two comprehensive victories, England were ready to do battle in their first Test match in Brisbane. The now obsolete Exhibition Ground was the scene of the first ever women's Test match and the tension was palpable. With fifteen hundred spectators looking on, the jittery Australians only managed to put 47 runs on the board in the first innings. We are already familiar with the exploits of Myrtle Maclagan who took 7 for 10 with her accurate spin bowling on a drying pitch. Spin was very much the queen of the match as England in turn suffered at the hands of Australia's spin bowlers and only Maclagan's 72 and Archdale's 32 saved them from a similar scoreline. Australia restored some dignity in their second innings and rallied to 138, with Essie Shevill scoring a patient 63 not out. Essie's married sister, who went by the splendid name Fern Blade, also played in this match. However, 138 was not enough and England won comfortably by 9 wickets.

Australia's wicketkeeper, Hilda Hills, suffered a broken nose in their first innings and retired hurt for the rest of the match. Perhaps Miss Shevill's rudimentary mask wasn't such a bad idea after all.

In these early Tests the women's game adopted the laws of the men's game as issued by MCC with one exception, the size of the ball. The men's ball weighed in at 5½ ounces and the ladies' at approximately 5 ounces and this has remained so to the present day. In the 1930s the men were still playing Tests with no time restrictions as this was reckoned to obviate the need for a side to declare an innings. It was becoming less practical, however, since matches could drag on for days, often with no end in sight. (The longest Test match on record, between England and South Africa at Durban in 1939, lasted twelve days. It only ended when England had to make a mad dash to catch their boat home. The match was abandoned as a draw and, unsurprisingly, this was the last 'timeless' Test ever to be played.) Sensibly, the women opted for three-day Tests for the 1934/5 series, which allowed them both to honour their busy match schedule and avoid dropping dead from exhaustion.

The second Test at the Sydney Cricket Ground boasted an impressive array of cricketing sisters for Australia, namely Margaret and Barbara Peden and Essie and Irene Shevill. Had their sister Fern not been dropped for this match, the Shevill family would have been even better represented.

The women were naturally delighted to play at the famous Sydney Ground and crowds swelled to an average of 4,500 over the three days. The result was another easy win for England by 8 wickets, with Maclagan showing her full might with the bat by scoring the first century (119) in women's Test cricket as well as contributing to a record first-wicket partnership of 145 with Snowball (71) – this remained a record in Australia until 1976. Snowball donned the gloves to help demolish the Australians, stumping four batsmen in an innings, a feat never bettered for England. Joy Partridge was the bowling star in Australia's second innings, taking 6 for 96.

In the third Test in Melbourne there were signs that Australia were starting to catch up with England. The fast-improving Aussies seemed to have the measure of the England batsmen and bowlers, and their queen of spin, Peggy Antonio, caused pandemonium in English ranks when she took 6 for 49 in England's first innings. Petite and dark-haired, Antonio dominated the 1930s with her masterly leg-spin and the Australian press loved her, christening her 'Girl Grimmett' after the great Clarrie Grimmett. For the first time, a Test match proved to be an evenly balanced contest and the game finished in a draw. Australia might well have won had time been on their side. Again, England's superstars Maclagan and Snowball were the only ones to get going with the bat, with a 50 and 83 not out respectively, but England failed to seize the advantage.

There was a suggestion that the ashes of the stumps used in the final Test match in Melbourne should be placed in a silver urn, so as to create a physical presence, but the Australian Women's Cricket Council was against the idea, preferring the idea of 'mythical Ashes'. So there would be no repeat of that black day (for English cricket at least) in August 1882 when the original 'Ashes' were born.

In fact, the Test series between England and Australia only became known officially as the Ashes in the women's game in 1998 when a ceremony took place in the Harris Gardens at Lord's. A miniature bat, signed by the England

and Australian Women's Cricket Squads, and a copy of the WCA Constitution and Rules Book were consigned to the flames and the ashes were sealed in a trophy, to be known henceforth as 'the Ashes'. This trophy was also in commemoration of the dissolution of the WCA, originally formed in 1926. This trophy and the replica urn were made from a 300-year-old English yew tree that had been blown down in the great storm of 1987.

England had been a real hit in Australia and the team left Australia for New Zealand with a degree of reluctance. A farewell dinner was thrown for them by the Victorian WCA, as Grace Morgan recorded in her diary:

'This was all very nice but was tinged with sadness as we were loath to leave Australia. However, from what we were told our visit had been thoroughly appreciated and has helped Australian women's cricket considerably.'

Once in New Zealand, the England women took the country by storm, demolishing teams wherever they went. Women's cricket in New Zealand was very much in its infancy and the home teams' raw inexperience was testimony to that. England sailed through their matches in Auckland, Wanganui, Wellington, Canterbury, Otago and Invercargill, winning by enormous margins and being met by enthusiasm and interest by Kiwi cricketers and the public alike.

The New Zealand team, which had only been in existence for two years, were completely outclassed by England in the only Test, played at a chilly Christchurch. England's daunting 503 for 5 declared proved too much for the fledgling NZ, who could only muster 44 and 122 in their two innings. Records galore were made by the English batsmen: Snowball smashed 189, her century coming in 115 minutes (a record) and at that time the highest score by a woman. Hide, with 110, crept into the record books as part of the highest second-wicket partnership of 235 with the unstoppable Snowball. Maclagan, never out of the limelight, took 5 for 22 in New Zealand's dismal first innings. Poor old New Zealand even lost their captain, Symons, to injury and were one bat short in their second innings. It was a superb team effort by England and a fitting way to end the tour. The 'mythical Ashes' sailed home with England. Twelfth man and generous-hearted diarist Grace Morgan commented on this Test:

> Betty A declared at midday when the total was 503 for 4 [*sic*] wkts. New Zealand were dismissed a second time before tea for 122. They batted much more confidently this time but during the day three of their team got hit in the face by the ball – not because of body-line!

Despite the obvious dominance of England in both Australia and, more starkly, New Zealand, this tour gave both countries an immense boost with press coverage and crowd attendance beyond their dreams.

## Aussies Sail to England

In 1937 it was Australia's turn to visit England for the first time and there was much hype and speculation before their arrival. Money was, as ever, tight for the WCA and an absolute minimum of £1,000 had to be found to cover the travelling, hospitality and entertainment costs in England. Our dynamic English ladies prepared well in advance and managed to raise £150 beyond the £1,000 target. Knitting, selling chocolate, and donations from village cricket clubs did the trick.

Thirteen of the sixteen-strong touring team to arrive at Southampton in May 1937 had faced England before on their home soil in 1934/5. Two years had passed and a mature and improved side was keenly awaited by the English. Unlike the England touring party of 1934/5, these Australians were kept on a short leash and there was to be no messing about, as their 'Tour Rules' reveal:

- No member shall drink, smoke or gamble while on tour.
- No girl may be accompanied by her husband, a relation or a friend.
- Writing articles on cricket during a tour is strictly forbidden.
- While on board ship, no girl shall visit the top deck of the liner after dinner.
- Members of the team must retire to bed by 10 p.m. during the voyage.
- Members will do physical drill on deck at 7.15 a.m. daily except Sundays.

Under the captaincy of Margaret Peden, these disciplined troops were Peggy Antonio, Nancy Clements, Elsie Deane, Mollie Flaherty, Winnie George, Patricia Holmes, Amy Hudson, Marie Jegust, Nell McLarty, Barbara Peden, Hazel Pritchard, Kathleen Smith, Sue Summers, Alicia Walsh and Alice Wegemund.

In contrast to Australia's team of 'old hands', England had gone for fresh blood with seven debutantes making an appearance at the first Test at Northampton. A transformed Australia squared up to England and won this first Test by 31 runs. The Aussies amassed an impressive 300 runs in the first innings and the crowd feasted upon the fluent, graceful batting of Hazel Pritchard. She knocked up a stylish 87 'with her own inimitable delicacy of touch', ably supported by the powerful Kath Smith, who scored 88. Our own heroine Myrtle Maclagan replied with 89 not out, and Snowball made a valiant 72 in the second innings, but the slow, high-tossed leg-breaks of Peggy Antonio brought about England's demise: she took 9 wickets in the match.

The two teams were so well matched that almost all of their matches were in the balance until the closing stages. The turn of fortunes and roller-coaster of emotions from both sides gave us cricket at its best.

The Blackpool Test produced another closely fought battle and this time England came out on top. Maclagan hit the headlines with her 115, the first female century on English soil, and Hide shone with the ball, cleaning up the Australian batsmen with match figures of 8 for 58. Australia were not shy with the bat either, with sterling efforts from Pritchard, Smith, Holmes, George and Barbara Peden, scoring 302 and 126 in their two innings. Peggy Antonio produced another superb display of spin, taking 8 wickets from only 23 overs. The gloves were handed over to Australia's replacement keeper, Alice Wegemund, for this Test, and she made a cracking debut with a record 7 dismissals in the match. Eileen Whelan (now Ash), the last surviving member of the

1937 England side, took 3 for 35 in the second innings. We will hear more of Eileen's adventures later.

Despite bad weather, the Oval Test proved to be just as dramatic as the previous two. Holmes made a sparkling 70 in Australia's first innings but England's Davis was a major thorn in their side when she took 4 for 10 in only 4 overs. Lady fortune had firmly landed in the England camp. The batting giants Maclagan, Hide and Snowball were at their blistering best and initially England's order appeared impenetrable. However, day three saw Australia rise from the ashes as McLarty and Antonio delivered canny, pinpoint-accurate bowling to stifle England's progress. Marjorie Pollard, a pioneering enthusiast of the women's game, wrote about the 1937 tour for the official magazine, *Women's Cricket*, and her take on the mastery of these Australian bowlers makes interesting reading:

> England 227 for 3, had as their plan of campaign a rapid 130 odd runs before lunch. Splendid thought. But, the plan miscarried, for the very simple reason that Australia this morning were a totally different side as compared with yesterday afternoon. If I live to see more accurate bowling than that of McLarty's, I shall be surprised. If I see a cleverer spin bowler than Antonio I shall not only be surprised, but a genuine disbeliever.

It was a painful and trying morning for England's batsmen and it yielded only 80 runs. Australia's fielding didn't miss a beat and Snowball missed her century by one miserable run after a spectacular run-out. Time now became the enemy and Hide had to declare at lunchtime when only 100 runs ahead. The Aussies had the final afternoon to bat at their leisure and Hazel Pritchard made a calm 66, Antonio 37, Kath Smith 45, and this steady stream of runs took them out of the woods to 224 by the end of the day. Both sides had triumphed in their way and a draw was the inevitable result. The crowd of nearly 7,000 punters got more than their money's worth and the press couldn't have been more enthusiastic. Even the sceptics were silenced. One pleasantly surprised man was overheard saying: 'I thought they'd bowl lobs, but by Jove, they can play.' A droll Harold Griffin cartoon strip of the time bore the caption: 'Hard-hitting Hazel at The Oval, Australia's female Bradman, who makes boundaries look as easy as dabbing on lipstick.'

Other press comments from the summer of 1937 include these glowing accounts:

Those who had not before watched first-class ladies cricket, expected to see them attempting to achieve something beyond their power. They must have left the ground amazed at what they had seen.

Their technical efficiency, liveliness and enthusiasm, made the thought of a [men's] county match seem humdrum.

There was a lesson to be learnt by men who, relatively, potter about at the game.

As so often, Major Pridham has some insightful and complimentary words for the Australian 1937 players:

Mrs Margaret Peden – She made a change of bowling for

that last over of the match – and the tour; a big but justifiable risk, worthy of a Winston Churchill.

Miss Patricia Holmes – Her score of 200 (retired) at Basingstoke v. West of England – the first time a woman cricketer has ever played an innings of 200 – was a wonderful physical feat.

Hazel Pritchard – earned the title of 'The Australian lady Bradman'. This was no idle compliment.

Peggy Antonio – She was capable of spinning the ball more than any other woman bowler. She also proved herself to be the best all-round player in women's cricket.

Mollie Flaherty – The fastest bowler yet seen in women's cricket, she had a fine and vigorous action, technically good enough to satisfy the shade of Walter Brearly.

Nell McLarty – Would any man have expected that a girl could keep a perfect length for hours at a stretch? Steady.

Kathleen Smith – As a batswoman she was described as having the most vicious pull-drive in women's cricket.

A staggering 10,000 spectators turned up to Mitcham Green to watch the final fixture of the tour, a match attendance that spoke volumes for the admirable spirit and quality of play these ladies achieved throughout their season in the sun.

As war loomed, however, high hopes of a second visit to Australia and New Zealand for 1939/40 were dashed when the tour was cancelled. It would be another eleven years before England would take up their bats in anger again.

**Post-War Revival**

When that day seemed to have arrived in the winter of

1947, it was a false start: a ship could not be found to take the England team to Australia and New Zealand, and so the trip was postponed for another year. Britain was still suffering from post-war aches and pains but morale was high and our cricketers wanted to enrich their lives once again with good cricket and better times. The England men had already received a thumping from Bradman's boys both home and away, so the ladies were keen for a glorious victory to lift the nation.

Under the captaincy of veteran Molly Hide, the team set sail on the Orient Line's *Orion* in October 1948. Old-timers Maclagan, Snowball, Morgan, Brown, McEvoy, Whelan and Lowe made the cut, together with young guns Wood, Birch, Wilkinson, Duggan, Sanders, Robinson, Johnson and Joy. Netta Rheinberg went as their player/manager. The *Australian Women's Weekly* had plenty to say about the approaching England players, all of it complimentary: 'Veterans of the first and second Test teams, and youngsters who learned to bat and field while menaced by Hitler's Luftwaffe, the team has plenty of confidence and is dead keen to put up a good show in Australia.'

Despite wobbly sea legs, the girls made quick work of the All-Ceylon XI at the Tamil Union Cricket Ground in Colombo. The Ceylon team had been cobbled together from scratch with five Europeans and six Sinhalese girls, who had gamely thrown themselves into a crash course in cricket over the few weeks before England's arrival. It was not a serious match but the crowd of 8,000 were particularly zealous in their appreciation, as described by Netta Rheinberg in her tour diary: 'At the end of the game, the crowd rushed on to the pitch and mobbed us! I was quite anxious as I watched a sea of brown faces approaching and wondered whether to give the order to "beat" it.'

Highlights of the game were Molly Hide's century and Megan Lowe's hat-trick with her canny spin. The Ceylonese girls had much to be heartened by, their natural aptitude for the game evident in their wrist play and sharp eye. Another high point was when a surprising discovery was made as the England girls went out to inspect the wicket. They had a long chat with the head groundsman who turned out to be a sari-clad grounds*woman*, and also extremely good at her job.

By the time the tourists reached the Adelaide Oval for the first Test match they had a fine tally of results under their belt. Meandering across the western and southern states, Queensland and New South Wales, they had played eleven matches in all, winning seven and drawing four. In a game against the Combined Australian XI at Perth they came face to face for the first time with the Gargantua that was Betty Wilson. She flung herself about the field taking stunning catches and then unleashed her superior bowling on the unsuspecting English. Her batting was even more devastating, knocking up a breathtaking century, together with another talented centurion, Una Paisley. This was more than a little sobering for the English women, now well aware that the Tests would be no easy ride.

The Australian public showed their vast appetite for women's cricket when 20,000 men and women showed up for the Adelaide Test. Betty Wilson did not let them down: she smashed her way to the first century by an Australian woman in an international against England. Hot on her heels, Una Paisley, the Aussie captain, cut and drove her way to 46 and built a 115 partnership with Wilson at lightning speed. A dangerous pair, indeed. Wilson was unrelenting in her destruction of England and she took the batting line-up apart, claiming six victims for only 23 runs. Special mention goes to Whiteman, too, who was involved in six dismissals in England's second innings. Paisley and Hudson confidently stroked their way to 173 for 5 declared in Australia's second innings. England hadn't a hope in hell and lost by 186 runs.

Australia dismissed England for less than half their first innings total at the Melbourne Test and eventually left England 309 to win in four and three-quarter hours. The golden pair of Maclagan (77) and Hide (51) played a match-saving partnership before leaving it to the rest to block for King and country. Huge sighs of relief from the England camp when the clock struck six o'clock and the rubber was saved for the final match of the series at Sydney.

England needed an outright win in Sydney if they were to prevent the 'mythical Ashes' they had held since 1934 being claimed by the Australians. For once, Molly Hide won the toss and England were first to open their account with the bat. Alas they scraped a flimsy 172 with only Hide and Wilkinson making any inroads. The Australians pounced like panthers in the field and Schmidt starred in the slips, taking three fine catches. Hudson, Laughton and Paisley batted soundly and took Australia to 272, a confident 100 runs ahead of the Brits. When the menacing clouds finally broke on the last day, England lost their chance to go for the win. Hide battled on in chilly, slippery conditions in between rain breaks and finished with an admirable 124 not out, making her the first woman to score a fifty and a hundred in consecutive Test innings. Neville Cardus, the well-known cricket writer and music critic, who was there on the day, compared her to Denis Compton, and the Sydney Cricket Ground Trust was so impressed that they hung a photograph of Molly in the pavilion, the first 'sheila' to be honoured in this way.

But this was well and truly Australia's Ashes. They were the superior side throughout the series and had the edge on the English in every facet of the game. They deserved to win with their skilful, athletic fielding and devastating spin bowling from an array of first-string bowlers in Craddock, Paisley, Wilson and Hudson. In sharp comparison to England, Australia batted right down the order, while England depended too much on its big stars to win matches and needed greater depth.

England's domination of the 1930s was in a post-war decline and all those years of inactivity brought on by the war had taken their toll. But at least nothing had dampened the spirit of these ladies and the vitality and sparkle with which they played would have made MCC, those champions of 'the spirit of cricket', extremely proud.

### New Zealand 1949

England were little troubled by New Zealand and won the only Test in Eden Park, Auckland, by 185 runs. Back in 1935, England had thrashed the Kiwis by a colossal 337, so there was a marked improvement in their play fourteen years on. In her only Test appearance for New Zealand, their off-spinner Gooder, had match figures of 8 for 73 in 39.2 overs.

### Willow to Willow with Eileen Whelan

Our only living debutante from 1937 is the vivacious Eileen Ash (née Whelan), who, in 2011, became the first woman Test cricketer to reach the age of 100 not out. I had the pleasure of meeting this spry, quick-witted lady in her 102nd year at her home perched on a hill, with sweeping views over Norwich. Not one to be left behind by technology, she asked whether the bossy lady on my Satnav had got me to her house without any trouble. Then, spying my iPhone, she asked if I had an iPad as well and expressed disappointment that she hadn't been given one for Christmas.

There was nothing disappointing about Eileen. She made her debut for England in the first ever women's Test match played on English soil at Northampton in the 1937 Ashes series. She earned her place as a specialist medium-pace bowler, taking 10 wickets in her international Test career at an average of 23.00.

Eileen was immersed in cricket from the moment she drew breath, with six uncles and two brothers, all of whom played the game. Her proud father liked to tell people at their local cricket club, where Eileen used to play with her two brothers: 'The girl's better than the two boys and she's a much better fielder.' Her poor brothers didn't stand a chance. At five she was given her first cricket bat by her enthusiastic parents and she took the bat to bed with her that night. Some things never change.

She made her mark in that first Test series in England by

taking four wickets in both the first and second matches and her place was cemented for the proposed 1939 tour to Australia. We know that war intervened and broke her heart at the peak of her powers. As cricket took a back seat during the war, she worked in security for the Civil Service, playing only a handful of games for the Red Cross.

Eileen was one of the lucky ones to board the *Orion* in 1948 bound for Australia in the company of the much-vaunted Mary Duggan, Molly Hide, Myrtle Maclagan and Betty Snowball. This fearsome combination of personality and talent was stretched to the limit when they came breast to breast with the omnipotent Betty Wilson. Eileen described the team's reaction to Wilson: 'We were all terrified of her; she was just so efficient and powerful.'

Eileen stressed how much she always loved fielding and she was singled out by the Australian men's captain Lindsay Hassett in 1949 when he walked straight past England captain Molly Hide to congratulate Eileen on a supreme performance in the field. She attributes some of her love of bowling to the Essex and England fast bowler Kenny Farnes, as she spent her teenage years admiring his elegant action at Leyton Cricket Ground at Ilford. Sadly, Farnes was killed in the Second World War.

Eileen still keeps a shiny cherry in her bureau at home and often tosses it from one hand to another, rekindling memories of her sparkling playing days. She showed me her grip and talked me through her bowling: 'We didn't "swing" the ball in those days, but "swerved" it and I could move it both ways. I had a sneaky slower ball which was a leg-break and always the fifth ball of the over so as not to confuse the keeper.' In today's game, she would never have got away with her sneaky fifth ball of the over because video analysis would have exposed her cunning. More disguise and variety is demanded of bowlers these days in a world ruled by technology.

Eileen remembered with relish her time in the sun in Ballarat, near Melbourne, playing against a Victorian County XI: 'I had the time of my life scoring a quick 104 and then took 5 wickets for 10 runs, every one of them clean bowled, and all the schoolboys clamoured for my autograph.'

Her passion for the game is as fierce as it ever was and she is glued to Test cricket on the telly whenever possible, even if it means dragging herself out of bed at four in the morning to watch England take on India. She was overjoyed to be made an honorary member of MCC in 2011 and made a beeline for the Pavilion to watch the England women play India, and even had a stroll out to the middle during an interval: a thrill she never thought she'd live to experience, seventy-five years after making her debut for England. She took in the men's South Africa Test, too, and is now looking forward to an action-packed Ashes Test series from the best seat in the house. Eileen and I have a date in the diary to meet in the Pavilion for a glass of something special. Her spirit is indomitable.

## The Golden Fifties

Women's cricket experienced a golden age in the 1950s as cricket thrived in the post-war gloom; there seemed little else on offer for sporty ladies to savour. It was a decade which saw five Test series: in 1951, England v. Australia at home; in 1954, England v. New Zealand at home; in 1957, England v. Australia and v. New Zealand down under; and in 1958, England v. Australia at home.

England wanted the Ashes to return home but it was not to be. The 1951 series finished 1–1 and saw the coming of age of Betty Wilson with bat and ball, and veteran Myrtle Maclagan once again showed the world that she was still the number one England all-rounder. Mary Duggan stole the show in the third Test at The Oval with her devastating bowling during Australia's second innings. Duggan took two nine-wicket hauls in this series and her outstanding international reputation was set in stone.

England welcomed New Zealand for the first time in 1954, led by Rona McKenzie from Auckland. The poor New Zealanders were almost washed away by persistent, drenching rain throughout the tour with summer barely showing its face. The honours remained with England: they took the first Test at Headingley, and the last two were drawn. New Zealand number one all-rounder Phyl Blackler ended the tour with a lively run average of 52.66 and a bowling average of 13. Further mention must go to Joyce Clothier of New Zealand who scored 37 not out in an excruciating five and a half hours in the second Test at Worcester. She saved the game for her country, but pity the poor spectators who, if they were sensible, took the opportunity to catch up on some kip.

The England team made their third journey to Australia and New Zealand in the winter of 1957/8. For a change, New Zealand was their first port of call, but not before a spot of bother in the Panama Canal. Handicapped by a paralysing tropical rainstorm, their liner RMS *Rangitane* collided with a freighter. Five days were needed in a sweltering Balboa to patch things up. No one was hurt but the dreadful weather would haunt the England party throughout the trip and they were labelled 'the Rainmakers' by their opponents.

England took six of the 1948/9 tourists to support the new blood in the side, with a new captain in Mary Duggan. The first Test at Lancaster Park, Christchurch, saw a marked improvement from New Zealand since the two countries had last met nine years earlier. They made 223, their highest score against England, and, for the first time ever, were in a position to declare in a second innings, which they did at 177 for 7. Jean Coulston surprised the visitors with her impressive fast bowling and Mary Duggan named her 'an outstanding player'. Duggan experimented with her spin bowling for the first time in a Test and duly reaped the rewards in New Zealand's first innings. She then scored a quick-fire 108 but Robinson's 65 was too laboured and the English ran out of time. It could only be a draw.

New Zealand put up another valiant effort in the second and final Test at Eden Park, Auckland, mainly thanks to Paton's match-saving innings of 77 not out when all around her were dropping like flies. New Zealand were hanging by a thread but they didn't let England take the win. Speight was their star bowler in this game and she finished with match figures of 6 for 66. Wilkinson's first innings score of 90 was her highest in Test cricket and gave England the foundation it needed. New Zealand was all at sea against the slow bowling of Mary Duggan and she snapped up seven easy wickets in the match very cheaply. But, for the first time, England had failed to beat New Zealand.

'The Rainmakers' brought their bad luck with them to the first Test at North Oval, Sydney, when not a ball was bowled in the entire three days thanks to a downpour. Things went from bad to worse when the unrelenting heavens washed out the first day's play at St Kilda, Melbourne, in the second Test. By the time they eventually made it to the middle the wicket was in a wretched state and the batsmen had an equally wretched time. Australia were bowled out for 38, their lowest score ever recorded, and Mary Duggan finished with astonishing figures of 7 for 6. Any celebrations were short-lived as England bested Australia in the low-score stakes by prodding and poking at Betty Wilson's off-breaks until she dismissed them, taking 7 for 7, and demolished the last three England wickets with a hat-trick. England all out for 35. The wicket firmed up for the second innings and Australia were able to put a respectable score on the board of 202 for 9 declared. England clung on desperately for a draw but it was a moral victory for Australia.

In complete contrast, a sun-baked deck produced a batsman's heaven for the third Test at the Adelaide Oval – a refreshing change from the bogs they'd been faced with so far. Wilson continued to play like a dream and hit 127 to record the highest Test score in an Ashes series. Not to be outdone, the ever-dependable Cecilia Robinson made a plodding 102 in just over six hours, the slowest on record. Wilson fizzed away with the ball and took 6 for 71 in England's only innings of 325. A run-fest but, again, no result in the offing.

Unusually, the teams were awarded a fourth Test at the WACA at Perth to make up for the damp squib that was Sydney. Another plumb hard wicket in perfect conditions invited runs and England's openers Driscoll and Robinson put on 95 together, their highest opening partnership of the tour. The foundations were laid and England eventually declared on 253 for 6. Australia were 280 for 7 in reply with fine knocks from Batty and Dalton, and Robinson, reliable as ever, reached 96 not out in England's second innings of 188, leaving Australia 162 runs to win in just under an hour. Time was the winner yet again with another draw to end the tour. Five draws in a row really proved that more time was needed for the chance of a result. Bring on the four-day game...

For England, this was Duggan's series, but a number of other players made their mark on this tour: Ruth Westbrook, England's keeper, made her debut and showed grit with gloves and bat, and Joan Hawes hit the international scene with her controlled and accurate bowling. Ruth went on to marry England Test cricketer Roger Prideaux, the pair having met at the Advanced Coaching Course at Lilleshall, and they have the distinction of being the only married couple both to have played Test cricket.

## Sixties Satisfaction

England had plenty to be satisfied about in the swinging sixties as they sailed through the decade without losing any of their fourteen Tests. Their faraway eyes were firmly fixed on South Africa, where they opened their sixties account with a four-match Test series. Wild horses couldn't keep them away as they saved the £250 needed per player to pay for their passage on the *Pretoria Castle*. Led by a young and thrusting 23-year-old Helen Sharpe, they won the series 1–0 after romping to victory in the third Test at Durban by 8 wickets. England did not have the opposition entirely under their thumb, however, as the South African debutantes gained first innings leads in the first and last Tests, showing promise for the future.

The Australians returned in 1963 and England were out of time in the final innings of the first Test at Edgbaston, and the day ended with a drawn match. Despite a run of wins under their belt in warm-up matches all over the country, Australia's batting was disappointingly sedate and their captain, Mary Allitt, bored the crowd senseless. Only a policewoman from Darwin, Australia's number nine Pat Thomson, managed temporarily to interrupt the humdrum batting with a brisk 30 runs. Their second innings was just as dreary but time waits for no one and England's target of 200 in 105 minutes was beyond the bounds of possibility. A giant yawn for all concerned as another draw came to a close.

The popular seaside resort of Scarborough in Yorkshire hosted the second Test and dutifully served up a delightful cocktail of wet, windy and foggy conditions in the prevailing gloom. When 'mist stopped play' on the third day, the Australians were on the verge of a nineteenth nervous breakdown as they were robbed of an innings' win. You can't always get what you want as a team but individuals can still shine and Miriam Knee, a future Australian captain, had a scorcher of a game, scoring 82 runs and taking 8 wickets in the match. Poor visibility came to the emotional rescue of the English when play was delayed until lunchtime and they then stonewalled, drawing the match by a whisker after hanging on by a thread at 93 for 9.

Some girls have all the luck and Mary Duggan departed the international scene with a bang at The Oval when she dominated England's first innings with a terrific 101 not out. This was the first century scored by a woman at The Oval. Nobody could get her off her cloud and she followed up with 7 wickets in the match. Rachael Heyhoe pinched some of her limelight by smacking the first ever female 'six' in a Test. Duggan made a bold declaration in their second innings, giving Australia a tempting 210 to win in four and a quarter hours, asserting 'nothing ventured, nothing gained'. Duggan and Sanders ravaged the Australian middle order and England won the match (and the Ashes) by 49 runs. It turned out to be their last win against Australia for forty-two years.

Fortunately I've run out of Rolling Stones song titles to weave into my 1960s section without going completely over the top. The Stones are mad about cricket so I thought it only right and proper to include them. Did you spot the eleven songs? It's only rock 'n' roll but I like it, like it, yes I do.

We're at Scarborough again. The year 1966 brought the New Zealanders over and their first Test was played at the Scarborough Cricket Ground. A side bursting with youth, under fledgling 24-year-old captain, Patricia McKelvey, contained only one player, the redoubtable Phyllis Blackler, who had experienced playing conditions in England before. To try to beat England in the series was therefore a tall order indeed. England were not short of raw talent either and also boasted a new captain in Rachael Heyhoe. All seemed right with the world on the morning of 18 June 1966 as the sun shone brightly over that part of Yorkshire.

Heyhoe was clearly unfazed by her debut as captain and hit a fluent 113 in the first innings, and set a new third-wicket record stand of 121 with her capable vice-captain, Edna Barker. England declared on a healthy 273 for 6 and New Zealand replied with an uneventful 178, with opener Judi Doull making a circumspect 74. Debutante June Moorhouse of England then earned her corn, taking 4 for 38 in her first Test. The Kiwi batting dragged on in both innings and, when the inevitable rain arrived, both the batting and the conditions weighed against any chance of a positive result. All these draws were getting a bit tedious.

New Zealand carried their sober run rate into their first innings at the second Test at Edgbaston, but they more than compensated for this in the second innings when they amassed a record score of 300 for 7 declared, Brentnall's 84 not out being the record highest score for New Zealand against England. Although the game ebbed and flowed intriguingly, and nail-biting run-outs had spectators on the edges of their seats, sadly they had to make do with another draw.

New Zealand were rapidly improving with every Test and the final contest at The Oval was undoubtedly the tourists' game. In particular, three Kiwi ladies really stood out for their exceptional performances: veteran Phyl Blackler flashed a quick 68 and produced a record fifth-wicket partnership of 93 with Carol Oyler (67 not out); then Burley stunned England by taking 7 for 41 in the second innings on an innocuous Oval pitch.

On 5 runs for 3 wickets overnight on the second day, the future for England looked bleak, but some serious blocking and predictable stoppages for rain ultimately deprived the Kiwis of their first win against England and the series duly finished 0–0. One English newspaper reported, 'It is doubtful if England could have survived had 45 minutes play not been lost through rain. At close of play New Zealand could surely be forgiven for thinking that God is an Englishwoman.'

Jos Burley, New Zealand's bowling heroine at The Oval Test, happens to be something of a jack of all trades. Having initially qualified as a schoolteacher and swimming coach, she now trains horses in Cambridge – 'the town of trees and champions', famous for its thoroughbred stud farms – on New Zealand's North Island. Her horse Happyto Keepa won at the Taumarunui Cup in 2011 and the delighted 68-year-old Jos had told the *Waikato Times* two weeks before the race that 'Happyto Keepa will win at Te Rapa first-up'. Just as with her bowling at The Oval, she was bang on the money.

The 1968/9 tour of Australia and New Zealand saw England flying to their destination for the first time. If this was a milestone of sorts, another was surely the introduction of the eight-ball over. I have no idea why the powers that be thought eight balls were better than six: perhaps they felt the bowlers were getting fed up with changing ends so frequently...

The 28-year-old debutante Enid Bakewell scored her maiden Test century at Adelaide, and England flaunted their superior batting power with a total of 270. In reply, the Australians were painfully slow but the England bowlers lacked the penetration to finish them off. They gradually amassed 339 for 7 declared which killed the game as time was in short supply. With both sides needing to bat again in roughly three and a half hours for a result to be achieved, a draw was inevitable. Nevertheless, four Australians passed the 50 mark with Lynn Denholm on 93, and two century partnerships were forged. But it was all too slow and the crowd's interest dwindled to nothing. Rachael Heyhoe took advantage of the meandering pace of the game for a bit of batting practice and scored 76 and 68 in her two innings. The Australians had the bowling edge, however, and Miriam Knee finished with figures of 8 for 68 in the match.

Next on the agenda were searing temperatures of 104°F and bushfires in Melbourne. The blazing heat must have agreed with the players, though, as they put on a much better show for the punters. Rachael Heyhoe and Edna Barker rallied England with a third-wicket partnership of 137, and Edna chalked up her maiden Test century after ten years in the England side. Miriam Knee saved Australia's skin by contributing a fine 96 when they had been 53 for 5. In the field, Anne Gordon bowled her socks off and equalled Betty Wilson's record of 10 wickets in a match, taking 5 for 61 and 5 for 57. England really should have won this match but they put down too many chances, despite the fact that 20 out of the 30 wickets had been pouched.

Australia picked up the pace in the next game at the North Sydney Oval and were eventually all out for 213. Heyhoe and Clifford were the only significant run makers for England, while Kutcher (5 for 49) and Gordon (4 for 57) made short work of the rest of the team. Bray, 69 not out, and Parker with 60, allowed Australia to declare on 210 for 3, and England were set 231 to win in two and a half hours. They made a brave go of it but the game petered out into a draw.

England had done the necessary, however, and the Ashes stayed at home. For England, Rachael Heyhoe had been dynamic with the bat throughout the series while Miriam Knee was the Aussies' golden girl, heading the batting and coming a close second to Anne Gordon in the bowling averages.

On, then, to New Zealand, where the damp, slow wickets were more similar to English wickets early in the season and in stark contrast to the fast Australian pitches of the previous few weeks. The English girls coped well at Wellington in the first Test, although rain intervened and ruined the latter stages of the match. It ended in a draw but not before New Zealand captain Patricia McKelvey made history by scoring 155 not out, the highest individual score by a man or woman at the Basin Reserve Test Ground. New Zealand posted a towering 302 on the board, their highest total ever. For England, Bakewell, in superlative form, not only took five New Zealand scalps in their first innings, but knocked up 124 in a total of 340 for 7 declared. According to a local newspaper at the time it looked as if New Zealand needed to tighten up on their catching: 'In thirty minutes, the New Zealand women's cricket team undid the work of a whole day, dropping four chances and letting England get away to a good start in their first innings.'

Records continued to be set in the second Test at Christchurch with opening bat and Auckland schoolteacher Judi Doull scoring her first century and cementing a record first-wicket stand of 128 with Janice Stead. For England, Enid Bakewell smacked 114 runs, her second consecutive Test century, before her 5 for 56 in New Zealand's second innings put England in a convincing position. She was matched by some fine wicketkeeping from Shirley Hodges, whose lightning reactions saw her stump three victims in a row off Bakewell's spin. Hodges managed five dismissals in this innings in support of the England bowlers.

England were set 173 to win in just over two hours and it was game on. They battled against the clock, and the tenacious batting of Bakewell (66 not out), Disbury (41), Heyhoe (37) and Barker (24 not out) saw England through to victory by 7 wickets with four minutes to spare.

Cornwall Park, Auckland, was the scene of the third and final Test. Unsurprisingly, England fielded an unchanged team and posted a cool 293 for 9 on the board, with heavyweights Bakewell (52), Heyhoe (88) and Barker (51) in tiptop form. Pace bowler Mary Pilling was the pick of the England bowlers with 4 for 53 as New Zealand were scrambled out for 192. In the true spirit of the game, Heyhoe then declared on a tantalising 150 for 4, giving New Zealand a target of 251 in 225 minutes. This was gettable, and dangerously so, and Doull, McKenna and Coe had England in a cold sweat before the devastating duo of Hodges and Bakewell once more plundered the New Zealand batting and wrapped up the innings for the tourists. Still, New Zealand had reasons to be cheerful: their 214 in three hours was a notably plucky attempt to go for the win. If the plaudits ultimately went to England's batsmen, with both Bakewell and Disbury passing 1,000 runs on tour during this match, New Zealand were proud of their gutsy team, despite losing the series 2–0. Kiwi cricket writer Don Cameron commented:

> New Zealand lost the final Test against England at Cornwall Park but won a great victory for women's cricket. In a hectic and thrilling finish the England Women's Cricket team ended their tour by beating New Zealand … In a brave effort the New Zealanders went pell-mell for victory and even if they cast away the last six wickets of their second innings they did themselves and the game proud.

## Stayin' Alive in the Seventies

The West Indies had yet to be granted Test match status and they were keen to prove themselves worthy of it. England, led by Rachael Heyhoe, headed out to Jamaica in 1970 to play an unofficial Test series. The West Indian girls impressed crowds of thousands with their high standard of play and England were invited back to Jamaica again in 1971, playing three games. They also took in Trinidad and Tobago for a triangular tournament, and Trinidad won the Hayward Trophy, generously donated by the cricket philanthropist Jack Hayward. It was carnival time and the England girls enjoyed a non-stop party.

The 1970s was a high-profile decade for the women's game with the effervescent Rachael Heyhoe still at the helm and the patronage of millionaire Jack Hayward much in evidence. As we have seen, thanks largely to these two individuals the first Women's World Cup took place in 1973 and hosts England beat Australia in the final by 92 runs.

The Australians were back in England again in May 1976, with the sides so evenly matched that the series ended in three draws. Rain interfered with the first Test at Old Trafford and both captains relied heavily on their pace bowlers, who were responsible for 80 per cent of the overs bowled. Runs were spread evenly across the teams and Heyhoe Flint (now married) hit her first ton against the Australians, and her overall third in Test cricket.

Edgbaston delivered a hard, fast wicket, the sun blazed all day, and this time it was Australia's turn to produce a centurion when Margaret Jennings notched up 104 at a snail's pace 303 minutes, Australia's all-time slowest. England then challenged Australia to score 235 in 175 minutes to win, not impossible on such a firm batting track. The Aussies had a bash but fell short, finishing on 169 for 6 at close of play. Bakewell was England's Player of the Match with another extraordinary all-round performance with bat and ball.

The sizzling summer continued into the last Test at The Oval where a four-day match was staged for the first time between the England and Australia women. E. M. Wellings, a distinguished cricket journalist, had proposed a four-day Test back in 1968 after a stream of interminable draws. The dry spell of '76 created hard, flat wickets which were unlikely to produce a result and a four-day Test looked as if it might well be the answer to deciding a series.

The match turned out to be a real feat of endurance for England and they scored a paltry 134 in the first innings. Karen Price made a glittering debut for Australia against England with five wickets to her name by the end of the match. When their turn came to bat, the Aussies kept their eye firmly on the ball, focused on winning their first Test series against England for twenty-seven years. Lumsden made 123 in 278 minutes and the great Henry Blofeld remarked that at times her batting resembled that of her fellow country-man Ian Chappell. Australia amassed 379 runs, 245 ahead of England, and had the luxury of two whole days in which to get them out. A bullet-proof position, it seemed.

Eyes were popping at England's statistics in their second innings: all out for 326 in an innings lasting ten hours and forty-eight minutes, with 157 maidens bowled out of 264 overs. Captain Heyhoe stonewalled her way to 179 in eight and a half hours, saving her country's bacon, and England closed their innings 81 runs ahead. The final Test, and the series, was drawn.

Australia and England played their first official one-day international series in 1976, consisting of forty-over matches, and England took the upper hand, winning the series 2–1. One-day international limited-over cricket was a relatively new phenomenon at the time and not one the purists were ready to embrace. The first ODI in the men's game was played in 1971 at the Melbourne Cricket Ground when the first three days of the third Test between Australia and England were washed out. There was outrage in the late 1970s when Australian entrepreneur Kerry Packer established the World Series Cricket competition and coloured pyjamas, floodlights with a white ball, on-screen graphics, on-pitch microphones and multiple camera angles appeared for the first time. Traditionalists considered it to be a vulgar circus and a sacrilege to the game, but Packer was a man way ahead of his time.

As we have seen, South Africa were left out in the cold in the 1970s once the sporting boycott had been imposed against apartheid. There was some activity during this time when a privately sponsored team of women players from England calling themselves 'the Unicorns' toured South Africa twice between 1974 and 1976. These women were the first rebels to defy the international ban on cricket but received very little publicity. This was well before the men embarked on rebel tours in the 1980s and created enormous controversy around this very sensitive subject.

In 1979 the West Indies came to England for the first time to play a Test series. The Windies had already whetted their appetite at home against Australia in 1975/6 and away to India in 1976/7, drawing both series. They didn't fare so well on English soil, though, going down 2–0 in the series. Enid Bakewell, flaunting her superiority once again, scored 68 and 112 not out and took 10 wickets at the final Test at Edgbaston as England cruised to victory. The Windies skipper, Pat Whittaker, deserves a specific mention as she anchored her team in both the batting and bowling departments. Another star in the making was the Windies keeper, Yolande Geddes-Hall, whose remarkable skill behind the pegs claimed 7 dismissals in the series.

## One Vision: the Eighties

By 1984 the New Zealanders were well overdue a visit to England, fifteen years having passed since their last Test meeting. By this time, one-day internationals were firmly in the fixture card and three ODIs were scheduled in addition to the three Tests.

Debbie Hockley, a mere twenty-two years old, captained the tourists and only one member of this youthful side had played in England before. New girl Janette Brittin made a startling entrance in this series, scoring a phenomenal number of runs for England, amassing 338 altogether in the three Tests. (Her ODI tally was just as spectacular, with 258 runs at an average of 129.00.) She opened her international account with 144 not out at Headingley at the first Test and from then on her momentum was unstoppable. These burgeoning Kiwis were not shy with the bat either, and Dunning's 71 kept their head above water and gave them a draw.

There was another draw at Worcester where New Zealand were just not attacking enough in their first innings to make it interesting. Brittin continued her supremacy with 96, and Kiwis Rattray, Turner, Clark and Signal all made their first half-centuries.

For the first time Chaucer's Canterbury and its beloved lime tree hosted the final Test between England and New Zealand. Hodges, for England, made her highest Test score with 158 not out. Captain Hockley scored 107 not out to balance the books for New Zealand, and followed that up with 62 in the second innings. A lot of runs were scored, but a lack of bowling penetration on both sides produced another draw and thus the series itself was drawn. Why on earth did they dispense with the four-day Test experiment of 1976? It's human nature to want winners and losers rather than placid draws.

At least the ODI series provided us with firm champions as England crushed New Zealand 3–0.

The year 1984 marked the Golden Jubilee of Test cricket for the women's game. Australia had played England in the first ever Test match in Brisbane in 1934 and now, fifty years later, it was time to salute the occasion. The exhausting itinerary contained five four-day (hooray) Tests and three ODIs plus ten other warm-up matches. England's first captain of 1934/5, Betty Archdale, spun the coin at the WACA Test in Perth to kick off this Jubilee series in style. Australia's firepower Debbie Wilson, Denise Martin and captain Sharon Tredrea were the world's fastest bowlers and they were straining at the leash to get at the England batsmen. The ball duly zipped around but our girls coped well with the onslaught and piled on 290 runs, with vice-captain Jackie Court making 90. In the first Australian innings their openers would not budge: Verco and Emerson put on 97 together for the first wicket and Kennare's blast with the bat pushed the score along to 251 all out. Brittin then cut, pulled and drove her way to a lightning quick 112 off 137 balls and England were able to declare on 242 for 9, giving Australia a sporting chance to score 282 in roughly four and a half hours. The Aussies made a slow start, despite their number three, Kennare, hitting a majestic 103. The England bowlers failed to make the breakthrough and, with Australia finishing on 209 for 8, another draw was chalked up.

The Adelaide Oval had not been put at the women's disposal since 1957/8, an indication that they were not always treated with the respect they deserved, but this time round they had the pleasure of playing the second Test there. England were tumbled out for 91, their lowest score since Melbourne in 1958, Karen Price tormenting them with 4 for 22, and then Emerson's century putting Australia in a winning position, 171 runs ahead of England. England had plenty of fight in them, though, and Watmough (70) and Edney (50) put on most of the runs to edge their team 125 ahead of the Aussies. On paper, Australia had a leisurely five and a half hours to coast to victory, but Starling's pace and perseverance produced a career best of 5 for 36 and Australia faded. Faced also with McConway's canny spin, they collapsed to 120, five runs behind the target. This is what Test cricket is all about – these moments of intense drama are certainly worth waiting for. The crowd were on the edge of their seats until the nail-biting climax. 'England Win a Thriller' was the headline splashed across the British papers the following morning.

The Australians were determined not to lose at any cost at the Gabba in Brisbane. This match was a run festival, with England scoring 275 in their first innings and Australia playing out a marathon innings of 326 for 9 declared. The Aussies had prudently taken their time, and had thus removed almost any chance of an England victory. The girls had plenty of opportunity to show off their batting dexterity to the crowds with Jan Southgate's 74 and Hodges' 95 for England, and Emerson (84), Reeler (59) and Larsen (52) pumping up the grand total for Australia. A flat wicket delivered the second draw in the series and England were still up 1–0.

The women graced the turf at Grahame Park Cricket Ground, Gosford, New South Wales, for the first time for their fourth Test outing. The invincible duo, Verco (48) and Emerson (58), supplied Australia with a first-wicket stand of 114, establishing a new record. Captain Thompson closed their first innings on 232 for 8 and then demolished England for 140. Australia's 153 for 9 declared set England 246 to win with plenty of time in the bank. England crumbled once again, with only Brittin (65) making significant runs, and Martin and Fullston inflicted the most damage to the Poms with career bests of 4 for 24 and 4 for 53. An emphatic win for Australia by 117 runs.

It was fitting that Bendigo, Victoria, should host the final Test as it was here that the first recorded women's match in Australia took place in 1874. At the time, the *Bendigo Advertiser* reported: 'The match evoked great enthusiasm and was watched by a large crowd, feelings being rather mixed about this new and daring innovation in feminine activities.'

Coming into the game, honours were even between the two countries and both teams had everything to play for. This match promised to be a scorcher despite the reputedly placid Bendigo wicket. Australia batted beautifully with Kennare's 104 setting up the home side for victory. Aussie Thompson bowled out of her skin in the first innings with career best figures of 5 for 33 to keep England in check. Australia required 116 to win, with all the time in the world to get it. They cruised through to a 7-wicket victory, winning a Test series against England for the first time since 1948/9, so they had much to celebrate. They had never before won two Tests in a series, let alone two in a row. A triumph against the odds and personal satisfaction for captain Raelee Thompson.

Probably the star of the series was Australia's Jill Kennare, whose two centuries rivalled Betty Wilson's same achievement in 1958. She followed up with two more centuries in the ODIs and Australia won that series 3–0. Aussie star number two was Denise Emerson, sister of Australian Test bowler of the seventies and eighties Terry Alderman, who hit 121 at Adelaide, with 453 runs in the series, outscoring her team-mate Kennare, who was on 347 runs, and Thompson topped the Australian bowling averages with 18 wickets. England's best player was Jan Brittin, who scored 429 runs, with Southgate, Hodges and Court next in line. Avril Starling was England's premier bowler with a haul of 21 wickets, the most by an England player in a series, overtaking Myrtle Maclagan's 20 victims in 1934/5 and Mary Duggan's 20 in 1951. Starling equalled Betty Wilson's world record of 21 wickets, although Maclagan, Duggan and Wilson all achieved their feats in a three-Test series to Starling's five.

India made their first visit to England in 1986 with the weight of the world on their shoulders, with reports that the Women's Cricket Association of India had issued an ultimatum: lose the series and your funding will be removed.

Despite India's captain Kulkarni denying the existence of such a threat, their desperate delaying tactics were a monumental pain in the backside. Their batting may have been the dullest on record but they certainly won first prize for drama queens of the universe. The England team and the poor watching public were subjected to sit-down protests, time-wasting, sponsorship rows and a tirade of speeches. The Indians played the diva card to new extremes.

Their intentions were clear from the first Test at Collingham near Leeds as they stared defeat in the face. England were well on course for victory with opening pair captain Hodges (68) and Cooke (117) putting 149 on the board, chasing 254 to win. India then unashamedly started whinging about being dazzled by windscreens of parked cars and bowled just eight overs in the penultimate hour of the match. They then wasted an agonising amount of time readjusting the field to the left- and right-handed England openers. The batsmen, meanwhile, stated that they were not remotely bothered by any glare but it didn't make a jot of difference. The Indians then parked their backsides on the pitch and refused to budge until all the vehicles in the car park had been moved. Where, you may ask, were the umpires when all this was going on? For their part, the substantial crowd made their feelings quite clear about such poor sportsmanship, and the Indians were roundly booed. Cooke and Court made a valiant effort with a dynamic 104 in the last 20 overs but the match petered out into a draw with England just 25 runs short of the target. Slow left-armer Gill McConway summed up the intense irritation felt in the England camp:

We were robbed. We had all sorts of gamesmanship from India – the imaginary glare and what have you. It was frustrating: we should have won. The umpires lacked the experience of dealing with individual situations and I felt very, very, very frustrated – but at least it gave us plenty of space in the newspapers.

The malcontent on the pitch seethed into post-match commotion, with the Indian players slow-handclapping the umpires as they left the field. England's chairman, Cathy Mowat, responded by criticising the Indians in her speech, at which their team manager threatened to boycott the rest of the tour if she didn't make a public apology. Mowat would not back down, however, and it took England's president Audrey Collins, an expert in the art of diplomacy, to pour oil on the very troubled waters. India's paint-drying tactics continued to dominate the series.

In the second Test in Blackpool, Sandhya Agarwal took a colossal six and a half hours to score 132, and the lifeless wicket only made matters worse. India took almost two days finally to declare on 426 for 9. In their first innings, the England batsmen did their utmost to clatter a speedy 350 for 6 declared, with Jane Powell accelerating to 115 not out, but when India ground their way to 176 for 2 in four hours, a draw was inevitable.

Agarwal took an eternity in stretching out her innings of 190 from 523 balls in nine hours and twenty minutes at the final Test at Worcester. The crowd (what was left of them) were taken to new realms of boredom in this match, never before experienced by mankind. Still, Agarwal did break

Betty Snowball's record by one run; it had stood for fifty-one years. In fact, back then Betty had deliberately thrown away her wicket at 189 as she thought the crowd would appreciate a change of scene! This was Agarwal's second century of the series and team-mate Rangaswamy acknowledged her achievement: 'The 1986 tour was Agarwal's series. She frustrated the England players with her slow batting, but performed incredibly well for us.'

Brittin and Hodges both made centuries in the first innings, taking England to 332 for 7 declared. McConway's clever bowling rewarded her with 7 for 34 in India's first innings: 'You just had to keep tempting them, find greater variation. My fingers got quite sore.'

England made the most of their second innings in the limited time and Sarah Potter became the fourth centurion of the match as England declared on 253 for 7. Of course, time ran out and the series was drawn. The Indians had got what they wanted and funding remained in place.

Despite the apparent animosity, by the end of the series both camps were mixing well off the field and England's spirits were lifted when they whitewashed the Indians 5–0 in the ODI series. They didn't meet again until the World Cup in 1993 and it was another thirteen years before India were invited back to British shores to play a Test match in 1999. The women's game in India has survived into the twenty-first century against all the odds and this can only be a good thing for women's cricket.

Australia landed on British soil in 1987 brimming with confidence, having won the 1984/5 Ashes series 2–1. The Australian side were a sleek unit, superfit and spot-on in the field. The phenomenal number of catches taken by Australia in the three-match series showed off the superiority of their fielding: 28 of the 42 England wickets to fall went to catches. The Australian slip fielders were outstanding and their coach, Peter Bakker, remarked on their nimble work in the field: 'Our fielding and catching has developed a lot over the years and most of the state sides put a lot of time into fielding.'

England were comprehensively outplayed by Australia in the majority of the tussles, going down in the Test series 1–0 and losing the ODIs 2–1. Australia bagged their Test win in the first match at New Road, Worcester, winning by an innings and 21 runs. Highlights were Haggett's maiden century of 126 for Australia, the highest score by a woman on her debut, and England's left-armer McConway producing yet more of her magic, taking 6 for 71.

Australia's diminutive Denise Annetts polished off Agarwal of India's record of the previous season with a considerably more entertaining 193 in just over six hours in the second Test at Collingham. The five-foot Annetts hit a whopping 30 fours and fashioned another world record in a 309 partnership with opener Lindsay Reeler (110 not out). Sadly, the great British weather did for much of the match and the teams had to settle for a draw. Rain must have played its part in the third and last Test at Hove, too, as there was no play on the fourth day and another draw was the inevitable result.

Unrelenting rain meddled with the ODIs as well and the game at Lord's was reduced to 31 overs with Australia winning by 70 runs. The Guildford match was abandoned and England won at Canterbury by 6 wickets. Australia took the series on run rate.

England may have made the final of the fourth World Cup against Australia in 1988 but Janet Brittin described their performance on the day in unflattering terms: 'It was like watching paint dry and then playing in glue when you got out there.'

England floundered on the MCG wicket and failed to penetrate the ring on this slow and low track. The Aussie spinners Lyn Fullston and skipper Lyn Larsen inflicted their worst on the England batsmen as they limped to 127 all out. Zero atmosphere in the vast and barren MCG added to their torture. The Aussies then played a carefree innings, rocketing past the England total with the loss of only two wickets.

## Slipping in the Nineties

It was all drama at the first Test against New Zealand at Auckland in January 1992. While Graham Gooch's men were living it up a couple of miles down the road on their way to winning their first one-day international, Helen Plimmer's girls were breaking run-scoring records in their first Test against the White Ferns. Run machine and BA stewardess Janette Brittin and bank clerk Carole Hodges both made half-centuries and smashed a third-wicket partnership England record with their 129 runs. England declared on 356 for 9 on day two but not before another world record was set between Janet Tedstone and Suzie Kitson, with a ninth-wicket stand of 99. There is nothing more frustrating for the opposition than the tail-enders

taking the game away from them. The cursed rain intervened and by the last day New Zealand were 214 for 9,
desperately trying to avoid the follow-on. Nancy Williams
had retired hurt earlier in the innings after being walloped
on the head by a wild return from mid-off. After a trip to
hospital she stoically returned to the crease.

England claimed their first Test victory in New Zealand
since 1969 when they beat the Kiwis by 4 wickets in the
second Test at Cook's Gardens, Wanganui. Kiwi captain
Debbie Hockley hit a tenacious 79 in the first innings but
her team were very much on the defensive. Jo Chamberlain
dismissed five of them in the first innings, and then
followed up with 3 for 42 in the second to help remove
New Zealand for 104. England required 172 for victory
and Carole Hodges set the tone with her 48 and was later
named Player of the Match.

England wicketkeeper Lisa Nye stole all the headlines
on the opening day of the last Test at Pukekura Park, New
Plymouth. Her quick hands took eight dismissals in one
innings, overtaking the men's Test record of seven. Girl
power! Opening bowler Chamberlain continued her reign
of terror and took another 5-wicket haul and, together
with Hodges' four victims, removed the home side for 142.
England replied with a controlled 228 for 7, with Watson
(70) and Hodges (96) making hay (as it were) while the sun
shone. But it didn't last, rain once again had the last word
and the final day was written off for a draw.

Australia were brought over to New Zealand for the
triangular series, and they found themselves against
England in the final. The compact Denise Annetts scored a

magnificent century as the Aussies amassed a total of 282 for 4 in their 60 overs. Alas, it was all in vain as the heavens opened and the match was abandoned. There was some consolation for the Australians as they were awarded the series thanks to a superior number of points in the qualifying games.

The English roses were well and truly smothered by the Australian gladioli in the first ever women's five-day Test. The agile footwork of Annetts helped her make 148 not out, and Aussie skipper Lyn Larsen hit her highest Test score of 86 in their first innings. With thunder brewing on the horizon, Australia snatched England's last wicket in the nick of time to win the match. An overjoyed Larsen felt the win more than justified the decision to stage a longer Test: 'I think it's very important to continue with the five-day Tests. If you look back through the records there have been so many draws, and nobody is interested in them.'

The England men were having a dismal time of it with the Ashes in 1993, and Graham Gooch fell on his sword in the fourth Test at Headingley when Australia won the Ashes in devastating style. Four days later, the England women won the World Cup at Lord's, an achievement that went some way towards easing the nation's grief at losing the cherished Ashes.

However, the tournament had been fraught with setbacks before it had even started. Two weeks before the first ball was bowled, funding was still not in place. Fortunately, the Foundation for Sport and the Arts came to the rescue with a £90,000 grant and a number of high-profile individuals chipped in with generous gifts. Finances were still tight, though, and the players themselves had to roll the wicket and remove the covers at Ealing, a disgraceful way to treat any national side.

The media had largely ignored the competition but once England had made the final, to be staged at Lord's, the country sat up and took note. MCC had assisted in underwriting the event, and were pleasantly surprised when a crowd of 5,000 turned up, giving them their largest paying attendance of the year for a match not involving Australia.

Janette Brittin top-scored for England with 48 and became the first woman to score 1,000 World Cup runs. She described the surge of emotion as she walked out to bat: 'Never before have I gone out ... with tears in my eyes, caused by the wonderful ovation from the members who lined our path through the Long Room, followed by the crowd's reception as we walked out to the middle.'

England made 195 for 5 from their 60 overs, before New Zealand crumbled to 128 all out in 55 overs. Jo Chamberlain, a van driver from Leicester, was named Player of the Match for her blistering 38 off 33 balls and for her flair in the field. As Chamberlain returned to the Pavilion, Sarah Potter recalled the reaction of the members: 'Even the normally reserved elderly gents massed in the members' stand stood to show their approval.'

These women had proved themselves to the world and it was a sharp wake-up call for the administration of the women's game. Sarah Potter, a former vice-captain of England, was brutally frank in her description of the situation:

Progress has been held back by lack of hard cash and column

inches, and buckets of male condescension. The sport in England staggers along in unnoticed crisis. Tours teeter on the edge of humiliating cancellation; players selected for their country are expected to have deep pockets, sympathetic employers, squeaky clean shoes and an inordinate patience about the sweet old dears who mostly run the game.

England made their way to the subcontinent in November 1995 unsure of what to expect, particularly in the stomach department, but the players were overwhelmed by the interest they generated from the cricket-mad Indian public. Huge, excitable crowds followed them around the country and Indian TV, radio and the print press had the whole tour of three Tests and five ODIs well covered. Every match was held in a principal stadium with first-class outfields and wickets carefully prepared for the Indians' masterly spinners. Cricketers have always been treated like gods in India and the England team needed tight security to keep them at arm's length from overzealous fans.

The Indians were a polished and youthful team and this tour revealed plenty of fresh talent. Spin bowling runs through their veins and eighteen-year-old Neetu David's fizzing leg-breaks saw her take 12 wickets, with her 8 for 53 in the second Test stealing the show. All-rounder Sangita Dabir had a corker of a tour, scoring 213 runs, taking 15 wickets and holding on to 7 catches. Wicketkeeper and proficient opening batsman, 21-year-old Anju Jain, amassed 313 runs and made 15 dismissals. India looked set to be the main threat to England in the ODI arena for the 1997 World Cup when they won this one-day series 3–2.

Tragically, the Indian captain, Purnima Rau, lost her husband to a viral infection days before the start of the tour. She bravely continued with the captaincy but, understandably, her form suffered and vice-captain Pramila Bhatt took over the reins from the fourth ODI onwards.

England were bristling with experience with nine of the 1993 World Cup champions in the squad. The first ODI in Delhi was a comfortable win for England by 9 wickets with a composed Brittin and Daniels knocking off the runs. The tables turned in Guwahati when England failed to chase a tantalisingly low score of 85 thanks to their inability to handle the wizard spin of the Indians.

A rowdy crowd of 15,000 greeted them at Patna for the third ODI and for some unfathomable reason hurled missiles at the England fielders; one player was even hit by a brick. Despite the attempted decapitation of the England fielders, the tourists romped home by 41 runs thanks to Brittin's earlier key innings of 81.

The Indian bowlers were on top at Lucknow and Indian captain Bhatt took 4 for 25. Openers Jain (65) and Chopra (50) guided their team to victory by 9 wickets with a new Indian record first-wicket partnership stand of 123. The Indians had levelled the series.

The Indian top order was little troubled by the England bowlers in Madras and chased down 146 with the loss of only 3 wickets. This accomplished team had taken the ODI series 3–2.

The Calcutta Test was cut short by freakish weather and four sessions were lost to the rain with a draw the only possible outcome. Despite the broken concentration, Brittin managed 84, and Jain was named Player of the Match for her 110.

The next match was a real humdinger, as reported in the WCA's magazine *Wicket Women*: 'The second Test at Jamshedpur saw exciting cricket with control swinging from one team to the other. England eventually won in the penultimate over taking the last wicket when India needed only 2 more runs to win.'

Hyderabad was the location of the last Test which culminated in a heroic last-wicket stand from Stock and Taylor. Both finished the match on 9 not out and survived 40.5 overs, including 26 maidens, to secure England the draw and the series by 1–0. Your average American will stare at you in disbelief when you patiently try to explain that a Test match can last as long as five days and sometimes end with no result. In a way, it just doesn't make any sense on paper. You have to be there to experience the subtleties and nuances of this intensely strategic game really to get it. You have to give it proper time and complete concentration in order to grasp the significance of a rearguard action such as the one put up by Stock and Taylor. It can sometimes be soul-destroying to watch but, equally, it can turn the best of us into quivering wrecks as the agonising minutes tick by and your country's fate seems to hang in the balance.

Unhappily, England extended their poor form in the ODI format when they went down 3–0 to New Zealand in the summer of 1996. Of that series, the less said the better. On a more positive note, three Test matches were scheduled to give the women a decent look at the long game. The first Test at Scarborough was a monumental run festival with

Barbara Daniels knocking up 160 and Kathryn Leng keeping her company with 144 to heap 414 runs on the board. Not to be outshone by England, New Zealand racked up a staggering 517. Kirsty Flavell redefined the meaning of the word endurance as she occupied the crease for over nine hours and became the first woman in Test history to score a double century. World records kept coming as New Zealand overtook England's record total of 503 for 5 made against the Kiwis in 1935. Daniels and Leng formed a world-record sixth-wicket partnership of 132 to keep the statisticians on their toes. Despite the fact that records were smashed left, right and centre, the almost inevitable draw was the end result.

The next Test at Worcester was a sodden affair with much of days two and three affected by rain. Nevertheless, Withers of New Zealand walked away with figures of 6 for 73 and Hockley hit a fine 115. The inclement weather once again meant a draw was the only possible outcome.

Kiwi captain Sarah Illingworth did not hesitate when she won the toss and elected to bat in the final Test at Guildford. The White Ferns had commanded with the bat throughout the tour and they did not disappoint in Surrey. In their opening innings of 362 for 5 declared, the top order was unrelenting with Fruin (80), Hockley (65), Flavell (97) and Drumm (62) in the ascendancy. Janette Brittin was the only Englishwoman to pass the fifty mark and England were bowled out for 271. In the second innings, Drumm punished England's bowlers with a flamboyant 112 not out to put New Zealand on top. They then reduced England to 160 for 8 but were denied their first ever Test win against the hosts by an effective rearguard action between Sue Redfern and Clare Taylor (not to be confused with Claire Taylor, mentioned earlier), who produced a ninth-wicket stand of 65. A relieved England were shepherded to a draw. An acutely disappointed Illingworth defended her decision to take the new ball soon after Taylor and Redfern came to the crease: 'I have no regrets. You have to fancy the new ball against tail-enders and the spinners have no problems using the new ball. We just couldn't make the breakthrough. We are obviously very disappointed.'

South Africa emerged from their period in the wilderness after the official international boycott was lifted. They celebrated their return to international cricket after a 25-year absence with a tour of Ireland and England in 1997. The tourists had three victories against Ireland to their name, having never played the one-day format, before they arrived on English soil for the five-match ODI series.

Sue Redfern wrapped up England's first ODI at Bristol with her best figures in a one-dayer of 4 for 21 to give the home team a comfortable 79-run victory. The Western Province all-rounder Helen Davies was the only South African to put up a fight with a dogged 64.

The precocious teenager Charlotte Edwards overwhelmed the Taunton crowd with her maiden century in only her second one-day international for England, but the match turned into a white-knuckle finale with Anina Burger of South Africa hitting the winning runs off the last ball. The tourists kept pace with the run rate of five an over thanks to a solid opening partnership of 105 between Linda Olivier (60) and Denise Reid (56) and a quick-fire 48 by Helen Davies.

Lord's provided the stage for the final ODI and England rose to the occasion with a seven-wicket victory giving them a 2–1 lead in the series. Cricket nut and former Prime Minister Sir John Major was among the spectators and voiced his admiration of the day's play: 'There has been a very high quality of cricket played here and the entertainment value is as good as any men's cricket. Anyone who thinks they won't see good cricket at a women's match had better come and watch and see how wrong they are.'

England got as far as the semis in the sixth World Cup in India in December, where they lost to New Zealand by 20 runs. The final was quite an occasion, with 60,000 spectators showing up to see Australia beating the Kiwis at Eden Gardens, Calcutta.

England donned pyjamas for the first time at home against the Aussies for the ODI series in 1998. Despite their fetching electric blue outshining the rather unflattering Australian yellow and green on the catwalk, the England girls were taken to the cleaners in a 5–0 whitewash. In England's defence, they pushed hard in the first three games but went to pieces in the last two. Superstar Australian captain Belinda Clark, already a force to be reckoned with, hit an unbeaten 95 at Scarborough and passed 2,000 runs in one-day internationals, becoming only the third woman to do so. The Scarborough match was battered by rain and, when they got to Derby, Alan Lee of *The Times* described the pitch as a 'suet pudding'. However, the Australian batsmen Lisa Keightley (59) and Melanie Jones (58) made light of it, and England's batsmen fell short of the 204 target by 64 runs.

Injuries dominated the game at Hove when England's number one batswoman, Jan Brittin, broke and dislocated a finger and was dropped right down the order to number nine. (She had already injured the same finger in 1996.) Superstar of the future Charlotte Edwards' knees let her down here and she had to call for a runner in the person of Barbara Daniels, but she still managed a noble 75 runs. Again, Australia's total was beyond England's reach.

England were without Brittin and Edwards in the fourth ODI at Southampton and they were sorely missed. Australia caught up with England's meagre total in only 25 overs with 8 wickets in hand.

Australia had a field day at Lord's and Keightley's 113 not out was the first female century at the home of cricket. This is the chart-topping dream of any batsman from anywhere in the world. Clark contributed 89 to Australia's 256 for 1, and only England captain Karen Smithies passed the half-century mark, with scant support from her team-mates. This time, a crushing defeat by 114 runs.

Jan Brittin motored past Rachael Heyhoe Flint's world record of 1,594 Test runs when she scored 146 in England's first innings at Guildford. Edwards chipped in with 53 and England were all out for a mammoth 414. Australia went one better on this flat, hard wicket when Joanne Broadbent smacked 200, toppling Denise Annetts' eleven-year Australian record of 193, but fell 4 runs short of Kirsty Flavell's world record set two years earlier. Jones (131), Price (80) and Keightley (56) all joined the party, and Australia piled on a world-record 569 to beat their own record by 44 runs, made against India in 1984. England batted second time round with Edwards (77) and Brittin (59 not out) in the runs once again, the match ending in a draw.

The super-competitive Aussies badly wanted a result and this was reflected in their first-innings declaration of 306 for 3 at Harrogate. Wall-to-wall runs were made by both sides and Jan Brittin's second successive hundred put England in a safe position. In the end, rain destroyed any chance of a result, turning the wicket into a lake.

Hungrier than ever for a win, Australia were unlucky with the weather once more in the last Test at Worcester. Another first-innings mountain of runs from Australia saw them declare on 427 for 4. This innings featured a stunning maiden Test century from Karen Rolton, her 176 not out including the game's only six, and another Clark ton of 136 to swell the score. Rain washed out day three so stalemate ruled once more in the match and the series at 0–0.

Jan Brittin, of course, won the Vodafone England Batswoman of the Series with her 450 runs, Charlotte Edwards emerged as Player of the Series and Clare Taylor grabbed the bowling honours.

Anjum Chopra came back to haunt England at Old Trafford in 1999 when she won the first ODI for India.

This left-hander from Delhi played a faultless innings of 52 and India scraped through with only three balls to spare. Chopra once again blew away the opposition with a match-winning century in the second ODI, and her second-wicket stand of 104 with keeper Anju Jain teed up India for victory. Clare Connor provided some relief for England with a final-over hat-trick and earned herself Player of the Match. England failed to chase India's total of 213 successfully and lost by 86 runs.

England captain Karen Smithies may already have lost the series 2–0 but she restored some pride to her team with an unbeaten 110 at Trent Bridge. Facing the final delivery of the match and needing four to win, she went aerial over mid-wicket to hit the winning boundary and England won by 3 wickets.

The first day of the Test at Shenley belonged to Charlotte Edwards. As England's star batswoman she had disappointed with only 15 runs in the last three matches so she was due a big score. She duly chalked up 108 for her maiden Test century and shared a 134-run partnership with her captain, Smithies (57). England felt confident enough to declare on 123 for 9 in their second innings, setting India 252 to win in 83 overs. India off-spinner Purnima Rau took 5 for 24 and was largely responsible for putting the brakes on England. England's confidence soon evaporated as India's openers Aheer and Jain put 121 on the board, putting the visitors firmly in the driving seat. However, the scores soon took a U-turn and India tumbled to 223 for 8. England could taste victory, but it was not to be: India grimly hung on for a draw.

## The Noughties and Beyond

The England winter tour down under in January–February 2000 was a major disaster for the English. The ever-widening gulf in the batting ability between Australia and England was glaringly apparent in this four-match ODI series. England's coach, Paul Farbrace, summed up the superiority of the Aussies: 'We also have to recognise that the Australians are miles ahead of us. They are fitter and stronger than any other side in women's cricket, added to which they were in the middle of their season.'

A crestfallen Karen Smithies relinquished the captaincy to vice-captain Clare Connor at the end of the Australian leg of the tour. Despite the 4–0 annihilation it was not all doom and gloom in the England camp. England's bowling and fielding were still up there with the best of them and they had the finest wicketkeeper in the world in Jane Cassar.

The Aussies asserted their dominance from day one when Lisa Keightley creamed 127 not out off 115 balls to help Australia beat England by 86 runs. There was at least a ray of sunshine for England when Cassar became the leading wicketkeeper in women's ODIs when she stumped Therese McGregor for her fiftieth dismissal.

Australia swiped all the gold medals in the final ODI at Newcastle when they smashed 299 for 2, their highest total against England, and a record opening stand of 179. Player of the Match went to Belinda Clark, who cracked an unbeaten 146 off 151 balls, and England were sent into orbit as they were thrashed by 220 runs.

The women thus went on to New Zealand with their tails between their legs and the Kiwis took full advantage of England's fragile mental state and further knocked the stuffing out of them with a 5–0 demolition job. The England squad thus faced a major overhaul on their return home in preparation for the South Africans that summer.

It was a different England that found its form again in the five-match ODI series against South Africa in the summer. England started with a bang, winning the first match at Chelmsford by 20 runs to end the run of defeats begun in the winter. They went two up in a reduced-over match at Trent Bridge but slipped up at Canterbury when South Africa snatched victory from the jaws of defeat in the last over. England took the honours in the fourth ODI at Taunton with Edwards (96) and Daniels (95) scoring freely around the ground. It was a satisfying win with which to take the series.

England's fresh young team next travelled to New Zealand in November 2000 with oodles of enthusiasm and spirit but they lacked the experience in knowing how to go on and win a game. They lost 3–0 in an ODI series designed as a warm-up for the World Cup the following month.

Once the big occasion arrived, a raw England hoped to survive an intense week of three internationals in five days against Sri Lanka and big guns Australia and New Zealand. Needing to win all three matches to guarantee a place in the semi-final of the World Cup, England dealt positively with Sri Lanka but the pressure placed on them and the maturity of the two favourites were too much for them. The White Ferns ultimately went on to win their first world title against Australia in front of a home crowd in an electrifying final.

Next on the agenda for England were the Ashes at home in the summer. Unsurprisingly, the Aussies took the ODI series 3–0 against an England side in the midst of rebuilding. Veteran Karen Rolton won all the acclaim for her blistering batting performances to see off a sharp England bowling attack, and Australia called the shots in the two Ashes Tests with zingy pace and consistency from the world-class Fitzpatrick as well as hard-hitting batting from the prolific Rolton, Goszko and Keightley. Debutante Michelle Goszko astonished everybody at the Denis Compton Oval at Shenley with a record-breaking debut innings of 204 and matched the highest ever score by a woman. Fitzpatrick cleaned up the England order in the first innings with 5 for 29, before England captain Clare Connor replied with 5 for 65. Australia powered through to win by an innings and 140 runs.

A merciless Fitzpatrick nabbed another 5-wicket haul in England's first innings at Headingley, finishing with 9 wickets in the match, and in a breathtaking display that earned her the Player of the Series award, the mighty Karen Rolton hit a massive 209 (a new record) from 313 balls, including 29 fours and 1 six. England were not about to roll over, however, and superstar Claire Taylor responded with a tremendous 137 to give the home batting order some much needed substance. Australia were forced to play a cameo second innings and won by 9 wickets. England may have lost both series but they had unearthed some bright new stars for the future.

England went from one hammering to another as India took them to task in the ODI series in January 2002 with a crushing 5–0 defeat. England were missing four or five of their key players and so a number of young guns were making their debuts and, thrown into the chaotic melting pot that is India, they had a tough time of it.

Nine days earlier, the solid duo of Atkins and Thompson had broken the world record for an opening partnership at the only Test in Lucknow, their colossal 200-run stand providing the backbone of the England total of 314 all out. Sadly, this auspicious start did not give England the win they wanted as driving rain and bad light prevented anything more than 68 overs on days two and three, and the match was drawn. England captain Clare Connor was, however, heartened by her team's effort: 'The performance in this Test match has given the whole team a lot of confidence, and Caroline and Arran were simply world class. It's a psychological victory for us that we protected our lead, and taking 6 wickets for 10 runs this afternoon ensured that we finished ahead.'

England next hosted a women's tri-series in July 2002 against India and New Zealand and, with the winter blues firmly behind them, dismissed India to face world champions New Zealand in the final. Alas, the top dogs remained on top as England collapsed to 98, losing by 63 runs, for a fifteenth successive defeat against the White Ferns. The Kiwis now reigned supreme, having won 26 of their last 33 ODIs. This was an era in which the inbred killer instinct and sheer self-belief of both the Australians and the Kiwis really came to the fore. Between them they conquered the world.

A transformed England met India at Beaconsfield Cricket Club in August for a compensation ODI, the Shenley Test having been abandoned due to severe weather. The original schedule had been a two-Test series. England's fresh ammunition came in the shape of fast-bowling teenagers Isa Guha and Laura Spragg, and the batting showed more depth, too. Openers Edwards and Leng made a match-winning stand of 92 to point England towards victory, and they beat India by 6 wickets. India's innings had been stunted to only 118 by the promising seam attack of Guha and the wily slow bowling of Connor. With victories against India in the first match of the tri-series and now at Beaconsfield firmly in their pocket, England's diabolical winter in India was consigned to history.

The England middle order were the heroines of the first innings of the Test at Taunton with Laura Newton top scoring on 98. Neetu David, the bane of England's winter tour, caused the most trouble with her spin and took 4 for 71. Day three belonged to nineteen-year-old Mithali Raj from Jodhpur with the highest score in the history of women's Test cricket. She surpassed Australia's Karen Rolton's 209 of the previous year with 214 glorious runs, and India were eventually all out for a grand 467. That left England to save the match with a dignified rearguard action on the last day. Edwards and Connor provided the bulk of the protection as the game drifted to a draw. England did not have the best of runs in the 2003 Women's World Series in New Zealand, when they lost their first five games against India, Australia and the home side. Australia stamped their authority on the tournament by remaining unbeaten as they went into the final. England desperately needed to restore some pride and so went into their last group match against India with their tails up. Charlotte Edwards returned to form with an unbeaten 79 and the top order showed a vast improvement, taking England's total to 208 for 4. The Blue Lions, as they were now known, nearly had their newfound confidence shattered by their old nemesis, Mithali Raj, who replied with a dominant innings of 98. Still, England stuck to it and splendid fielding and outstanding bowling saw India tumbled out as they won with the final ball of the match. Captain Clare Connor put the team's victory down to self-belief: 'We always believed we could win today. We talked about the need to post scores of 200 plus and everyone showed a lot of character in the closing stages.'

England faced India again the following day in the third-place playoff and, this time, Kathryn Leng was England's leading batter with a career best of 80. On a spinner's wicket, Connor and Harper royally defended their total of 191 and returned home with a 90-run victory. This was a major turning point in England's fortunes as they progressed up the world rankings from fifth to third place.

In February, the Ashes took England fast bowler Lucy Pearson to new dimensions when she rocketed to an 11-wicket haul in the second Test at the Bankstown Oval in Sydney. She joined Australian superstar Betty Wilson in equalling the world record and, of course, was named Player of the Match.

The first Test at the Gabba, Brisbane, was not quite so arresting for England, although it did have its moments. England managed to dismiss the home team for a trifling 78 in their first innings, Australia's third lowest Test total of all time. They had seized the initiative with glowing bowling performances but let it slip as their batting let them down and the Aussies recovered to win by 5 wickets.

England failed to cash in on Australia's low-scoring first innings in the second Test and the Aussies took a significant lead in their second innings, although England fought back well to secure a draw. The fifth-wicket world-record partnership of 136 by Lisa Sthalekar (120) and Alex Blackwell (58) allowed Australia to retain the Ashes. England had certainly had their chances to win matches and showed resilience with the bat which had been previously lacking. The gap, it seemed, was closing between them and Australia.

The music of Bryan Adams and Eminem provided the soundtrack as England blasted their way to a win at the first ODI against South Africa at Chelmsford in the summer of 2003. The top order showed true professionalism with Edwards making a conscientious 64 and Claire Taylor powering to 51 to push the total to 273. Debutante off-spinner Rosalie Birch scored 30 not out at number nine, and took a tidy 3 for 21 to give her Player of the Match. England blew South Africa away by 175 runs.

In the second ODI at Bristol, however, South Africa took control as teenage prodigy Johmari Logtenberg knocked up 61 and Terblanche hit 79. Laura Newton (68) made a promising start for England but South Africa's bowlers ground them down to a crucial final over with Clare Taylor and Lucy Pearson needing 14 to win. It was not to be, South Africa prevailed and the series was level at 1–1.

Sophia Gardens, Cardiff, provided the ground for the deciding match. Old-timer Pearson and new girl Birch restrained the South African batting order to a total of 147 and then Newton and Claire Taylor guided England to victory with the loss of only one wicket.

Teenagers ruled the first day of the Test at Shenley with fourteen-year-old Logtenberg (74) and Charlize van der Westhuizen (83) putting on 183 together. One of England's own teenagers, Helen Wardlaw, bit back by suppressing the South African top order with 3 for 31, then Claire Taylor took full advantage of the flat track by scoring a majestic 177, her highest total ever, as she and teenager Lydia Greenway notched up 203 for the fourth wicket. England amassed a daunting target of 497, their second highest Test total of all time. Super-ambitious South African captain Alison Hodgkinson ensured her team stayed in the game by occupying the crease for four hours during her 95 runs, steering South Africa to 285 for 8 by close of play on the last day. The batting paradise in the baking heat at Shenley was wittily described by Lucy Pearson, when she 'admitted to *Test Match Special* listeners that the wicket showed a striking resemblance to the adjacent M25 and Hodgkinson made the most of it'.

The teenagers made way for the veterans to come up with the goods in the second Test at Taunton. Pearson conjured up both bounce and movement on a particularly placid wicket and, with another fine display from Wardlaw, South Africa collapsed to 130. Claire Taylor (131) and Lydia Greenway (66) embarked on another fruitful stand, and young Birch contributed 62, to take England to 455. England then polished off the South African batting to take the game by an innings and 96 runs, thus winning a Test series for the first time since 1979. It had also been more than two decades since they had enjoyed the spoils of victory in both the long and short forms of the game against tourists. The blend of youth and experience had finally fused to generate dynamic, positive and compelling cricket.

South Africa endured another pummelling by England on the winter tour in February 2004. Hard-hitting wunderkind Logtenberg gave South Africa short-lived glory when she punched 67 runs for a one-wicket win to launch the ODI series in Port Elizabeth. England then bulldozed their way to a 4–1 series victory with 380 runs coming from the bat of Charlotte Edwards and 11 wickets taken by spin-sensation Rosalie Birch.

The cocktail of youthful raw talent and wise maturity worked wonders against the visiting Kiwis in the ODI series in August 2004. By the fourth match, England had wrapped up the series 3–1 with captain Connor and Edwards both making half-centuries. Edwards, at only twenty-four years old, passed 2,000 runs in ODIs during her innings, and eighteen-year-old Isa Guha claimed her first 5-wicket haul in a one-dayer.

The women beat the men to it when England played New Zealand in the first ever Twenty20 international. The Kiwis put on a first-rate show for the seagulls at Hove as they beat England by 9 runs. Birch was the pick of the England bowlers, but her 4 for 27 was all in vain.

In the solitary Test at Scarborough, Rebecca Rolls hit a super 71 but the tail refused to wag and NZ were all out for 215. England's openers, Edwards and Newton, both struck centuries but the rest of the order failed to capitalise on this phenomenal start and the tourists curtailed their hosts to a mere 70-run lead. Rain thwarted England's progress on day three and interrupted day four as Maia Lewis secured the draw for the White Ferns with a useful 60.

In the weeks leading up to the 2005 Women's World Cup in South Africa, England arrived early and played two ODIs against the hosts to whip themselves into shape for the big event. The South Africans looked fragile as England quickly got among the runs and wickets and boosted their faith in themselves with two comprehensive victories.

England fought their way into the semis and picked up two splendid records along the way: the highest total of the tournament, 284 for 4 against Sri Lanka, and the highest individual score, 136 from an electric Claire Taylor in the same match. England, ranked second, faced firm favourites Australia in the semis, the Aussies having won the last sixteen encounters between the two teams. It was always going to be tough, and as if on cue Australia completed a straightforward 5-wicket triumph against their old adversaries. Leading from the front, the invincible Belinda Clark hit a classy 62 to guarantee her country a place in the final. The England attack lacked venom and their injured star pace bowler, Lucy Pearson, could only watch from the sidelines. Australia remained undefeated as they trounced India in the final and roared to their fifth world title.

While the men were having a corker of an Ashes series in 2005, the women were at it, too. The first Test at Hove was saved by England's Arran Brindle (née Thompson) with her maiden Test century of 101 not out. The Aussie tail failed to wag in their second innings and Clare Connor's figures of 4 for 68 were thoroughly deserved. A draw took them to the second and final Test at Worcester with everything to play for, and in a fairy-tale ending for England their twenty-year wait for the ultimate prize was over: the Ashes were regained as they won convincingly by 6 wickets. The women, it seemed, had taken their motivation from their male counterparts, as Clare Connor told journalists: 'We've been watching the guys and been inspired by their fight and the way they're playing. The girls are over the moon.'

Katherine Brunt was beaming with pleasure as she was named both Player of the Match and the Series, after her 9 wickets in the match and her integral first-innings half-century.

The ODI series against Australia was just as gripping as the two best sides in the world did battle at Taunton with the series level at 2–2. Connor admitted that clinching the series on top of their Ashes glory would be 'beyond their wildest dreams'. Until winning consecutive matches to level the series, England had not won an ODI against Australia since 1993. This turned out to be the nail-biter to cap them all as Australia's gutsy bowlers, particularly veteran Cathryn Fitzpatrick, snatched a 4-run victory with only three balls to spare.

All-round star Karen Rolton then put the seal on Australia's tour with a 7-wicket victory in the only T20 match to take place. She really cut loose and hit a stunning 96 not out from just 53 balls, with Australia romping home with fourteen balls remaining.

Charlotte Edwards made her debut as skipper in the 2005

winter tour of Sri Lanka where they rolled the hosts over in two ODIs, and the next port of call was India, where they played only one Test but five ODIs. Michael Vaughan's England boys had been saved by bad light in the Faisalabad Test, but the women's game in Delhi looked more encouraging. England's batsmen were resolute as the Indian bowlers gave nothing away on a slow pitch with plenty of turn and Birch and Harper dug in to steer England to a draw.

The Indian captain, Mithali Raj, was both confident and upbeat about facing England in the ODIs, having beaten them in the World Cup earlier in the year. Her confidence was justified as the Indians, in their element, stormed to a 4–1 series win.

It wasn't long before India were knocking on England's door back home in the summer of 2006, kicking off their tour by obliterating their hosts by 8 wickets in India's first ever Twenty20 outing. Rumeli Dhar hit a dream 66 not out off 69 balls and was named Player of the Match. India and Twenty20 seemed to be made for each other. England punched back in the first Test at Grace Road, however, leaving India clinging on for a draw. Dhar and Sharma put on 77 for the seventh wicket, quashing any thoughts of a victory for England, and India were saved.

There was another fight to the death at Taunton in the second Test where England were made to eat humble pie as India forced the follow-on for the first time ever. England were on the back foot throughout the match following their meagre 99 in the first innings. Jhulan Goswami took two 5-wicket hauls in the match and left India needing just 98 for the series victory. They made it comfortably with 5 wickets to spare.

England exacted their revenge by reversing the away defeat inflicted on them in the ODI series over the winter. India simply did not put enough runs on the board, with England on fire in the field and a business-like attack from the bowlers.

England wintered in India again in 2007 but only managed third place in the one-day Quadrangular tournament in Chennai. Australia trampled all over New Zealand to clinch the title while England did battle with India in the playoff. Both Taylors hunted down the competitive Indian total of 219 to great effect, with Claire finishing on 77 not out and Sarah 52. A solitary triumph for England.

South Africa were found wanting in the Twenty20 arena when they were stuffed by both New Zealand and England on the same day at Taunton in August 2007. However, South Africa provided a useful warm-up for the Twenty20 series between England and New Zealand. Edwards and Sarah Taylor batted crisply in the first two matches and gave England a 2–0 lead in the three-match series. Their dour winter in India was soon forgotten.

Aimee Mason (now Watkins) caused England all sorts of trouble in the one-day series, helping New Zealand towards a conclusive 3–0 lead in twinkling Blackpool. Her phenomenal contribution with the bat spelt curtains for England, even though some pride was restored with a 3–2 end to the series.

And now to Australia. Clever thinking at the MCG had the women playing their Twenty20 match as a curtain-raiser to the men's Australia v. India game. This guaranteed large crowds and boosted media exposure: the crowd swelled to 27,000 and Channel Nine included the women in their highlights package. Despite England losing by 21 runs, they were thrilled to have the women's game promoted far beyond anything they'd seen before.

England fared better in the ODIs with an electric start to the series, beating Australia by 56 runs. They hadn't won an ODI on Australian soil for nineteen years so this was something to celebrate. Lydia Greenway and Jenny Gunn built a healthy 80-run partnership to help establish a total of 233 for 6 in that first game.

Aussie twins Alex (101) and Kate Blackwell (57 not out) turned it into a family affair at the MCG the following day and posted a formidable 240 on the scoreboard. In their innings, England floundered at 24 for 3, never really regained their composure and were all out for 156.

They then headed off to Sydney at 1–1 where rain washed out the third ODI, but the fourth game was a rip-roaring success for England. Edwards, playing her hundredth ODI, hit a nifty 70 not out to chase down Australia's 177, and Claire Taylor played a supporting role to build a match-winning partnership. New kid on the block, the seventeen-year-old Australian Ellyse Perry, worked wonders with the ball, knocking out both England openers: clearly a talented all-rounder and one to watch out for.

Steph Davies was flung in at the deep end when she made her international debut for England in the vital last ODI with England 2–1 up. She rode her early nerves to take 4 wickets, including 3 lbws. Aussie openers Alex Blackwell and Nitschke continued to dominate with the bat and contributed generously to a total of 211 on a five-day-old wicket. Two hundred and eleven was a big ask for England on such a battered pitch and they fell 41 runs short. Ellyse Perry once again radiated talent and took three crucial wickets for Australia. At 2–2 England hadn't won but they hadn't lost either. The Aussies had won every ODI series against England since 1976 so in many ways this was a result.

At last, for the purists out there, we come to the Ashes Test. Charlotte Edwards knew that she had to win eight sessions to secure the win and that's what she was gunning for. This meant that England needed to be on top for more than two and a half days' play out of four so it was a bold call. England only had to draw to retain the Ashes but they were hungry for blood and played with tremendous spirit. In fact, they monopolised nine sessions and brought home the Ashes in style. Isa Guha had a golden match with figures of 9 for 100, taking 5 for 40 in the first innings, and well and truly earned her Player of the Match award. England bowled Australia out for 154, followed by a record partnership of 159 between superstars Claire Taylor and Edwards herself. Taylor scored her second half-century of the match to propel England to a 6-wicket victory. However, it was not all plain sailing for our heroines. Lisa Sthalekar threw a spanner in the works with her flight and guile and then hit an entertaining 98 in Australia's second innings, but it was not enough to save them. What a shame the men got more media coverage in their 5–0 Ashes defeat than the women did for their glorious victory. An elated Edwards said: 'I'm delighted, almost lost for words. To beat Australia in Australia is a fantastic feeling. We had always said we would come out here and aim to win this match in order to retain the Ashes and that's what we did today.'

England landed in New Zealand on a high, oozing with confidence. They blazed through the country as they took the ODI series 3–1 to conclude one of the most thrilling and successful tours ever down under. Claire Taylor was in scorching form with the bat and was voted Player of the Series, an award decided upon by the head coaches of each country.

The West Indies meandered through Europe in the summer of 2008 with a handful of wins under their belt. They easily rolled over Ireland and the Netherlands but were brutally undone by England as they crashed to 41 all out in their only ODI against the hosts. Most of the young West Indian players had not played international cricket before; it goes without saying that they learned much from these experiences.

South Africa were next in line for a drubbing as a ruthless England took the ODI series 4–0: an unblemished record for the season so far by the girls in blue. With an ever-growing appetite for limited-overs cricket, and with three Twenty20s being fought between the two sides, once again England ruled the roost with a 3–0 series win. This was all in preparation for the World Twenty20 in 2009 and South Africa had some work to do.

Next on the conveyor belt of limited-overs clashes was India, who went 3–0 down in the ODI series before having their Twenty20 contest washed out at Taunton. They were even denied a consolation victory when England then won the fourth ODI and rain ruined the last fixture.

Edwards and her invincible soldiers had made a clean sweep of wins in this grand-slam summer and they were more than ready to take on all-comers at the World Cup in Australia the following March. My only criticism would be that Test cricket was heartlessly brushed aside in favour of a summer crammed with nothing but limited-overs cricket; being a traditionalist I would like to see Test cricket make a comeback to the women's game.

England could do no wrong in the 2009 World Cup in Australia and they held their nerve in the final to beat New Zealand by 4 wickets. After three previous attempts at World Cup glory, England captain Charlotte Edwards finally lifted the $35,000 trophy and, boy, did the tears flow…

Bravo to the ECB for setting an example to other nations by investing in women's cricket for more than a decade. Their backing reaped rewards as the England girls nailed the World Cup and the Ashes by the summer of '09 – and there was more to come.

In the final of the 2009 World Twenty20 against New Zealand at Lord's, England so outclassed the Kiwis that it was more like watching the amateurs playing the professionals. The England powerhouse systematically destroyed its opponents, bowling them out for 85. Katherine Brunt delivered the fireworks with the ball, removing the White Ferns' top order with a career best of 3 for 6, then England coolly knocked off the runs and won by 6 wickets. Kiwi captain Aimee Watkins was in despair about their performance: 'Everything we tried turned to custard,' she said.

The staging of the tournament as a double-header with the men's final in the afternoon was a complete success. Anyone who was anybody in the world of cricket witnessed the best of these women's matches and the impact on the press was unprecedented. The England women had achieved the double as champions of two World Cups in the same year and the flag of St George reached stratospheric heights in women's sport.

But nothing lasts forever, it seems. England came crashing down to earth when the Australians began their tour with a sensational win at their only Twenty20 match in the summer. England looked exhausted and they needed to find some of that old dynamism for the next five ODIs and the climactic Ashes Test.

Mercifully, it didn't take the England girls long to refuel and for the killer instinct to return; they took the ODI series 4–0, with the fifth match falling foul of the weather. Despite the whitewash, Australia fought tooth and nail, with two of the games going to the last ball. A pink ball was used in the match at Wormsley (the Buckinghamshire home of Sir Paul Getty had its own cricket pitch) for the first time in an international game, in support of the breast cancer campaign.

The men's and women's Ashes ran in tandem as the England men clung on for a draw in Cardiff to begin their series. The single Ashes Test played by the women at Worcester reached the same conclusion by the end of the last day, with rain bringing the match to a premature close. Australia had been in the depths of despair in their first innings at 28 for 5 as tough Yorkshire lass Katherine Brunt tore through the top order, taking 6 for 69. Jodie Fields then played a gritty captain's innings of 139 and lifted her team out of trouble. Her partnership with debutante Rachael Haynes (98) formed a world-record fifth-wicket partnership and Australia were eventually all out for a respectable 309. England found themselves in a similar predicament to Australia at 59 for 5 but dug deep with gutsy fightbacks from Morgan, Gunn and Marsh helping England to grind out a total of 268.

The West Indies delivered a bombshell when they claimed both the ODI and the Twenty20 series against the double world champions in the Caribbean at the end of 2009. They went into the third and last ODI at 1–1 and it was a close call. The Windies were struggling at 66 for 6, pursuing 177 for victory, when Deandra Dottin and Stacy-Ann King came together and breathed new life into the chase. Their seventh-wicket stand of 87, together with Taylor's 43, sealed the win by one wicket. The self-belief of these West Indian women had overcome the Goliath.

It would appear that our world champions were on a downhill slide when they lost the ODI series to India in Visakhapatnam in February 2010. Mithali Raj, in attacking form, hit her third consecutive half-century to give India a clear 3–1 lead in the five-match series. It's always a tall order to beat India on the subcontinent and England had yet to overcome them in an ODI series, but some of the old magic was restored in the Twenty20 series as Laura Marsh steered England to a series win with her unbeaten 47 in Mumbai.

England had a disappointing time in the 2010 World T20 in the West Indies when they failed to get beyond the group stage, and Australia knocked them off the number one spot when they met New Zealand in the final. England would spend the next few months nursing their damaged pride and licking their wounds before facing New Zealand on home turf in July. A low-scoring game at Hove decided the Twenty20 series in New Zealand's favour, though England's Danielle Hazel upset the Kiwis' top order with an artful display of slow bowling.

As an aperitif to the ODI series against New Zealand, England travelled to face Ireland in a one-dayer. England were the big fish in a small pond and Edwards and Marsh racked up a vast total of 274 for 7. Ireland never looked threatening with the bat, although Laura Delany made a classy 43 off 90 balls.

It was paramount that this momentum be carried through to Taunton for the first ODI against New Zealand. England managed this by a whisker, winning by one wicket, thanks to a responsible 70 runs from Edwards. The hosts sealed the series in the fourth match at Barnsley, where local girl Brunt bagged 3 wickets in front of her home crowd. The Taylors (Claire and Sarah) were back in form with a stand of 98 and the team coasted to victory, winning by 9 wickets. Welcome back, England.

England were on song again in Colombo when they secured a tight win in the first ODI in November 2010. Faithful servant Claire Taylor churned out 73 runs, making this her twenty-second half-century in her tally of ODIs. For Sri Lanka, Deepika Rasangika bowled some destructive left-arm seam and sent four of the England batsmen back to the pavilion, but Taylor and Gunn patched up the England innings to help them finish on an inviting 192. Sri Lanka scrambled to reach the target but a middle-order collapse settled their fate and England squeezed a win by a snug five runs.

The second ODI was an anti-climax in more ways than one as rain washed out the game. England captain Charlotte Edwards was keen to crown her 142nd ODI as the most capped player in women's international cricket with a win, but it was not to be although she did mark the occasion with a career-best bowling performance of 4 for 30.

Sri Lanka put up little resistance in the T20 series as England motored through the three matches to a 3–0 clean sweep.

A jubilant England had laid the groundwork for their tour to Australia in January 2011, which opened with a three-match ODI series. The Aussie women blasted their way through the first two matches thus taking the series. Edwards (90) and Knight (72) gave hope to the England cause in the second ODI but the onslaught inflicted by Lanning (103 not out) and Nitschke (70) proved too much for our bowlers as they cruised to a 9-wicket win. England were grateful for a consolation win in the final match in which Lydia Greenway played a relaxed innings of 59 with two immaculate reverse sweeps to please the crowd.

This final win boded well for the T20 series against the world champions as England sealed the win 4–1. Greenway was named Player of the Series for her crucial contributions in the first two matches to give England a 2–0 lead.

England went into the Ashes Test at Sydney with heads held high. Debutante Sarah Elliot and Australian captain Alex Blackwell crushed any hopes of England glory in the fourth day to gain a 7-wicket victory. Their match-winning partnership of 125 ultimately forced England to hand back the Ashes to Australia.

Hampshire's Rose Bowl was the stage for the Quadrangular T20 final. India and New Zealand had been knocked out to make way for England v. Australia, and England continued their unfaltering dominance of T20 cricket. The reigning queen of T20 internationals, Lydia Greenway, accelerated her score to 48 on a slow wicket, to build up England's total to 132 for 9. Holly Colvin dealt with Australia's top order and her top-quality bowling earned her Player of the Tournament for her 7 wickets. Australia continued to wobble and fell short by 16 runs.

England were in superb nick for the Quadrangular ODI series and met their old foes Australia in the final once again. T20 goddess Greenway hit a fluent 58 and Sarah Taylor smacked a rapid 43 to put England in a strong position. This time England's seam bowling did the trick as a hostile Brunt took a career best of 5 for 18 to prevent Australia reaching the 230 total. A sparkling summer for the England stars indeed.

England steamrollered their way through South Africa in October 2011 with a 3–0 whitewash in the ODI series. In the second match at Potchefstroom, Edwards (138) and Sarah Taylor (77) displayed true class to post an intimidating 314 on the board. South Africa scratched around but failed to keep up with the run rate and the series was in the bag for England at 2–0 with one to play. Greenway (63) and Knight (55 not out) provided the meat of the England innings in the final match and wonderwoman Greenway took Player of the Series.

It was no surprise when England reigned supreme in the T20 series with a 2–0 win. South Africa just failed to make enough runs in both matches and England comfortably reached the targets.

World domination spread into New Zealand as England made another clean sweep, winning 4–0 in the T20 series. Kiwi Morna Nielsen caused pandemonium in the England dressing room in Invercargill when she took 4 for 11, but it was not enough to throw England off course.

England's tyranny continued into the ODI series, giving them their fourteenth consecutive victory after a 3–0 thrashing of the White Ferns. Sarah Taylor celebrated her record as the youngest woman to reach 2,000 international runs when she scored an unbeaten 109.

In preparation for the ICC World Twenty20 in Sri Lanka in October, England played several Twenty20 matches with visits from India, Pakistan and the West Indies, but there wasn't a sniff of a Test match. England blew away the cobwebs against Ireland in June in a one-off T20, in which Edwards opened the season with 72 not out and Ireland were crushed by 51 runs.

England's tour de force in the T20 arena assured both victories against India. The memorable moments were Greenway's spectacular catches at backward point and deep mid-wicket, where she palmed the ball back into play to stop her momentum carrying it over the boundary. Captain

Charlotte Edwards talked of the team being 'completely in awe' of her fielding genius.

With Sarah Taylor, Lydia Greenway, Charlotte Edwards and Katherine Brunt in the team, England are undeniably the best women's international side in the world.

Both T20s against India preceded the men's domestic T2Os, which swelled the crowd, increased TV coverage and boosted the players. Sarah Taylor's enthusiasm for the double-header format was palpable: 'It's definitely more exciting when we play before the men.'

The year 2012 may have been a bumper one for Twenty20 but it left some of the players frustrated at not being able to test themselves in the longer form of the game. The last Test was played in Sydney in January 2011 and there is a strong desire to play more. A diplomatic Edwards said: 'We would love to play more Test cricket but we understand that's not where the game's going at the moment.'

Uncharacteristically, England lost the first two ODIs to India, but made a splendid comeback with a hat-trick of wins to take the series 3–2.

Pakistan were next in line for a pre-World Cup bash against England, but England were in a different league and finished with two consecutive wins in the T20s.

The gulf between England and the West Indies was made painfully clear in the five-match T20 series in September. The Windies went down 4–1 but a savage display with the bat from Deandra Dottin with 62 off 34 balls gave her team the win in the final match.

England were without question the favourites to conquer the World Twenty20 in October – a dead cert for the bookies.

Those familiar rivals England and Australia faced each other in a final which translated as the best team in the world versus the defending world champions. It was not a pretty game of cricket and nerves were frayed by the hype of a globally televised final and a substantial crowd. The Aussies bowlers nagged away and denied England any useful partnerships in their chase of 142. The pressure built and England buckled. Sixteen runs were required off the last over and, after a comedy of errors in the field, England needed an unlikely six to win. It was a messy finish that ultimately went Australia's way.

The Long Room, Lord's.

# MCC BOWL A MAIDEN OVER

**M**arylebone Cricket Club was founded in 1787 as a private members' club for gentlemen when Thomas Lord purchased a site in London, now Dorset Square, and established it as the Club's home venue. MCC was, in fact, a reconstitution of a much older club which probably began life in the early eighteenth century, possibly even before. This former club resided for a long period at the 'Star and Garter' on Pall Mall and had been known as 'The Noblemen's and Gentlemen's Club' or 'The Cricket Club'. It had strong sporting connections with the original London Cricket Club, the White Conduit Club, the Jockey Club, the Hambledon Club and various prize-fighting promotions.

The earliest known match to be played on its current site at Lord's Cricket Ground in St John's Wood was in 1814 and the magnificent grade II listed Victorian Pavilion was constructed in 1889–90.

MCC is the authentic headquarters of cricket and it ran the game worldwide until 1968. The Club remains the owner and maker of the laws of cricket and any changes to the laws must be reported to members at a General Meeting of the Club. It also fulfils an important role in championing the spirit of the game.

MCC has currently 18,000 full members who have access to the ground and the Pavilion for all matches, and it provides Lord's with a home ground for Middlesex County Cricket Club.

## The First Vote

So how did the ladies manage to break down the Pavilion doors of this male bastion after more than 200 years of a 'blokes only' cricket club? The stormy relationship between women and the world's most famous cricket institution really began with gusto in 1991 when the first vote was taken on whether to elect women as members.

As an aside, only two years earlier, MCC had witnessed a female assault on its members of a more colourful variety. During a Test match in May 1989 (one of the chillier summer months), a bouncy Sheila Nicholls stripped off and streaked across a velvet outfield at Lord's. She dodged determined stewards in hot pursuit and made it to just in front of the Pavilion where she completed her exposure with an athletic cartwheel. One member seated in one of the upper tiers was overheard to say, 'That reminds me, I need to mow the lawn.'

Ladies who love the game of cricket were knocking on the Long Room doors and felt they had the right to watch this beautiful game from the best seats in the house. A former England women's captain, namely Rachael Heyhoe Flint, set the ball rolling by filling in the daunting form and bravely applying for membership in 1991. Despite the backing of distinguished members such as Sir Tim Rice, Dennis Amiss, Brian Johnston and Sir Jack Hayward, the required two-thirds majority was not achieved and she was refused. Of MCC's 18,000 members, 2,371 voted for women and 4,727 against. With so many not bothering to vote, the MCC Committee had a lot of work to do to galvanise its troops into action.

This resolution, proposed by the then Mr T. M. B. Rice and Mr B. A. Johnston (Johnners to the rest of us), came to a head at the MCC AGM on 1 May 1991 with strong words being exchanged between both camps. Tim was concerned that women should not be stopped from becoming members of the best club in the world by 'blinkered, reactionary chauvinism'. He went on to say, 'I believe that MCC must be seen to have moved at least into the twentieth century before the beginning of the twenty-first century, or else by the end of the twenty-first it may not be the best club in the world.'

There were members concerned with having to build another loo and the impracticalities of mixed changing rooms ... I think they were rather missing the point. Johnners explained that there were already regular ladies' loos, with two very comfortable seats in them! How did he know? At times, this meeting was bordering on the farcical.

More stirring words came from a pro-ladies member: 'We have a Queen, we have had a woman Prime Minister, we are going to have a woman Speaker: the role of women is changing about us. I say we have our heads in the sand if we do not recognise the changes that are taking place.'

Hear, hear!

However, the old school had won the day this time. Bill Edwards, press officer for Saracens Rugby Club and long-time MCC member, was dead against the idea of ladies in the Long Room:

> I'm too old for change and I don't want the upheaval. Whatever spoon you feed in the sugar with there will always be problems. Look at the House of Lords – there are over a hundred women there now and they are putting a bust of Emily [sic] Pankhurst in the corner and even setting up crèches.

And all this after Margaret Thatcher, the Iron Lady, had governed the country armed with a lethal handbag. It is difficult to understand what Mr Edwards meant by 'too old'; at fifty-four, he was a spring chicken compared with members' average of sixty-one.

At that time the prevailing attitude of the members was the fear of a massed female invasion of their sacred 'gentlemen only' club. They treasured the escapism and comfort of their male preserve and had no intention of sacrificing this. Ladies were about as welcome as a West Indian fast bowler unleashing a lethal yorker smack on to your big toe.

Other county cricket clubs were unimpressed by the MCC members' reaction. Surrey and Nottinghamshire were vocal in their support of their own women members and the obvious benefits they brought to their clubs. The decision also sparked anger abroad from Diana Edulji, who had captained the Indian Women's cricket tour of England in 1986. She talked of being banned from the Pavilion at Lord's and was upset to be told she could only sit in the Tavern stand. She thought MCC should change their name to MCP – male chauvinist pigs. She remarked that Mrs Gandhi was a strong devotee of women's cricket and pointed out that up to 25,000 women attended major matches in India at some grounds.

## The Second Vote

The ladies may have been out for a duck in their first innings but the Committee were chomping at the bit to get them out to the middle again. MCC Members XI versus the Ladies XI was looking more like a timeless Test than a Twenty20 wham bam thank you ma'am. Seven years later, in 1998, it was time for a second innings.

In 1998 Colin Ingleby-Mackenzie became president of MCC and he was behind much of the impetus for change in this historic year. A dynamic and progressive Old Etonian, in his days as a dashing captain of Hampshire he was never known to have closed any door to a lady anywhere. Both Colin and the Committee reintroduced the proposal in the belief 'that the benefits lady membership would bring to the Club's activities in support of cricket in the widest sense are incontrovertible'.

Would this second vote invite the same reactionary backlash

or would the members unashamedly vote in favour this time? Rachael Heyhoe Flint had her doubts: 'Seven years on and I'm still not confident that there's going to be a majority. Last time 10,000 members didn't bother to vote and there needs to be a two-thirds majority.'

The more cynical among the membership argued that the Committee's sole reason for backing female membership was financial. The cost of the running and development of Lord's is immense and in the press it was reported that MCC had just been refused a £4.5 million lottery grant. The exclusion of women from its membership was certainly one reason given for this refusal. One long-standing member rather abruptly summed up the MCC debate: 'What's behind this is money. It's not a question of the two sexes. If it was, then this ballot wouldn't even have arisen. The Committee would have said to Rachael, "Sorry but this is a private male club." What I object to is that we're almost being held to ransom.'

Many members felt that MCC were being steamrollered purely by this financial issue: 'The concept of lady member-ship is merely a red herring. The Club is only interested in using the "women's issue" as a tool in order to generate additional finances, whether that be from the National Lottery or from a gang of commercial sponsors.'

The same member then added: 'There is no evidence that the absence of lady Members has any bearing on the Club's image; and there is also no evidence that women can make any positive contribution to the game of cricket.'

Of course, expense was a major factor behind the

Committee's proposal but certainly not the only one. MCC may be a private Club but it is in a public arena with a public responsibility. Why shouldn't cricket-loving ladies watch this game from the best seats in the house? Rachael Heyhoe Flint put it well: 'When I go to cricket, I want to watch, not spend my time in the bar drinking G&Ts or my head in the hamper looking for another bottle of chardonnay.'

Well, she could do both...

Amanda Heathcote, the 24-year-old PR consultant to the Professional Cricketers' Association, was exasperated by the situation and felt it was ridiculous to bar women, particularly those who had played for England. And the issue was not just about sexual equality but more about the nature of the game. At the time the women's game was being embraced by the ECB alongside the men, and MCC had an important role to play in supporting these endeavours to appeal to a wider audience. By this time the England women had twice won the World Cup and the numbers of female followers of cricket were very much on the increase. Stuart Weatherhead, the Club spokesman, said: 'The principal reason for reaching this decision was the positive effect it would have on MCC's public role which is now being re-defined as the ICC seeks to develop the game worldwide.'

A Special General Meeting was held for members at Lord's on 24 February 1998 to tackle, once again, the issue of lady membership. A carefully worded report was presented to the membership by the Committee and was bolstered with strong and persuasive arguments in favour of the fairer sex.

The report pointed out that the Committee had bravely stuck their toe in the water and experimented with members' reactions by introducing Special Regulations for a Women's One-Day International between England and New Zealand in June 1996. This allowed members to invite up to four guests of either sex into the Pavilion. This clever venture resulted in only a little grumbling from the members and was by and large considered a success. On the back of this, two more matches in 1997 were awarded these Special Regulations and not a peep was heard from the membership. The only other occasion at which women had been permitted to grace the Pavilion as spectators during the hours of play had been way back in 1966 for a match between Old England and the Lord's Taverners. Softly, softly, catchee monkey…

This meeting, chaired by the then president Colin Ingleby-Mackenzie, covered everything from the importance of the Club's public role to the state of ladies' lingerie in the Club colours: 'The members' shop at the moment consists of a lot of clothing in members' colours: we have shirts, we have pyjamas, we have boxer shorts, we have stockings. The mind boggles at what it will be like in twenty years' time, with twin sets, skirts and lingerie in MCC colours.'

Ludicrously, one member, in the belief that women didn't actually want to join MCC, felt that it was likely that few women would be able to afford the MCC subscription.

Another member was concerned about ruining the atmosphere of the Club:

If we were debating tonight whether to have fruit machines in the Long Room, I would vote against it because it would alter the atmosphere of the Club. If we were debating whether to wear shorts in hot weather and take off our shirts, I would vote against it because it would alter the atmosphere of the Club. Likewise, as the Committee say, having lady members would alter the atmosphere of the Club.

A rather more down-to-earth and realistic voice came from the pro-camp:

If the MCC wishes to have a voice in the world at large and to improve cricket, as we all know it can do, it must retain its respect and authority, and it cannot be respected and authoritative if it is a back-water cut off from the main stream of opinion in society.

So far, Her Majesty the Queen had been the only lady permitted to grace the Pavilion during the hours of play. Was this all about to change? Sadly not. The second vote on this issue in a decade had been a close call but once again a two-thirds majority had not been achieved. However, a simple majority had been reached in favour of women joining the ranks of MCC, so the tides were most definitely turning.

Those members staunchly against changing the rules of the Club felt the rarefied atmosphere of the Long Room had been preserved, but at what cost to the game? This was a major blow to the modernisers of the game and had stunted the growth of cricket when it had had a golden opportunity to blossom. Even Tony Blair, Prime Minister at that time (who apparently preferred football), was stirred into a reaction having received a number of letters from dismayed members of the public complaining about the outcome of the vote: 'Such a decision does not reflect well on the MCC or anybody else.'

Tony Banks, the then Sports Minister, also stuck his oar in by stating that the Lottery would have nothing to do with MCC until it changed its stance.

The Pavilion at Lord's was the only place in all of English cricket where there was a men-only rule during the hours of play. MCC members needed to buck up and join the twentieth century.

The hierarchy at MCC were far from defeatist and promptly distributed a questionnaire to members to try to establish the exact reasons why large numbers of them objected to female membership. In the February vote, both camps had been strongly represented with 60 per cent voting in favour of women's membership and 40 per cent against.

Some of these verbatim comments give us an accurate idea of the main reasons behind the majority of votes. Here are some examples of individual responses from the pro-camp:

'It's 1998 – the world has changed! We are a club with a public face and cannot afford to be sexist in any way. We will be a better club for the change and in reality it will make little difference.'

'They play cricket, they watch cricket, they make teas, they score, they support. They are part of the team!'

'It is ludicrous to exclude any section of society as we go into the twenty-first century. MCC will remain a laughing stock in society until women are treated equally.'

The main thrust behind the 'no-camp' appeared to be tradition: MCC was created as a men-only club and should remain as one:

'I don't like being "railroaded" by external pressure. I don't see why there should be women members. I'm a traditionalist – the atmosphere and nature will be altered forever.'

'The MCC is a unique club for men interested in all aspects of cricket. The unique atmosphere and ambience in the Pavilion is ideal for discussion and watching.'

'The MCC is essentially a men's club. I have come across very few women who are interested in cricket and I feel that those who are would be "out of place" within the confines of the Pavilion.'

There were rumours that other responses on this questionnaire made entertaining reading with Stone Age views such as the rattling of tea cups, the clicking of knitting needles or, shock, horror, the possibility of breastfeeding in the Pavilion all given as reasons to continue to bar women from MCC.

### Third Time Lucky?

With England hosting the Cricket World Cup in 1999, the MCC Committee was really feeling the pressure to be seen to support the game of cricket on all levels. A bold move was made to have another vote in September 1998, only seven months after the last one had fallen short of its target. The Committee armed itself with a formidable batting order with ECB chairman Lord MacLaurin, Sir Paul Getty and former England captain David Gower on board the Pro-Women XI. With MCC president Colin Ingleby-Mackenzie and president-designate Tony Lewis in the driver's seat pulling out all the stops to convince the membership to go with the women's vote it was looking more and more likely that the ladies would win the day. However, Rachael, once again, was not convinced the membership would roll over so easily so soon after the previous vote: 'Many of them feel they are being bulldozed into this and they cannot see why there is the indecent haste – after all, the Club has been around since 1787.'

Lord MacLaurin stressed the urgency of the situation and wanted to bring this home to the members: 'We desperately need to encourage youngsters – male and female – to take up the sport and do all we can to stimulate interest in the game and bring back the commercial support which is vital to the health of the game.'

The Committee went at it with all guns blazing by holding a series of informal meetings around the country for members and dished out a glossy brochure entitled 'MCC and the Future – Women Membership?' The MCC PR machine was at full throttle. There were some complaints that this brochure was not impartial, with quotations from the great and the good such as Richie Benaud, Sir Paul

Getty, Colin Cowdrey and David Gower all glowingly in favour of the admission of women. But most felt that the Committee had acted with honest intentions and were courageous in their approach in reflecting the views of the majority of members.

Once again, the motion 'Men and Women shall be eligible for membership' was debated at the Special General Meeting on 28 September 1998. Both sides of the camp were well represented with three members speaking for the motion and three speaking against on an alternating basis. The debate was then thrown open to the floor and sparked some spirited and stimulating contributions.

One member, involved in Broadhalfpenny Down, the home of one of the oldest cricket clubs in the world in Hampshire, used a chapter in a book by Diana Rait Kerr about Hambledon Cricket and the Bat and Ball to drive home his message. The book explains how William Barber, described as a useful change bowler, took over from Richard Nyren in 1771 and continued to look after the wellbeing of players and spectators, not forgetting the ladies, 'who were assured that they would be as much at home in the pavilion as if they were in their own drawing-rooms'. He goes on to add that Hambledon Cricket Club was the first law-making body for cricket in England, before MCC was even formed, and evidently it looked after the interests of women and made them welcome. Two hundred and twenty-seven years later MCC were a lone all-male bastion.

The resounding message from these pro-speakers was to appeal to the membership to put aside their prejudices for the greater good of MCC and of cricket. The issue is one between a private club and a public club.

From the anti-camp, more emphasis was thrown upon criticism of the Committee and their handling of the issue:

> I think we should vote firmly against the proposal. The arguments are spurious. Even if one is in favour of the entry of women, which I think is probably unwise, the handling of the issue, the propaganda, the spin that has been given to this tampered ball is distasteful to me and, I suspect, to many others.

The vote took place at the end of the meeting and 69.8 per cent were in favour. A two-thirds majority had been achieved and the resolution passed.

The whole procedure of admitting women to the Club caused major emotional turmoil within the hallowed walls of the Pavilion. After 200 years of 'chaps only', the membership had finally given in to good sense and good manners and flung open the Pavilion doors to the fairer sex – and the world did not collapse. The MCC Committee's weeks of intense campaigning had paid off and the image of MCC was not to be forever tarred with the brush of elitism and the prejudices of stuffy old farts, but was in tune with the modern world.

### The First Lady Members

Now any woman had the right to be nominated to join MCC, but there was a small problem of an eighteen-year waiting list to overcome. It was important that the women were treated exactly the same as the men and not given preferential status. Roger Knight, the then MCC secretary, made this point: 'I think the feeling would be that if someone applied to join the Club, whether a man or a woman, they should be treated the same. If we make the decision that men and women should have equal rights, we probably would not introduce positive discrimination.'

To accelerate a quota of ladies to the top of the waiting list for ordinary membership would really have been pushing their luck with the members and would have been unfair. However, MCC needed to be seen to be encouraging female members right from the outset and to put their money where their mouth was. This was achieved by MCC bowling a modest ten maidens through the Pavilion doors as honorary members. These ten ladies were chosen for their exceptional service to the world of cricket and thoroughly deserved to be members. And here they are:

- Betty Archdale, captain of the first women's touring team to Australia and New Zealand in 1934/5
- Edna Barker, toured Australia and New Zealand with England and won 15 caps in total and is a former captain of South of England and Surrey
- Audrey Collins, served as president of the Women's Cricket Association from 1981 until 1993 and whose playing career began in the 1930s and continued for over four decades

- Carole Cornthwaite, captain of the England team in 1986 and 1987 for six Tests and five one-day internationals and played in eighteen Test matches for England
- Jackie Court, represented England forty times
- Rachael Heyhoe Flint, who played for England from 1960 to 1979, gaining 45 caps, and captained the national team from 1966 to 1976 over twelve Tests and nine one-day internationals
- Sheila Hill, a qualified umpire who umpired the final of the first Women's World Cup between England and Australia and played cricket for Oxford University, Kent and East England.
- Norma Izard, the longest-serving senior England manager, managing twelve international tours before stepping down in 1993, and president of the Women's Cricket Association from 1994 to 1998
- Diana Rait Kerr, curator of the MCC museum from 1945 to 1968
- Netta Rheinberg, secretary of the Women's Cricket Association in 1945 and from 1948 to 1958 and player/manager of the England tour to Australia and New Zealand in 1948/9

Since then, MCC has granted fourteen more women honorary life membership in recognition of their services to cricket.

**First Lady Playing Members**
For those women who are keen players of the game there

is always the option of becoming a playing member. These women, like the men, would need to play five to ten matches for MCC over two to three years as probation-ary candidates in order to be eligible for a fast track to full membership. They would need to demonstrate that they played the game in the right spirit and performed to an acceptable level, i.e. a competent 1st XI standard. Playing members of MCC have a responsibility to represent the Club in the right way by spreading the gospel of this great game far and wide and by upholding 'the spirit of cricket' on the field by encouraging enjoyable competitive sport. To MCC's credit, all this was set in motion for women within months of the vote coming through.

The inaugural MCC women's cricket match, in which I was lucky enough to participate, was played at the Bank of England ground in Roehampton against a Surrey U-21 side in 1999. Wendy Watson, representing MCC, marked this historic occasion with a century. The match had a good turnout with the great and the good in attendance, including the then president, Ted Dexter, and members of the main Committee.

MCC now has over 100 women playing for the Club in more than thirty fixtures in a season, including successful tours to countries such as Luxembourg, the Netherlands, Trinidad & Tobago and Sri Lanka. This is something to be proud of.

MCC playing members are made up of a true assortment of cricketers from competent club players to internation-als who play together in the same team. The standard of the opposition they meet can vary tremendously: for example, they might play against other national teams or teams from schools, universities, clubs or the armed forces. There is often a training session run by the MCC players at schools just before a match, and sides will sometimes be put together with a mixture of MCC players and pupils so as to give pupils as much guidance as possible and so that they can benefit from a high standard of cricket. We have, for example, had matches in which England stars Claire Taylor and Caroline Atkins have represented MCC against schoolgirl opposition – offering a perfect opportunity for these girls to be inspired and to see how the game is really played. MCC will tend to opt for 'declaration' cricket rather than 'limited-overs' and will usually elect to bat first so as to keep games competitive.

MCC Young Cricketers are frequently selected to play in these games and their skill and expertise benefit those less experienced enormously. The MCC Young Cricketers programme was set up to nurture fresh talent with the superb facilities at Lord's offering expert coaching and intensive playing opportunities. These young people often go on to have successful careers in county and international cricket. Past megastars have included the likes of Sir Ian Botham, spin master Phil Tufnell and even Australia's Mark Waugh. Notably, MCC were the first cricket organisation in this country to pay female cricketers, thus producing the first female professional cricketers in England in 2003. Since its inception, this scheme has fostered such talent as Caroline Atkins, Beth Morgan and Steph Davies, all of whom went on to play for England. Atkins expressed her appreciation of her time at MCC:

> Being based at Lord's was a real privilege and it inspires you to work extra hard because you know so few get the chance and so many greats have played there. Scoring my first international century at Lord's was made all the more special by the years I trained there and longed to go out on the most famous cricket pitch in the world and show what I could do!

## A Female Playing Member's View from behind the Bowler's Arm

Stalwart playing members such as Sian Price have made more than fifty appearances for MCC. Sian has sat on committees, been on cricket tours and watched endless matches at Lord's. She is truly making the most of her membership, as are many other cricket-loving ladies. I went to her house in Kent to interview her and was greeted by her eighteen-month-old son Benedict dressed in an MCC sweater. Not a bad start...

Sian had the usual introduction to cricket in the garden of her parents' house playing with her older brother. It's in such places where the imagination can run riot; where the seeds of the great game are sown for ever; where we can play timeless Test matches and hit sixes into the neighbours' potting shed. At prep school Sian was fortunate enough to have a form teacher who played for the Sussex 2nd XI and was 'bonkers about cricket'. He got her playing in matches with the boys and she found that she more than held her own. Most girls of this age would be dragged off to play that rather mediocre game rounders, but Sian was lucky enough to be given the chance to play cricket, an altogether more challenging and stimulating game which was more or less off-limits to girls in those days. She was less fortunate at her all-girls senior school where only conventional girls' sports were played and so cricket disappeared from her world for a time. It was not until she went up to Cambridge as a post-graduate student reading Theology that she encountered the game again. There Josh Leppard, a fellow theologian and Middlesex 2nd XI player, coached her and got her out in the middle once more. She really got stuck in and won a half-Blue.

Once the vote had gone through at MCC, Nigel Laughton, who was then the European Cricket Development Officer there, wasted no time in despatching a membership form to Sian. She then tracked down three members of MCC who lived in her village, and many gin and tonics later she had the necessary signatures and letters needed to complete the rather daunting membership form. One of her proposers had actually voted against women joining but had a change of heart once the vote went through!

Sian's first game for MCC was against Oxford University Women in The Parks, and many more games followed at other first-rate venues. MCC players are truly spoilt in that they get to play in some marvellous grounds around the country and all over the world. Both Sian and I were tourists on the inaugural MCC Women's tour to Holland in 2001 against the Dutch national women's team. She also toured Sri Lanka in 2006 where the locals put up a good fight to draw the series and the tourists struggled in the searing heat and harsh conditions.

I asked Sian what her typical day at Lord's entailed on a major match day. She summed it up succinctly: 'An early start reading the papers on the train, then hog some seats at the ground, take in the atmosphere with plenty of strolling about and bumping into mates between the hours of play. Plus a determined effort not to hit the alcohol before 11 a.m.'

Sounds to me like a typical day at Lord's for the majority of members. Perhaps chaps and ladies are not quite as dissimilar as first thought...

We talked about our initial experiences and feelings when we first entered the Pavilion and Long Room as full members. Those early days were somewhat intimidating with a Pavilion heaving with blokes, not all of whom were happy with our presence. There was plenty of staring and quite a bit of tutting; members would sometimes ask if we were lost and one or two even demanded to see our passes. Refreshingly, though, there were some who would make a point of telling us how delighted they were to see ladies in the Long Room and how pleased and relieved they were with the result of the vote. A bit of a mixed bag really.

On one of my first excursions into the hallowed Pavilion in 2003 I was involved in a clash with a particularly cantankerous old goat. I was standing at the end of the Long Room watching a Test match and minding my own business when a red-faced, handlebar-moustached fossil, fresh from the Bowlers Bar, stumbled in, took one look at me and roared: 'You're a woman! We don't have women at MCC! What are you doing here?'

A packed Long Room fell deathly silent and all eyes were on us. I carefully explained that women had been members since 1998 and asked if he had been living in a cave all this time. He then blustered and flustered and huffed and puffed at me and demanded to see my MCC pass. I pointed out that he was not a steward and asked if he would please leave me alone. That was when my knight in shining armour came to the rescue in the form of main Committee member, His Honour Nigel Peters QC, who asked this twerp to leave. He did not go quietly so Nigel had to manhandle him out of the Long Room, down the stairs and out of the door. I could still hear him shrieking outside.

Nigel raced back, offering profuse apologies, and invited me to join him in the Committee Room for the rest of the day. By the time I entered the sanctity of the sacred Committee Room I was surrounded by Committee members asking if I was the girl who had been attacked by the man with a moustache. Word travels fast. I was handed a glass of champagne and led to a sumptuous leather chair with a superb view of the cricket where I sat for the remainder of the day's play. I was in heaven and later enjoyed a cocktail party hosted by the Committee for all of the England and Zimbabwe players.

This was the year of Tim Rice's presidency and, having spotted me in the Committee Room, Tim told me in his charming way what a delight it was to have a lady member present. He asked if I'd had a good day and when I told him of my encounter with the moustache he looked absolutely mortified and promptly invited me to spend the day in his box on the Sunday of the Test. Of course, I said that I'd love to but was sorely disappointed as England proceeded to stuff Zimbabwe inside three days so there was no play on the Sunday. A few days later I received a letter from Tim asking if I'd like to play for his team, the Heartaches, and go on a tour to Cornwall. The tour was a blast and I have enjoyed a close friendship with Tim ever since. And to think that all this came about thanks to my crusty old friend with the whiskers.

Fifteen years on, things have settled down with barely a squeak of protest from the membership. The number of ladies in the Pavilion is still fairly small but those who do turn up are true cricket lovers enormously enthusiastic about the game. And most of these ladies come armed with a considerable knowledge and are more than capable of taking on any members in a lively discussion about the state of the game. Sian would go as far as describing MCC as a 'home from home'.

### Female Infiltration into MCC Hierarchy

MCC is a complex machine made up of a number of principal committees with sub-committees reporting to them. The main Committee is the big chief and it is responsible for the entire management of the Club. It's pretty tough to get voted on to the main Committee with the likes of cricketing legends, former prime ministers, Oscar winners and lords and knights of the realm on board. Once again, as we have seen,

Rachael Heyhoe Flint smashed the glass ceiling and became the first woman to serve on this impressive Committee in 2004. Her election on to the Committee was never a matter of tokenism. 'I come from a business background where we treat people as customers and clients and not just paying punters, and I hope to bring some of that to Lord's.'

Full Committee members serve a period of three years before they have to retire for at least a year before being eligible for election once again. The membership wanted Rachael back and she served her second stint from 2008 to 2011. She is currently sitting on the main Committee for a third time and is a Trustee of the Club. A very distinguished lady indeed, she has achieved a great deal for MCC.

The Club has embraced ladies at all levels with other female members making their contributions across the board on Finance, Marketing, Arts and Library, Membership and Cricket Committees. I sit on the Membership and General Purposes Committee which discusses every aspect of the Club. Part of my role is to serve on a Disciplinary Panel and meet with errant members. Inevitably, there are gags about whether I take a run-up when I'm dishing out six of the best or if I'll be wearing my thigh-high leather boots ... *Fifty Shades of Grey* has a lot to answer for. I love the banter. Misdemeanours range from gate-crashing MCC bridge matches and scoffing all their food and drink to unacceptable and aggressive drunken behaviour. It really isn't cricket, but on the whole the 18,000 membership are a decent bunch who have a deep love of the game and come to Lord's in the right spirit.

The year 2013 is an unprecedented one for MCC main Committee as they will find themselves with more than one lady in the Committee Room. This year, two of us will be joining Rachael in the higher echelons of MCC. As I mentioned earlier, it is a difficult job to get elected as you're often up against pretty tough competition with high-profile names in the running. Ideally, you want a good cross section of disciplines represented on the Committee and two or three female voices would give it a healthy balance.

## Ten Years On...

By September 2008, MCC had 67 full lady members, 272 Associates and 410 candidates for membership. MCC Women's playing membership had taken part in almost 200 games across the country and abroad. The low number of full lady members at this point attracted some criticism from various women's and equality groups. Dr Katherine Rake, director of the Fawcett Society, which campaigns for equality, said: 'Paying lip service to equality is not enough. Funders and sponsors should be looking at how they're delivering equality in their membership as well.'

Those of us right in the thick of things at MCC tended to disagree with this rather over-the-top attitude to equality. We just want to be treated fairly, on a par with the men. Fast-tracking women just for the sake of balancing the numbers would have created unnecessary discord. Rachael put it well: 'Having waited two hundred and eleven years to acquire membership, that's the one thing I stressed throughout the nine-year campaign: we didn't want any favours. The process for becoming a member is exactly the same as the men, and why shouldn't it be?'

The tenth anniversary was celebrated with a black-tie dinner in the Long Room and a good old knees-up.

## MCC Maidens Timeline

- 1976 First women's match at Lord's: England v. Australia one-day international
- 1993 England Women's Cricket team wins World Cup at Lord's
- 1998 MCC votes to admit women as Club members
- 2001 Women's Varsity Match played at Lord's, on the Nursery Ground, for the first time
- 2003 MCC's Young Cricketers programme includes female players for the first time. Gillian Richards became one of the first female MCC Young Cricketers
- 2004 Rachael Heyhoe Flint becomes the first woman to be elected to the MCC Committee
- 2006 Claire Taylor hits 156 not out v. India – the highest ever individual score in a one-day international at Lord's
- 2006 England's Andrew Strauss and Charlotte Edwards unveil plaques to mark the second Lord's ground, used between 1811 and 1813
- 2007 First international archery tournaments at Lord's – China v. GB v. India. Won by India women and GB men.
- 2009 MCC member Claire Taylor is the first ever female *Wisden* Cricketer of the Year
- 2009 Tenth anniversary of women members at MCC

## Female Reflections from Lord's

The days of chivalry are past, as we are often told,
And ladies are no longer woo'd by knights in armour bold,
They like their menfolk modern, and they call their fancy free,
But there are no lady members of the MCC

A husband has no more the right to call his wife a slave,
The women wear the trousers now, and make the men behave,
They play lacrosse and hockey, and are powerful off the tee,
But there are no lady members of the MCC

Parliament has ladies in both parties, Left and Right,
They do not like bad language, so the men must be polite,
They all have had a vote, indeed, since 1923,
But there are no lady members of the MCC

Women play their cricket with both credit and renown,
They bat with skill and science, and they bounce their bumpers
down,
Their fielding is a pleasure, and as neat as it could be,
But there are no lady members of the MCC

The day will come (or will it come?) – I hope that I'll be there –
When Lord's will see the ladies playing cricket on the square,
The faces in the Tavern are a sight that I must see
When the ladies win the toss against the MCC!

– Heather Wheatley

Stafanie Taylor. An explosive batsman and gyrating queen
of the West Indian team, Taylor is an inspiration to
budding girl cricketers in the Caribbean.

# CUTTING EDGE

**At Home with the Boys**

Sarah Taylor is an über-talented England wicketkeeper-batsman who was the cause of a huge rumpus in the male-dominated world of cricket. At the start of 2013 she was having informal talks with Sussex County Cricket Club about the possibility of playing for the men's 2nd XI county side later in the year. And if she is good enough, why on earth not? In my mind it is simple: you pick your best team irrespective of colour, race or sex. It couldn't be more straightforward.

There are those, however, who worry that this just reinforces the abiding view that women's sport will always be judged against men's, rather than on its own merit. Marjorie Pollard, a forthright and formidable lady, was one of the founders of the Women's Cricket Association in 1926 and held unwavering opinions on, God forbid, mixed cricket:

> We do not want, wish or hanker after games of cricket with
> men. That suggests that we are adverse to men. I would kill

that thought immediately. But it is sound and sane to realise from the start that men and women cannot play team
games together or against each other ... I am not suggesting
that the standard of women's games is so far below that of
men's that they cannot play together or against each other. I
think that the standards are different – just that – different.

These comments are to be found in Marjorie's book,
*Cricket for Women and Girls*, first published in 1934.
She may have had a point back then when the officially
organised women's game was in its infancy and prevailing attitudes were more of the Victorian kind; but we now
have a very different breed of female cricketer and we live
in a very different world. Since the WCA merged with the
England Cricket Board in 1998 and pumped money into
the women's game and Sky television gave it far more
airtime over the past decade, we now have an incomparable female on the cusp of going professional.

It is not a question of impoverishing the women's game
or purely making a point by measuring women against the
standards of men, but one of lifting women's cricket to a
new and spectacular level. With this will come prestige and
popularity, which can only enhance women's presence in
the world of sport.

England's captain, Charlotte Edwards, waxes lyrical on
the subject of Sarah Taylor, claiming that she is the best
batswoman in the world and 'can be as good as she wants
to be'. In the meantime, Taylor has a hell of a lot of work to
do in stepping out of her comfort zone and elevating her

extraordinary talent into uncharted territory. The real test comes this summer at Walmley Cricket Club when she plays in the men's Birmingham Premier League. Only then will she be a viable consideration for the Sussex 2nd XI. If she is successful, she will go on to take women's cricket to unimaginable heights.

Taylor, together with many other women cricketers, is no stranger to the men's game; in fact she learned her craft in a male environment. As a former pupil at Brighton College she averaged 41 in the boys' 1st XI and took over the gloves from the older and first-choice male wicketkeeper. She was picked on merit and there was nothing more to it. Current England team-mates Holly Colvin and Laura Marsh all went through the same system at Brighton and were all coached by former England captain and ex-pupil Clare Connor.

Another England star, Arran Brindle, hit a century in the men's Lincolnshire Premier League, and England players often play against the top boys' public schools as they consider this a standard similar to their own. Men's 2nd XI county cricket is not a world away from this.

On seeing Taylor bat for the first time, one dazzled England coach remarked, 'she hits the ball like a man, that's rare in women's cricket'.

Mike Selvey, writing in *The Guardian*, was also taken by her superior batting: 'As a batsman, Taylor is a rarity in women's cricket in that she has a well-developed offside game: her cover driving last summer was as exquisite as any that came from the bat of Hashim Amla or Ian Bell.'

Her main challenge will be to adapt technically and mentally to the men's game. She will have to cope with the longer game in the premier league, learn to handle a larger ball and face up to the considerably faster bowling. There will be no holds barred and rightly so. Selvey felt that her real trial lay in dealing with pace: 'The adjustment she would have to make would largely be in terms of pace – from the seamers, an extra 10–15mph above what she would normally be used to taking – and maybe the degree of turn spinners might get and the pace at which they're bowled.'

Taylor has the potential so let's wait and see.

### Amateur or Professional?

Women's cricket has come a long way from its humble and largely ridiculed beginnings but it still has a long way to go. Gone are the days of having to buy your own blazer and cap and sewing on the England badge, yet, even today, most female international cricketers exist in a halfway house of semi-professionalism. Charlotte Edwards' own career has seen huge development in the England camp since she made her debut in 1996, two years before the ECB took over the women's game. She remembers her first appearance with fondness – albeit with a large dollop of amateurism:

I still remember that day like it was yesterday. We didn't have a sponsor, I didn't even wear three lions on my shirt. But that doesn't take away from what a feeling it was to make my England debut. I've still got the blazer and cap I paid for, and they were brilliant days.

Since then there has been a vast amount of investment and the majority of the current England players have contracts with the cricket charity Chance to Shine as coaching ambassadors. This role allows them time to play and train on a salary and is the closest women cricketers have got to becoming full-time professionals. Their work for CTS is invaluable in inspiring the next generation of schoolgirls. Some of the England squad are employed by the MCC Young Cricketers programme or are part of a university cricket academy, which grants them the freedom to play and train for most of the year.

England are now the number one side in the world and Edwards readily admits that a big reason for this is the increased investment being poured into their game: 'You're only going to get the success if you invest money.'

England have unparalleled financial support and Australia are a close second. They have a whole team of experts behind them, from head coach to the assistant coach, media manager, physiotherapist, data analysts, specialist skills coaches and strength and conditioning staff – a far cry even from ten years ago when Claire Taylor, one of England's most prolific batsmen, had to supple-ment her cricket career with a full-time job in IT. More recently, England have come further down the line in terms of performance fees and other remunerations, but the professional expectations and demands put upon them still do not match the payment.

Other countries lag behind England but they are making slow progress. Major players New Zealand and India are still underfunded as their national boards have yet to inject more investment into their management. Sri Lankan players now receive a match fee and modest contracts, linked to the military, have been introduced. Key players in the West Indies team are on annual retainers but funds have recently dried up – it is to be hoped that this does not hinder their recent world-class successes. Pakistan have yet to hit the big time but they can boast the highest number of contracted female players in the world. In February 2013 they posted their highest ever World Cup score of 192 against India.

Both Anjum Chopra and Lisa Sthalekar, captains of India and Australia respectively, were keen to point out to *Time Out* that, while there have been dramatic improvements in the infrastructure of the women's game with access to the best facilities, coaching and increased funding, it is tough to survive as individuals. Sthalekar talks about 'a fine line between semi-professional and professional' as the International Cricket Council and the national boards make more demands on the players but do not adequately reward them financially. Talented players are having to retire prematurely, according to Sthalekar, and it is a crying shame:

The age bracket they kind of stop [at] is 25–26. At the state level, a lot of girls aren't earning any money at all, so it becomes an expense. And it's like, 'Do I keep doing this? It's the game that I love. Or do I find a career that's going to pay the bills?'

She goes on to say:

Are we going to go for more cricket? If we are, they've got to start paying us more. If not, then they've got to take away some of their expectations. The game has become extremely professional and their expectations from the athletes are of professional athletes, but we are not paid professionally.

These women are endlessly compromised by their need to develop a professional career away from cricket. It was a sad day for cricket in 2012 when England's star bowler Isa Guha hung up her boots at the peak of her powers at only twenty-seven years old. Charlotte Edwards summed up this sorry state of affairs: 'If we played for money we would be playing different sports.'

These ladies cannot survive on love alone.

The disparity between the male and female players was made painfully clear when the ICC paid a US$100 daily subsidy to their male players and only US$60 to the women in the 2012 World Twenty20. This easily avoidable blunder was further reinforced by the blatant and corresponding inequality in prize money on offer: US$1 million for the men and US$60,000 for the women.

It has taken an inordinate amount of time for the

women's game to get to the stage at which it finds itself because it has been hidden away for so long. The recent explosion of media coverage on television and in newspapers, magazines and online has thrust the game on to the world stage. The 2009 World Cup was the first tournament to receive global televised coverage. This blanket exposure has done much to challenge prejudice and raise awareness and, crucially, the consummate skills of the leading players have proved without doubt that women's cricket is worth watching. This puts enormous pressure on the players to perform as they are not just playing for themselves and the team, but for the very survival of their game.

The ICC has a strong commitment to developing the global women's game and has made great strides. The next logical step would be to ensure that women's cricket is included in the TV broadcasting rights negotiations of member countries, but this has yet to happen. Funding is a constant challenge and the ICC and players alike realise that limited-overs cricket has to be the future, for the time being at least, if they are ever to achieve full professional status. T20s are particularly TV-friendly and work well as a double-header with the men's game to maximise the in-house crowd and remote viewers. Right now, the fifty- and twenty-over formats of the game are the perfect vehicles to promote women's cricket and there has been a strategic shift in this direction. Once women have conquered this arena maybe then they can return to their roots and face the ultimate challenge of Test cricket.

Notably, women are starting to make waves in the

traditionally male preserve of cricket administration. In 2012, Jackie Janmohammed made history when she became the first female to head a country board in Kenya. Closer to home, Lisa Pursehouse was appointed Chief Executive of Nottinghamshire County Cricket Club, the first lady to run a county. MCC have been proactive for the women's cause and invited Charlotte Edwards to join its high-profile World Cricket Committee, three years after the accomplished ex-England captain Clare Connor was appointed to the ICC board. Other significant benchmarks include Enid Bakewell's induction into the ICC's Hall of Fame in 2012, and England's Arran Brindle being a torchbearer in the 2012 London Olympics. Melbourne Cricket Club have finally followed the example of their namesake MCC and created their first women's team. All this brings vital recognition to the women's game and its importance should not be underestimated.

Funding, facilities and exposure are gradually on the up for women's cricket and bit by bit the game is moving in the right direction. The 2013 World Cup in India showed just what investment could deliver, revealing the cream of women's talent to be right up there with most of the men.

## Salad Days

So, who are the cricketing poster girls out there exhilarating and motivating the young girls of today? One such blossoming role model is Australia's seventeen-year-old Holly Ferling, who could be seen strutting her stuff at the World Cup in India. She is the perfect role model for the next generation of girl cricketers. Her gangly teenage awkwardness is offset by her sensational pace bowling, generating speeds of up to 120kph. She also looks the part with her golden locks gathered together with a white ribbon in a charmingly unkempt style, and her fresh young looks and giggling demeanour do much to capture the heart of every spectator.

Holly, however, is no normal teenager. At fourteen she struck gold when she took a hat-trick with her first three balls in men's grade cricket in Kingaroy, Queensland. She is the first girl to be awarded Queensland Junior Cricketer of the Year and has even impressed Australian cricket idol Jeff Thomson with her flair.

Ferling made her international debut in the 2013 World Cup in a group stage match against Pakistan and delivered respectable figures of 2 for 10. If she admires anyone in particular it is her fellow team-mate 22-year-old Ellyse Perry, who went down with a stomach bug before the Super Six game against England. Ferling was caught off guard when she was told she would replace her idol Ellyse in this high-profile battle against the old enemy. It was an overwhelming prospect for her, as she recalled:

> I found out probably an hour before the game. We were trying to give Ellyse as much time as possible for her to be well. It was just instant nerves and I was like, 'Oh my God, I am playing against England!' It was unreal and I was just excited to get another game.

She overcame crushing nerves on the field to gain instant

success with her first delivery. With long hair flying, the long-limbed Ferling struck again in the first over of her second spell and took the scalp of Greenway, the game's top scorer. Her lively bounce off the deck brought her 3 for 35 in only her second international, and that flush of intense pleasure at her own achievement was endearing.

The importance of female role models in the game cannot be understated. Holly Ferling's youthful aspirations were fuelled by her admiration for Perry, and without such an influence she might not have reached the dizzy heights of international cricket. Her words speak for themselves:

> I've always looked up to her. To do what she has done at such a young age is an incredible feat and I don't think it will ever be done again. To play alongside her against Pakistan and then to train alongside her and to be in the team environment with her is just an incredible feeling.

It is now Ferling's turn to inspire budding schoolgirl cricketers around the world.

It is right, too, to make a fuss about Ellyse Perry. At sweet sixteen she became the youngest Australian to play senior international cricket when, in July 2007, she made her debut in an ODI. She is a double international, having represented her country in both cricket and football, and has the distinction of playing pivotal roles in both World Cups. While playing for the Matildas, the Australian women's football team, her golden boot creamed the ball into the top left-hand corner of the net against Sweden in the 2011 Women's World Cup. No wonder she is universally loved.

When Australia trounced India in March 2012, Perry took her second international 5-wicket haul and was surrounded by a posse of adoring young Indian girls demanding photographs and autographs after the game. No other female cricketer gets this level of attention. Already a superstar in the eyes of many young girls around the world, Perry is charmingly modest about her impact on others:

To me sport and physical activity have been a huge and beneficial part of life and have given me a lot of joy. In that respect, if I encourage young kids to become involved in sport that is something I would feel quite glad about. Sport is something I am passionate about and it does make a difference in people's lives.

Her fighting talk in Mumbai reveals to us what makes a 24-carat champion tick:

What I love about sport is just the continued challenge about it – you're never as good as you can be. And that is what really motivates me and excites me about playing. The good thing is you can always come back, the next ball, the next day. You can keep working on things. I do enjoy the challenge of trying to get better and I do get competitive.

More recently, she stamped her authority on the men's game when she became the first woman to play in the highly competitive Sydney grade cricket league. Her take on the men's dressing room makes entertaining reading:

> I have never heard a bunch of boys carry on with so much rubbish. There is a lot of bravado. The boys really embrace the sense of fun and mateship. They are willing to give each other a bit of stick but they are also willing to take it and that transfers on-field quite nicely.

In May 2012, Perry's football club, Canberra United, issued an ultimatum: either commit fully to the club and give up cricket or ship out. Thankfully, she chose cricket and the game is all the richer for it. This does not mean the end of her footballing days, though. Her mission is to continue to play both sports at the top level, and this will take careful planning to enable her to cope with the high demands and the lack of an adequate professional wage to support her. Fingers crossed that she will be able to sustain both sports for her country and continue to give her young fans plenty of thrills and inspiration to take up the game themselves.

Stafanie Taylor is the Caribbean's wonderchild and is arguably the best female cricketer to have materialised so far in this part of the world. She is streets ahead in runs scored and comes a close second to Anisa Mohammed in the wickets race. Taylor has been showered with awards, winning Women's Cricketer of the Year in 2011 and 2012 in the ODI category, scoring 514 runs at an average of 46.72 and taking 16 wickets at 13.12 with her potent off-spin over the 2012 season. And all this before her twenty-first birthday.

Taylor caused more of a stir by making the long list for the most treasured prize of all when the ICC opened the Cricketer of the Year award to both sexes. The chances of a woman ever claiming this trophy are remote, however, as emphasis has tended to be placed on ascendancy in the Test arena; with women barely touching the Test format, it is simply not a fair contest. Other ICC awards open to women are for Emerging Player, Spirit of Cricket and People's Choice, but not a single woman has even been long-listed for any of them. This is largely down to a lack of media attention and insufficient public awareness but it is up to magnetic young stars like Taylor to remedy this.

She was brought up on a diet of cricket in Jamaica, taking up the game at the age of eight, and went on her first cricket tour to Guyana when she was ten. She hit the international scene at seventeen, taking two catches and causing one run-out in her first ODI against Ireland. Her Twenty20 debut followed soon after and she cracked 90 runs off 49 balls to help overcome Ireland by 75 runs.

Taylor is composed and mature beyond her years and takes her responsibility as a shining example to future generations very seriously:

Cricket is not so popular. We are trying to get it more common among the girls, trying to get them in at a young age from school. Me being the figure out there for some of them, hopefully seeing me play or hearing about me can get them involved. They want to be like me, whether it is my personality or some other thing. I was that age as well. I look at it as being a role model.

Taylor's life outside cricket is intriguing and she is conscious of the need for women to develop a career away from the game:

I still go to school and I would love to be a forensic scientist. That is my dream really. I am working towards it.

She is only too aware that women's cricket in the West Indies is not marketed well enough and it is her job to make waves in the sport and increase exposure. The likes of Holly Ferling, Ellyse Perry and Stafanie Taylor hold the future of women's cricket in their hands – and the future looks bright.

## 2013 World Cup

The World Cup is the pinnacle of achievement in international cricket and its most cherished trophy. The tenth Women's World Cup was held in Mumbai and Cuttack in India in January and February of 2013, with eight teams participating – Australia, New Zealand, England, India (the hosts), Sri Lanka, West Indies, Pakistan and South Africa. At the tournament's opening press conference, Charlotte Edwards, captain of defending champions England, was keen to explain just how far the women's game has come:

Recent ICC events have shown that the game is becoming popular. I have heard we are attracting loads of young girls who want to play the game. That is the most important thing for us as players. I think we have changed people's perceptions about women's cricket a lot. Hopefully this tournament will be another step in hammering that message home.

The competition was broadcast live on television throughout and proved to be a mesmerising experience. The first bombshell struck England early on in their group match against underlings Sri Lanka. England stumbled at 29 for 3 but made a late recovery as Gunn and debutante Jones pushed the score on to 238, giving England the cushion they needed. Sri Lanka made an auspicious start with a century-opening partnership between Yasoda Mendis (46) and Jayangani (62) and the stage was set for the rest of the team to drive to glory. The captain Siriwardene embraced the initiative with a sprightly 34 and, later, the almighty all-rounder Kaushalya came in at number six and mercilessly attacked the England bowling. She drilled and smashed her way to 56, including five fours and three astonishing sixes. Batsmen came and went regularly until Sri Lanka needed 9 off the last over with 8 wickets down. The crowds' nerves were in shreds as Kaushalya hit a four and was then run out on the next ball. It all went down to the last delivery, with 5 required for the win, and keeper Mandora Surangika, with unshakeable confidence, sent it soaring over deep midwicket for six. With a squeal of pure joy she went down on her knees as her team-mates mobbed her.

The West Indies, the underdogs, captivated the crowds with their first-ever win over New Zealand in a Super Six match to elevate them to second place, and only one more win stood between them and the final, where Australia lay in wait. For once, Windies stars Taylor and Dottin did not take all the kudos as all-rounder Daley and off-spinner Mohammed contributed 45 runs for the ninth wicket to advance their team to 207. New Zealand then suffered a series of shocking lbw decisions: replays showed Sophie Devine's thick inside edge, Mackay and Broadmore's deliveries going down the leg side, and Browne was struck outside the line of off.

The Women's World Cup may be for the best players in the world but they were not afforded the best umpires in the world. Not one umpire came from the ICC elite panel and it showed. New Zealand were not the only ones to suffer – England were given two dodgy decisions in their Super Six game against Australia which they lost by two runs. Women's cricket is not, it seems, a top priority and operates on a tight budget and the use of costly equipment, such as the DRS (Decision Review System), is not viable at the moment. Had the DRS been in place a number of crucial decisions would clearly have been reviewed; who knows how the tournament would have turned out?

This may be a slight digression from the match itself but it does raise an important point. New Zealand made their own mistakes, too, with suicidal running between the wickets, and some effective swing bowling caused problems for their batsmen. The Windies won by 48 runs, putting their stamp on international cricket.

A chirpy West Indies came face to face with five-times

world champions Australia in their last Super Six match in Mumbai. The Windies produced another first when they beat Australia by 8 runs and consequently dealt defending champions England and 2009 runners-up New Zealand a fatal blow by removing all hope of a place in the final.

Against the Australians, the Windies were tottering at 59 for 5 in the nineteenth over as Ferling and Schutt bulldozed their way through the top order. West Indian heroine Deandra Dottin then came to the rescue and powered her way to 60, helping to take the West Indies to 164. On paper this looked like an inadequate total to defend against the Aussies' might, and Australia seemed perfectly placed for victory at 130 for 4, needing only 35 runs from 11 overs. Then disaster struck the Australians as Shanel Daley and Stafanie Taylor led the assault on the last 6 wickets, including three run-outs, for 26 runs. Windies captain Merissa Aguilleira knew exactly when to go for the kill: 'I felt some panic happening in their camp and that's the time we started to attack even more. We realised that as long as we bowl in the right areas, we can get wickets and that's exactly what happened.'

The West Indies were in the final for the first time in the history of the World Cup and they went bonkers, sprinting all over the outfield whooping and gyrating, in true Caribbean style.

Australia are old hands at World Cup finals, however, and know how to turn it on when it matters. Jodie Fields' aggressive captaincy paid off as she led her team to their sixth Women's World Cup success. Australia won the toss and batted first, leaving the West Indies to chase the highest ever total in a World Cup final. Openers Haynes (52) and Lanning (31) saw off the new ball and then Jess Cameron, Australia's number three, blasted 75 off 76 balls. When the Australian middle order slipped from 181 for 3 to 209 for 7 it was left to Fields and golden girl Perry to pump up the total to 259 with an unbeaten stand of 50 off 40 deliveries. The pressure and tension were evident as the Windies fielded below par and most of their bowlers turned in mediocre performances. The exception was seventeen-year-old leg-spinner Shaquana Quintyne who finished with impressive figures of 3 for 27 in her 10 overs.

Fields took the biggest gamble in probably the biggest game of her career when she selected Ellyse Perry. Perry had been on the bench for the last three matches because of a dodgy ankle injury and she was by no means 100 per cent. Fields went for the star quality of Perry in the hope that she wouldn't crack, and dropped the heart-broken teenage prodigy Holly Ferling. When Perry, on the verge of crumbling, pulled up in her first two attempts at bowling an intense look of doom clouded the face of her captain. But there is nothing soft about Ellyse Perry, and she painfully delivered the ball on her third attempt, before striking gold with the last ball of the over as Knight was given out to a slightly suspect lbw. On her tenth ball she took the wicket of danger woman Taylor, and with her fifteenth she had MacLean trapped lbw for 13. After only three overs her figures read 3 wickets for 2 runs.

Fields relentlessly targeted the Windies' best batsmen with her best bowlers and, when the powerful Dottin arrived at the crease, she brought Perry back into the attack. In the end Sthalekar, Australia's other premier fast bowler, terminated Dottin's innings and at 109 for 5 in the thirty-first over it was game over for the West Indies. They limped on to the forty-fourth over before Australia officially took the title of world champions once again.

The gap is steadily narrowing between the top four countries in the world – Australia, New Zealand, England and India – and the bottom six – West Indies, Sri Lanka, Pakistan, South Africa, the Netherlands and Ireland. These six need to play as much international cricket as possible against the big four to lift and develop their game and provide a broader horizon of competitive women's cricket. The gospel of cricket is being spread to schoolgirls all over the world thanks to the likes of Ellyse Perry, Holly Ferling and Stafanie Taylor – members of a special class of women at the forefront of the game. And many more will follow in their wake. Surely we are destined for even more dazzling days in the sun.

# ACKNOWLEDGEMENTS

The best cricket library in the world furnished me with almost everything that has ever been written about women's cricket – many thanks to MCC and its team of experts at Lord's.

Rather late in the day, I discovered that the Women's Cricket Association archives were sitting in a shed deep in the Lancashire countryside at the home of past England captain Carole Cornthwaite. I must thank Carole and her family for putting up with my invasion of their home, garden shed and photocopier for several hours on a bitter February day. The afternoon was punctuated by Mr and Mrs Cornthwaite dashing off to milk the cows.

Don Miles of www.womenscricket.net has been selfless in his quest to supply us with his splendid photos of England players, and only asked that a donation be made to the Sussex Women's Cricket Association in return.

The delightful centurion Eileen Ash (née Whelan) held court at her home in Norwich and relayed wonderful stories of her playing days in the first ever women's Test series in

England in 1937, and her adventures on the epic tour to Australia in 1948. Two hours of intense chat and countless photos taken by the talented Victoria Carew Hunt, and Eileen was still gunning for more.

My American real tennis pal and author Harry Saint painstakingly proofread the finished article, which must have been an arduous task for a man who knows next to nothing about cricket. I owe him.

Thank you to rock legend Mick Jagger for taking time out from his busy Stones tour of the USA for the endorsement of this book. I'll see them in Philadelphia.

I can't thank enough the team at Chance to Shine, led by the able Lucy Horitz, for their support and organisation of the promotion of this book. Fifty per cent of the proceeds will go to the charity's initiative, Girls on the Front Foot.

Many past and present England players have been more than helpful throughout the project and I thank them all. I am grateful, too, to Tim Rice for his contribution.

# PERMISSIONS AND PICTURE CREDITS

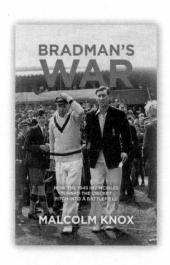